The Sacramental Church

Other books by John F. Nash

Quest for the Soul
The Soul and Its Destiny
Christianity: the One, the Many

The Sacramental Church

The Story of Anglo-Catholicism

JOHN F. NASH

WIPF & STOCK · Eugene, Oregon

THE SACRAMENTAL CHURCH
The Story of Anglo-Catholicism

Wipf & Stock
An Imprint of Wipf and Stock Publishers
199 W. 8th Ave., Suite 3
Eugene, OR 97401

www.wipfandstock.com

ISBN 13: 978-1-60899-789-3

Manufactured in the U.S.A.

*To St Mary's Episcopal Church
Asheville, North Carolina*

Contents

List of Figures and Tables

Preface

*T*HE *SACRAMENTAL* *CHURCH* IS the story of Anglo-Catholicism in Great Britain and North America. The book explores the historical, liturgical, and doctrinal foundations of Anglo-Catholicism, the circumstances in which it emerged, and what it offers today. Anglo-Catholicism is an expression of the Anglican faith that attaches great importance to the sacraments, especially the Sacrament of the Altar. It also emphasizes the sacred ministry that extends back to the time of Christ.

This book is written for the intelligent, non-specialist reader—one who wants a readable story but expects more than a shallow, superficial treatment and who welcomes opportunities for further reading. It is addressed to Anglo-Catholic laity and clergy, high-church Anglicans/ Episcopalians, members of other Anglican traditions, and all others interested in sacramental Christianity. The need for a new book is clear. The last comparable work, Bishop Charles C. Grafton's *The Lineage of the American Catholic Movement*, was published in 1911. More recent works have been more restricted in scope or hostile to Anglo-Catholicism.

The Sacramental Church cites the work of numerous individuals and, through liberal use of direct quotes, allows many of them to speak for themselves. It is in large measure their story. My job, to borrow a metaphor from John Mason Neale, has been to provide the "thread" on which the pearls are strung. The book is designed as a reference source as well as a narrative. The citations and bibliography will help readers find information of special interest.

All scriptural citations are taken from the King James Bible. Most of the Prayer Book quotes are from the websites of the Society of Archbishop Justus, a nonprofit organization in New York State, named for the fourth archbishop of Canterbury. Quotes from the *Tracts for the Times* (except Tracts 67–69) and many other references are taken from the "Anglican History" websites of Project Canterbury, an international volunteer organization. Our grateful thanks go to these organizations for their support of scholarly research as well as to the authors who shared their wisdom in the extensive literature on which this book draws.

Citing works from the Tudor and other early periods raises the issue of whether or not to retain archaic spelling. While doing so captures something of the spirit of the times—for example: "Of Baptisme, bothe publique and priuate" and "Lorde, nowe lettest thou thy servaunte departe in peace"—it impedes readability. Accordingly, modern English spelling is imposed on direct quotes, though no attempt has been made to alter words like "thee," "doth," and "bemost." Original punctuation, capitalization, and British spelling are preserved where applicable.

Much has happened in the few short years since I wrote *Christianity: the One, the Many*. How I became an Anglo-Catholic revolves around All Saints', Margaret Street, London, and the Lady Chapel at Ely Cathedral. It also involves Father Richard Shackleford, now rector of St Timothy's Church, Kingsport, Tennessee. That story must be told elsewhere.

The Sacramental Church is dedicated to St Mary's Church, Asheville, North Carolina. My sincere gratitude goes to Father Brent Norris, rector of St Mary's, who welcomed me into his parish and encouraged me in this project. Also to Bishop G. Porter Taylor of Western North Carolina who received me into the Episcopal Church.

I am indebted to the Rev. A. Charles Cannon, the Rev. Dr. O. C. Edwards, Jr., and Dr. David Moltke-Hansen for their very generous support and helpful comments on the manuscript. Rev. Cannon is former rector of St Thomas Episcopal Church, Coral Gables, Florida, and St Andrew's, South Carolina. Dr. Edwards is dean emeritus, Seabury-Western Seminary, Evanston, Illinois, and author of the award-winning *A History of Preaching*. Dr. Moltke-Hansen retired from the presidency of the Historical Society of Pennsylvania. I also acknowledge helpful suggestions from the Very Rev. William Willoughby, rector of St Paul's, Savannah, GA. What weaknesses remain in the book are entirely mine. My most sincere thanks go to Sylvia Lagergren, whose love and support made this project possible.

John F. Nash
www.sacramentalchurch.com
December 2010

Abbreviations

ACC	Anglican Church of Canada
AOJDD	Anglican–Orthodox Joint Doctrinal Discussions
ARCIC	Anglican–Roman Catholic International Commission
ASB	*Alternative Service Book*, Church of England, 1980
BAS	*Book of Alternative Services*, Anglican Church of Canada, 1985
BCP	*Book of Common Prayer*
BNA	British North America (the precursor of modern Canada).
CA	Church Association
CE	Common Era
CW	*Common Worship*, Church of England, 2000
ECU	English Church Union
ECUSA	Episcopal Church in the United States of America, more correctly known as The Episcopal Church
IALC	International Anglican Liturgical Consultation
IARCCUM	International Anglican–Roman Catholic Commission for Unity and Mission
ICAOTD	International Commission for Anglican–Orthodox Theological Dialogue
PECUSA	Protestant Episcopal Church in the United States of America
PECCS	Protestant Episcopal Church in the Confederate States
SEC	Scottish Episcopal Church
SPCK	Society for Promoting Christian Knowledge
SPG	Society for the Propagation of the Gospel in Foreign Parts
TEC	The Episcopal Church
WCC	World Council of Churches

The abbreviations listed above are restricted in this book to the stated meanings. Other terms, such as "Anglican Consultative Council" and "*Anglican Service Book*," are written in full.

1

Introduction

THIS BOOK'S TITLE REFLECTS the belief that Anglican Christianity is recovering its ancient heritage as a sacramental church—a church whose central act of worship is the Eucharist and whose mission is built upon the sacraments as well as on service to humanity. Offering the sacraments is itself a great service. Anglo-Catholicism is the force within Anglicanism making that recovery possible.

From a larger perspective Anglo-Catholicism emphasizes the transcendence of God and the mystery of Christ's incarnation. That timeless mystery cannot be captured by scriptural literalism or doctrinal formulas but is glimpsed through shared experience, enhanced by the aesthetic and dramatic dimensions of the liturgy.

Anglo-Catholicism in its modern form is the product of far-reaching initiatives in the nineteenth-century, collectively known as the Catholic Revival. The revival reclaimed for the Anglican faith features of medieval English Christianity that, over time, had either fallen into disuse or been suppressed. Its objective was not historical reenactment or reversing the outcome of the Reformation but restoring what rightly belonged to Anglican Christianity through its roots in the "catholic" church of late antiquity—practices and principles of contemporary importance and relevance. Anglicanism's claim to catholicity was not new, but the time had come to proclaim it with new vigor and act upon it.

This book tells the story of Anglo-Catholicism: how it came about, what it offers today, and why it has timeless appeal. A brief introduction to the Catholic Revival and Anglo-Catholicism follows, but first a few comments are in order concerning Anglicanism itself.

ANGLICAN CHRISTIANITY

The word "Anglican," from the Latin *ecclesia anglicana* ("the English church"), appeared in medieval texts, but it was first used to refer to the church and its members in the eighteenth century; the abstract "Anglicanism" dates from the nineteenth century. Today "Anglican" refers to the Church of England and the family of autonomous daughter churches that trace their origins back to the English church. Our story focuses on the Church of England, the Scottish Episcopal Church, the Episcopal Church in the United States, and the Anglican Church of Canada. Other authors are encouraged to tell the story pertaining to Australia, New Zealand, South Africa, and the many other places where Anglo-Catholicism has flourished.

The Church of England and more than forty other churches comprise the Anglican Communion. Their bishops meet every ten years at Lambeth Conferences, representatives participate in the Anglican Consultative Council, and primates—heads of member churches—meet annually. A few daughter churches, including the Reformed Anglican Church and the Fellowship of Confessing Anglicans, have seceded from the Anglican Communion. But they remain "Anglican." Anglo-Catholics are found both inside and outside the Anglican Communion.

The Church of England came into being as a freestanding religious entity in the 1530s, when the English bishops proclaimed their independence from Rome and King Henry VIII declared himself its "supreme head." The *Book of Common Prayer* of 1549 provided the liturgy in the vernacular English. But the episcopal structure and important beliefs and practices of the pre-Reformation church were preserved. English Christianity already had a tradition of more than a millennium, and that rich tradition molded Anglicanism as much as did the Reformation and subsequent events.

Anglicanism spread throughout the British Isles and, through colonial expansion, to many other countries. Some of them, like Canada and Australia, remain in the British Commonwealth, while the United States, South Africa, and others do not. Anglicanism also spread to countries with no historical links to England. For example, the Igreja Episcopal Anglicana do Brasil, the Province de l'Eglise Anglicane du Congo, and the Nippon Sei Ko Kai in Japan belong to the Anglican Communion. Anglicanism has strong English roots and has special relevance to the

English-speaking people, but it cannot be *defined* by ethnicity, language, culture, or colonial history.

Many definitions of "Anglican" and "Anglicanism" have been offered, but precisely what the terms mean in the modern context is a perennial topic of debate. Rowan Williams, current archbishop of Canterbury, described Anglicanism as a form of Reformed Christianity "grounded in the historic ministry of bishops, priests and deacons, and with the classical early Christian formulations of doctrine about God and Jesus Christ."[1]

Anglicanism is not homogeneous. The Church of England was built on principles of pluralism and inclusiveness and inspired similar principles in its daughter churches. Church parties emerged to promote particular shades of belief, preferences in religious practice, and attitudes toward civil government. "Churchmanship" became a major factor in ecclesiastical politics.

The English Reformation had broad popular support, but two main groups emerged: traditionalists, who wanted to preserve as much as possible of the medieval English church, and reformists, who wanted the Church of England to embrace Lutheran or Calvinist principles. Over time traditionalists became known as "high-church" and reformists as "low-church." High-church Anglicans preserved the thread of continuity with pre-Reformation sacramental Christianity that eventually found its way into Anglo-Catholicism. A third, centrist party, the "broad church," emerged in the nineteenth century.

Tension was not uncommon, but the parties generally tolerated one another, and commitment to church unity prevented squabbles from getting out of hand. The Catholic Revival provoked unusual tension, however, and Anglicanism was heavily polarized for more than fifty years. Thankfully, the turmoil subsided, and Anglo-Catholicism found its place within the general pluralism. Since then, other hot-button issues have arisen, and new parties have emerged to give voice to their concerns. Whether Anglican cohesion can be maintained remains to be seen.

Anglicanism's main cohesive force has always been the liturgy. In classical Greece *leitourgia* meant public service. But in Christianity "liturgy" acquired its modern connotation of collective worship. The liturgy involves both words and actions; hence the *Book of Common Prayer* included the script and also the *rubrics*, or "stage directions," for worship services. No matter how humble or informal, collective worship conduct-

1. Williams, R., *Anglican Identities*.

ed on a regular basis inevitably develops some degree of ritual. Anglo-Catholics favor more elaborate ritual or ceremony than others do.

Anglicanism did not have a founder, or "guiding hand," like a Martin Luther or a John Wesley. Neither does it have a comprehensive doctrinal canon, like the Roman Catholic dogmas or Calvinist confessions. Anglicans worshipped together and then reflected on the beliefs they shared. Anglican theology emerged from the liturgy—and is still doing so. The oft-quoted adage *lex orandi lex credendi* ("the law of prayer is the law of belief") provides a good description of the Anglican approach to doctrine, and we shall invoke it frequently in this story of Anglo-Catholicism.

The Prayer Book has gone through multiple revisions and has been translated into many languages as well as into modern English. It provided a common tradition on which Anglican daughter churches have based their own liturgies. Anglican liturgies are still scripted, rather than spontaneous, but now offer optional forms, especially of the Communion Service, to meet the aspirations of individual clergy and parishes. Anglo-Catholics look for forms that express their sacramental focus.

THE CATHOLIC REVIVAL

The most conspicuous outcome of the Catholic Revival was to restore the splendor of pre-Reformation ceremony to the Anglican liturgy. It will be instructive to contrast worship in the typical style of the eighteenth century with Anglo-Catholic worship today.

Styles of Worship

Anglican churches in, say, 1750 displayed all the puritan austerity of the post-Reformation era. Surviving medieval cathedrals and churches retained their architectural grandeur, but high altars had been removed, along with crucifixes and other images. Statues were defaced and murals or frescoes whitewashed over. Many of the old church buildings were also in poor repair. Some new churches had been constructed, and all the churches in North America were new; but their architecture was spartan, and decoration minimal. The dominant feature was the pulpit, a massive structure, towering over the pews and affirming the centrality of preaching in the religious consciousness of the time.

Worship followed the 1662 Prayer Book. The liturgy was standard-ized, with prescribed collects and scriptural readings for each Sunday and major festival. Devout Anglicans attended both morning and evening services. The Sunday morning service, which might last three hours, consisted of Morning Prayer, a sermon, and the first part of the Communion Service. The "evening" service, which might start as early as 3:00 p.m., included another sermon and Evening Prayer. It might also include baptisms, churchings,[2] marriages, and catechism classes for chil-dren preparing for confirmation and first Communion.[3]

Services were read by a clergyman, assisted by the parish clerk who led the responses to prayers and made announcements. The priest might wear a white surplice for Morning or Evening Prayer but changed into a black "Geneva" gown—similar to today's academic gown—for the sermon. The sermon, lasting about one hour, typically used the day's scriptural readings to encourage moral, socially acceptable behavior. Some priests composed their own sermons, but many read homilies written by promi-nent divines. Sermons were often dry, but they were generally optimistic in tone. Anglican clergy shunned the emotionalism of nonconformist preachers and the "hellfire" style of the Great Awakenings in America.

Two or three times a year the "Lord's Supper" would be offered, and the Communion Service would be read in full. On those Sundays, a simple Communion table was placed in the body of the church. No candles burned, unless they were needed for illumination, and no cross, flowers, ornaments, or images were permitted. Communicants knelt around the table—the only time laity or clergy made any kind of rever-ential gesture in church.

Today's Anglo-Catholic church is very different. Attention is fo-cused on the high altar. A cross and candles stand on the altar, which is draped in the liturgical colors of the day or season, or possibly stripped bare in penitential seasons. A tabernacle on the altar may contain the re-served Sacrament. The pulpit is placed to the side of the chancel or nave. The walls of the building may be adorned with religious images. Votive candles may burn before statues of the Virgin Mary and the saints.

The Communion Service—the "Sung Communion," or "High Mass," if the parish has the resources—is the main Sunday morning

2. The churching of women expressed thanksgiving for successful childbirth but also had echoes of primitive purification rites.

3. Gregory, "The Prayer Book," 96.

service. The faithful enter the church with reverence, genuflecting or bowing to the altar. They may bless themselves with holy water or may be sprinkled in the *Asperges* at the beginning of the service. Clergy, often more than one, wear ornate vestments in the liturgical colors of the season or festival. If a bishop is in attendance he or she most likely wears the traditional vestments of episcopal office: the cope and mitre.

Clergy, vested acolytes, and possibly vested choristers, process into the church, led by an acolyte carrying a cross. Bells are rung at key points in the service, and—except in Lent—incense creates a sacred aura in the chancel. Psalms and litanies are chanted, and the choir sings an anthem and leads the congregation in hymns. Announcements may be made of a retreat, a pilgrimage, or devotions like the Rosary. Confessions may be scheduled during the week. Special devotions like the Stations of the Cross may be offered during Holy Week. A Celtic Mass may be celebrated on certain festivals or even on a regular basis. References may be made to a religious order or community with which the parish has associations.

The Sunday Mass probably includes a sermon, but the focus is on the offering and consecration of the eucharistic elements, the breaking of the consecrated bread, and the distribution of Holy Communion. Virtually everyone in attendance goes forward and kneels at the altar rails to receive the Sacrament.

Casual visitors may see a resemblance to worship in Roman Catholic or Eastern Orthodox churches. Anglo-Catholic worship draws upon the catholic heritage shared by those churches. But Anglo-Catholics are *Anglicans*, owing loyalty to their Anglican bishops and primates. Like all Anglicans they affirm an essential connection to scripture, common tenets of faith, and a liturgy based on the *Book of Common Prayer* of their national church. The Catholic Revival reassured Anglicans that they could engage in ceremonial practices without endangering their faith or betraying their tradition.

Multifaceted Revival

The scenarios described above illustrate the impact of the Ritualist Movement and a related architectural movement. The latter, which began early in the nineteenth century, was prompted by recognition of the inadequacies of contemporary places of worship. It sought to revive the beauty of pre-Reformation church architecture and decoration, particularly Gothic styles. It encouraged the incorporation of chancels, high altars, and sacred images. The movement began almost simultane-ously in Britain and North America, but its focus became the Cambridge Camden Society. The society and its offshoots had a profound influence on church design throughout the Anglican Communion.

The Ritualist Movement began in the 1840s, again on both sides of the Atlantic. It sought to restore pre-Reformation ceremony to Anglican worship, particularly to the Mass. Elaborate ritual was reintroduced in inner-city churches as well as large cathedrals. The movement was strongly resisted by those who valued the style of eighteenth-century worship or who regarded ceremony as superstitious and "romish." But ceremony steadily gained acceptance and eventually became pervasive.

Those two movements sought to enrich the aesthetic and dramatic aspects of worship. Less conspicuous, but equally important, compo-nents of the Catholic Revival were concerned with theology, the church's sacred ministry, personal and collective holiness, and social justice.

The Tractarian Movement was initiated by a group of Anglican clergy at Oxford University. Beginning in 1833, members of the group responded to a crisis in the Church of England by writing scholarly tracts dealing with theological, ecclesiological, and other issues. The tracts broke little new ground, but they restated and reemphasized high-church positions on the regenerative power of baptism, the real presence in the Eucharist, and the church's sacred ministry. Deeper understand-ing of the Eucharist in turn strengthened resolve to celebrate the Mass in a beautiful setting with elaborate ceremony. The Tractarian Movement soon spread beyond Oxford and beyond England.

A less well-defined movement, which formed yet another aspect of the Catholic Revival, promoted holiness. One accomplishment was the restoration of Anglican religious orders. Another was the encourage-ment of spiritual disciplines, retreats, pilgrimages, and devotion to the Virgin Mary and saints. Finally, an unexpected side effect of the Catholic Revival was the emergence of a strong social conscience and develop-ment of a vibrant ministry to disadvantaged segments of society.

Broader Impact

The direct outcome of the Catholic Revival was the self-identification of certain parishes, clergy, and laity as "Anglo-Catholic." Equally sig-nificant was the quiet adoption by parishes throughout the Anglican

Communion of many of the same sacramental and ritual practices and the embrace of similar doctrinal principles.

Anglo-Catholic practices and principles have expanded to the point where they have become almost normative, testifying to the deep-seated hunger for a broader range of religious options than was once considered permissible. Most Anglican parishes now offer Holy Communion at least weekly. Clergy typically wear the chasuble, acolytes and choristers are vested, and bishops wear traditional regalia. Candles burn on altars or communion tables. Few Anglicans yearn for, or even remember, the austerity of the eighteenth century. Requiem Masses, religious orders, devotion to Mary, the Stations of the Cross, and even private confession are no longer considered alien. Anglicans now have choices that they denied themselves for 400 years.

Ceremonial worship has also spread beyond Anglicanism. Most Baptist churches have vested choirs. Vested ministers and choristers process into Methodist churches. Candles burn on altars in Presbyterian churches. None of those phenomena would have been possible two centuries ago.

ANGLO-CATHOLICISM

Sacramental Christianity

Christianity can very broadly be divided into "sacramental" and "evangelical" forms, based on style of worship and understanding of ecclesiastical responsibility.[4] Sacramental Christianity makes two interrelated claims: that Christ instituted sacramental rites through which divine grace flows to the faithful and that custody of those rites was entrusted to the apostles and their legitimate successors. Divine institution of the sacraments created the need for a sacred priesthood to administer them. Sacramental Christianity was the norm in the Middle Ages and today is expressed by, but not limited to, the Roman and Eastern Orthodox Churches.

Evangelical Christianity (from the Greek *evaggelion*, "good news" or "gospel") took early forms in the twelfth century and gathered momentum at the Reformation. Evangelicals attached great importance to the Bible, which they studied with emphasis on the "plain sense of the text," laying groundwork for the scriptural inerrancy of later times.

---

4. Liberal Christianity, which emerged over the last 200 years, may represent a third form.

They emphasized the individual encounter with Jesus and the conversion experience rather than the priesthood and sacramental worship. Evangelical Christianity remains strong in the modern world. Baptists make up the largest identifiable group of Evangelicals.

After the Reformation the Church of England, and in due course its daughter churches, straddled the sacramental-evangelical divide.[5] In consequence, tension developed between traditionalists and reformists, high- and low-church factions. Pluralism ensured that both sacramentally oriented and evangelically oriented Anglicans could find a spiritual home within the church. That pluralism can and should continue in a spirit of mutual acceptance. Nevertheless, the Catholic Revival gave Anglicans the opportunity to experience sacramental Christianity. Anglicanism is reclaiming its heritage as a sacramental church.

What is Anglo-Catholicism?

"Anglo-Catholicism" reflects the belief that the Anglican church is a branch of the "one, holy, catholic, and apostolic church" referred to in the Nicene Creed. *Catholicism* affirms the claim to the common, ancient heritage. *Anglo* refers to the church's English roots and distinguishes it from Roman Catholicism.

Anglo-Catholics view the sacraments as extensions of Christ's incarnation, instituted by him and entrusted to successive generations of the episcopate. They recognize all seven traditional sacraments but, in keeping with Anglican tradition, place greatest emphasis on baptism and the Eucharist. Anglo-Catholics believe that, through baptism, a child or adult is reborn and welcomed into Christ's mystical body, the church. They regard the Eucharist, or Holy Communion, as the central act of Christian worship and affirm the real presence in the Eucharist; they believe that communicants receive the body and blood of Christ. They may also believe that the Eucharist is a sacrificial act in which participants offer themselves to God along with the consecrated bread and wine.

Anglo-Catholicism certainly does not neglect outreach and service; indeed it was a forerunner in those areas. But primarily it is about worship. Anglo-Catholicism insists that recognition of a transcendent,

5. Lutheranism also straddled the divide, and some Lutherans have taken a similar course toward a sacramental form. It should be noted that *evangelical* has a different connotation in Lutheran churches. For example, the Evangelical Lutheran Church of America is not "evangelical" in the sense used here.

beneficent God creates an imperative to adore that God, either in its unity or in the persons of the Trinity. Anglo-Catholics appreciate the aesthetic and dramatic dimensions of ceremonial worship. The chancel, set apart from the rest of the church, is a sacred space, a holy of holies, a place of beauty, awe and expectation. The high altar, where the Eucharist is celebrated, is a focus of reverence. Sacred ceremony, performed tastefully and sensitively in a beautiful setting, is a fitting response to the mystery and glory of God.

Ceremonial styles of worship provide more perfect vehicles through which we can express our relationship to God and through which the divine presence can be felt and divine grace can flow to the world. Ceremony engages the senses and evokes a sense of reverence and transcendence. Through daily and weekly scriptural readings, special services, and liturgical colors that capture the mood of the season, worshippers share in the drama of Christ's birth, ministry, death, resurrection, and ascension, and the descent of the Holy Spirit at Pentecost.

Monasticism played a major role in pre-Reformation English Christianity. As a result of the Catholic Revival, Anglican religious orders were revived in the nineteenth century. While the religious life may seem anachronistic in today's world, it continues to provide opportunities for women and men to make lifelong commitments to renunciation, contemplation, and service in a context of communal living.

Many Anglo-Catholics would welcome closer contacts with the Roman and/or Eastern churches, but they greatly value their Anglicanism. Individual Anglo-Catholics have converted to Roman Catholicism or Eastern Orthodoxy, and vice versa. But there is no collective desire to submit to, or be absorbed by, another tradition. Until such time as Christian unity—or unity of sacramental churches—becomes a reality, each tradition has opportunities to make its unique contribution to worldwide Christianity.

Anglo-Catholicism has a special reverence for tradition, but it is motivated by more than nostalgia. Anglo-Catholics believe that their expression of Christianity is of timeless relevance, as applicable now as it was a hundred years, or a millennium, ago. The combination of the sacramental liturgy, personal spirituality, and service can fulfill a unique transformative role in the twenty-first century.[6]

6. Devotion, Ceremony, Healing, Service, and Renunciation—all within the purview of Anglo-Catholicism—are five of the seven paths of Christianity discussed in Nash, J. F., *Christianity*, vol. 2, 310–48.

STRUCTURE OF THE BOOK

A major thesis of this book is that Anglo-Catholicism should be viewed, not as a new phenomenon, but as the culmination of a process that began when Christianity came to the British Isles in the early centuries of the Common Era. The book focuses on the Catholic Revival and its outcomes. But Anglo-Catholicism, a distinctively English form of sacramental Christianity, cannot be understood without at least a brief review of this earlier history.

Chapter 2 traces the development of Christianity through the Celtic, Anglo-Saxon, Norman, and post-Norman periods. The medieval English church had weaknesses, which the Reformation sought to remedy. But it also was a vibrant expression of Christianity that encompassed the rich pageantry of worship in the great cathedrals, the lives of quiet contemplation and service in the monasteries, and the fervent devotion of the masses of ordinary people. When the English Reformers sought to reposition the church within western Christianity, they were conscious of traditions built up over a period of nearly 1,500 years—only about 400 of which were under the dominance of the Church of Rome.

Chapters 3 and 4 discuss the emergence of the Church of England as a distinct religious entity, and the spread of its traditions and ideals to Scotland and North America. Chapter 3 establishes a baseline of mainstream Anglican practices and beliefs as expressed in the English *Book of Common Prayer* and the Articles of Faith. Understanding that baseline is important before we discuss high-church and Anglo-Catholic divergence from it. Chapter 3 places emphasis on the *via media*, Anglicanism's middle way between Roman Catholicism and continental Protestantism. Together, chapters 3 and 4 show how Anglicanism adapted to different environments and changing political and social realities. They show how four national churches—the Church of England, the Scottish Episcopal Church, the Episcopal Church in the United States, and the Anglican Church of Canada—acquired unique qualities while honoring their common roots and preserving common traditions.

Chapter 5 traces the development of high-church Anglicanism from the Reformation to the early nineteenth century. It describes how a relatively small number of traditionalists were able to preserve, at great personal sacrifice, many practices and beliefs of the pre-Reformation church. High-church Anglicanism found its most complete expression in Scotland. The sacramental tradition was expressed in the liturgy of the

Scottish Episcopal Church, which then flowed to the Episcopal Church in the United States. Important elements of that Scottish/American liturgy later returned to reinvigorate worship in the Church of England and spread to most other national churches in the Anglican Communion.

Chapters 6 and 7 explore the multi-faceted Catholic Revival and the challenges it encountered. The former discusses the Tractarian Movement and the revival of Anglican religious orders. The latter discusses the architectural revival, the Ritualist Movement, and the work in social justice. Together the two chapters show how the Catholic Revival built upon the earlier "orthodox" high-church tradition. They examine the work of prominent individuals, their circumstances, and the resistance they faced. The Tractarians were persecuted, and a few came to see conversion to Rome as their only viable option. Ritualism met strong, sometimes violent, opposition but ultimately prevailed. Chapters 6 and 7 seek to capture the passion that motivated the Catholic Revival and the ways it surmounted obstacles to give expression to modern Anglo-Catholicism.

Chapter 8 explores what Anglo-Catholicism has become today and discusses major areas of Anglo-Catholic practice and belief. Liturgical research and ecumenical conversations strengthened Anglican worship and its theological underpinnings. Reports of ecumenical commissions reveal evolving theological understanding within Anglicanism as well as convergence with other sacramental churches. Chapter 8 continues the study of liturgies from different places and times, providing insights into the development of beliefs and attitudes concerning the Eucharist. The Communion Services of all four national churches now offer forms that express Anglo-Catholic principles and aspirations.

Chapter 8 also discusses how recognition of the glory of God creates the impulse for adoration. Anglo-Catholicism captures a strong sense of divine transcendence and pays special attention to the roles of aesthetics and drama in worship. Therein, we glimpse the divine glory— and perhaps anticipate a stage when humanity will fully be redeemed by the incarnation and redemption. The chapter ends by examining how devotion to Mary and the saints complements the worship of God. It shows that Anglicanism—and particularly Anglo-Catholicism—has established a middle way between past excess and neglect.

The "Reflections" section at the end of each chapter provides an opportunity to step back, view the pertinent issues from a larger perspective, and relate them to the entire story of Anglo-Catholicism.

2

The Pre-Reformation English Church

CHRISTIANITY CAME TO THE British Isles in Roman times, perhaps even in apostolic times. It faced enormous challenges, ranging from imperial persecution, to waves of foreign invasion, to a grim struggle between rival "denominations." This chapter traces the church's development through the Celtic, Anglo-Saxon, and Norman periods, to the Reformation. The isolation of the Celtic church gave way to integration of the English church into European Christianity and, for about four centuries, domination by the Church of Rome.

Christianity permeated all aspects of medieval life. Monasteries and cathedrals graced the English landscape, while the masses of people were swept up into popular piety in a highly stratified, paternalistic society. In the process the English church developed distinctive characteristics that laid the groundwork for the post-Reformation Church of England and eventually for Anglo-Catholicism.

EARLY CHRISTIANITY IN THE BRITISH ISLES

When William Blake exclaimed: "And did those feet in ancient time, walk upon England's mountains green: and was the holy Lamb of God, on England's pleasant pastures seen,"[1] he recalled a medieval legend that Joseph of Arimathea brought the boy Jesus to Roman Britain, perhaps even to Glastonbury.[2] Other legends assert that Joseph returned to Glastonbury in 65 CE and built a church dedicated to the Virgin Mary. (The locations

1. Blake, *Jerusalem*.
2. Taylor, J. W., *The Coming*," 224.

13

FIGURE 2.1: EARLY CENTERS OF CHRISTIANITY IN THE BRITISH ISLES.

of Glastonbury and other centers of early Christian activity are shown in Figure 2.1.) Yet another legend asserts that Ireland's first missionary was Altus, a soldier in the Roman army who had witnessed the crucifixion.[3]

Historians believe that Christian missionaries arrived in the Celtic lands of Europe's Atlantic seaboard sometime between the first and fourth century CE. Aside from legends, we have brief comments by Church Father Tertullian, Roman scholar Hippolytus, and other writers of the time. The first missionaries probably came from neighboring Gaul or North Africa, both of which owed their Christian lineage to the East. Rome was the capital of the Roman Empire, but it did not become a

3. Woods, *The Spirituality*, 49.

significant ecclesiastical center until the third century, and its dominance of western Christendom lay far in the future.[4]

The Ancient British Church

By the fourth century two forms of Christianity had taken root. In the area of effective Roman occupation, the main population centers of present-day England and Wales, close ties were maintained with the church in Roman Gaul, and Christianity adopted typical European patterns. The bishop of London served as primate of a traditional episcopate. Bishops Restitutus of London, Eborius of York, and Adelphius of Caerleon attended the Synod of Arles in 314. Provincial Latin, the vernacular language of Romanized Britons, was probably used in the churches.[5]

The Edict of Milan, issued in 313 by the Emperor Constantine, legitimized Christianity throughout the Roman Empire and ended state-sponsored persecution. In 380 Theodosius I declared Christianity the official imperial religion. The end of persecution was certainly welcome; many Christians in Britain had suffered martyrdom, including the saintly Alban. Imperial support was short-lived, however. The western Roman Empire was already crumbling, and in 410 the last of the legions and many Roman settlers left Britain. Picts and Scots soon invaded Britain from the North, and waves of German tribes: Angles, Saxon, and Jutes, flooded in from continental Europe.

The influx of pagans presented rich missionary opportunities. But the British church was ill-equipped to exploit them.[6] The episcopate collapsed, collective worship all but ceased, and church buildings were left in ruins.[7] Latin ceased to be spoken, and Old English replaced Gaelic as the vernacular language. The indigenous population migrated to other Celtic lands, including Brittany ("Little Britain"), or were absorbed into the new Anglo-Saxon culture.

4. By the time Christianity became the official religion of the Roman Empire, imperial power was centered on Constantinople. Challenges to the legitimacy of control of the English church by the Church of Rome in the late Middle Ages often appealed to British Christianity's independent origins. See for example Rankin, *A Handbook*, 17.

5. Thomas, *Christianity*, 80. Latin in the Roman provinces absorbed many indigenous words and pronunciations. Conversely, indigenous languages absorbed many Latin words.

6. Grafton, *The Lineage*, 64.

7. Reportedly some stone church buildings were restored by Augustine after his arrival in 597. Thomas, *Christianity*, 144–46.

England would soon be dominated by three large kingdoms: Wessex in the southwest, Mercia in the midlands, and Northumbria in the northeast. Kent, in southeast England, was settled by Jutes and remained an independent kingdom until the eighth century.

The Celtic Church

Elsewhere on the Atlantic seaboard Celtic Christianity took root. It was strongest in Ireland, which escaped Roman occupation, and in western Britain, where occupation was weak. It also gained a foothold in Brittany in northwest France and Galicia in northwest Spain. The Celts spoke Gaelic languages, but whether Gaelic was used in the liturgy is unclear. We do know that Latin was used in later times.

We may speak of a "Celtic church." But it had no centralized authority, and beliefs and practices probably varied from place to place. In some areas Celtic Christianity overlapped with the British church. Contacts with Christianity on the continent of Europe were mostly via Britain, and when the British church collapsed, those contacts became rare. The timing of Easter was determined by the Hebrew lunar calendar. In consequence, Easter in the Celtic church coincided with the Jewish Passover but not with Easter elsewhere in Europe, where newer formulas were used.

Hard facts concerning the Celts are scarce and often overshadowed by romantic speculation. We do know that Celtic society was built on a clan system in which extended families lived in village communities. Clans were ruled by petty kings or chieftains, and druids served the people's spiritual needs. With the coming of Christianity, priests replaced the druids, but the village structure remained largely unchanged. Communities were self-sufficient and had little interest in the larger world.

The great strength of the Celtic church lay in its monasteries. The earliest monasteries, which preserved the character of the village communities from which they evolved, housed whole families. Even when monasteries took on more conventional patterns of celibacy, "double monasteries" were common in which monks and nuns slept in separate quarters but shared work and worship facilities. Secular clergy and even some abbots were married.[8] Women enjoyed substantial equality in Celtic society, and privileges carried over into Celtic Christianity. Abbesses of

---

8. Woods, *The Spirituality*, 20. Secular clergy did not take monastic vows.

single or double monasteries exercised considerable power within their communities and sometimes over a wider area. Despite this semblance of liberalism, there was no laxity in spiritual discipline. Some monks, notably the *Culdees*, or "Servants of God," embraced ascetic practices as extreme as those of the Desert Fathers or the Stylites of Syria.

A diocesan episcopate had little relevance in a monastically based culture and a country without towns. Nevertheless, while contacts with continental Europe continued, efforts were made to build an Irish episcopate. In 431 Pope Celestine reportedly sent Palladius to be Ireland's first bishop.[9] He was followed by Patrick, a romanized Briton who had once been a slave in Ireland. According to tradition Patrick was consecrated by Bishop Germanus, probably at the abbey of Auxerre, Gaul, and established his see at Armagh in 433. Yet a well-defined Irish episcopate may not have existed before the eleventh century.

A stronger episcopate took root in present-day Wales, where a few Roman cities provided suitable diocesan centers. The first bishop may have been Dyfrig of Llandaff, around the turn of the sixth century. Legend recounts that Germanus consecrated him archbishop of Wales, but the timing is suspect. Dyfrig reportedly consecrated Deiniol first bishop of Bangor in 516.[10]

Ninian, another romanized Briton, who may have been a contemporary of Patrick's, brought Christianity to Scotland. After studying in Rome, according to eighth-century accounts, he founded a monastery at Whithorn in southwest Scotland. He converted the Picts of the lowlands, but they soon abandoned their faith. More successful was the Irish monk Columba (521–97), who established a monastery on the island of Iona in 563. Missionaries founded churches and monasteries at several other locations in the Hebrides, which had long been colonized by Irish settlers.[11] They also traveled to parts of the Scottish mainland. Columba reportedly reached Aberdeen and even visited the Orkney Islands off the northern coast.

Iona became the leading center of Celtic Christianity, even surpassing Armagh in importance. Its missionaries preached to the pagan Celts in northern Britain and, in due course, the Germanic settlers in England.

9. Ibid., 18, 49. Palladius may have died within a year.

10. Ibid., 40. Another date given for Deiniol's consecration is 545.

11. The Scots came from Ireland and intermarried with the Picts and other indigenous groups. "Scot" was later applied to all Scottish people.

In 635 Aidán, a Scottish monk from Iona, founded the famous monastery of Lindisfarne, off the Northumbrian coast. Iona, Lindisfarne, and the twin monasteries of Wearmouth and Jarrow, founded a century later, all became significant centers of spiritually, scholarship, and the arts. The seventh century represented the zenith of Celtic Christianity. But by then the church faced serious competition from the Southeast.

Augustine of Canterbury

Pope Gregory I sent his own missionaries into Kent, led by Augustine, former prior of a Benedictine abbey in Rome.[12] At the invitation of King Æthelbert, Augustine established a mission at Canterbury in 597 CE. In the "miracle at Canterbury," 10,000 people are said to have been baptized on Christmas Day. Augustine became first in the long line of archbishops of Canterbury. His papal mandate identified Canterbury as the metropolitan diocese of England, displacing the earlier primacy of London.

Conflict was inevitable as missionaries from Iona and Canterbury crisscrossed England, trying to win converts to their respective traditions. The pope had given Augustine authority over Christianity throughout the British Isles, but the Celtic abbots and bishops rejected it. In retaliation, the Roman missionaries declared Celtic baptisms and ordinations invalid.[13] They regarded the Celtic church as being in schism and confronted it over matters of authority, organizational structure, the timing of Easter, observance of the Sabbath, women's roles, and even such issues as the style of the clerical tonsure.

King Oswy of Northumbria convened a synod at the monastery of St Hilda at Whitby in 664.[14] The ostensible purpose was to resolve the timing of Easter; but it was widely understood that the outcome would determine Iona's or Canterbury's supremacy. Colman of Lindisfarne, Iona's representative, could not match the rhetoric of Canterbury's Wilfred. The latter reminded his opponents that they would meet Peter at the gate when they died. The whole of Christendom, he claimed, observed the day prescribed by Rome "except only these and their accomplices in obstinacy, I mean the Picts and the Britons, who foolishly, in these

---

12. Augustine probably took that name upon induction into the Benedictine order. Augustine of Canterbury is not to be confused with Augustine of Hippo.

13. Hardinge, *The Celtic Church*, 18–20.

14. Hilda (c. 614–80) was the double monastery's founding abbess.

two remote islands of the world . . . oppose all the rest of the universe."[15] Oswy was won over to the Roman cause, and Northumbria adopted Roman observances. Little by little the Celtic monasteries surrendered their autonomy and were brought under the Benedictine Rule.

By the late eighth century Roman Christianity had spread to most of England and Wales.[16] Celtic Christianity survived in Ireland, but in the ninth century it suffered increasingly from Viking raids, and many monasteries were destroyed. In 1155 the English pope, Adrian IV, gave King Henry II sovereignty over Ireland, and fourteen years later an Anglo-Norman army invaded Ireland at the "invitation" of the king of Leinster. Although much of the country remained under local rule, the invasion marked the beginning of English political domination that lasted until the twentieth century.

Although the churches and monasteries of Scotland also suffered greatly from Viking incursions, the Celtic church survived at least until the eleventh century. Efforts to bring the church into communion with Rome began with Queen Margaret (c. 1045–93), consort of Scottish King Malcolm III and sister of an Anglo-Saxon king. Malcolm's successor, David I, founded the first Benedictine monastery in Scotland, and Scottish Christianity was soon romanized. But Celtic culture survived into the eighteenth century in the clan structure and Gaelic language of the Scottish highlands. Efforts are now being made to revive it.

THE MEDIEVAL ENGLISH CHURCH

Canterbury's victory at the Synod of Whitby and improved travel and communications led to English Christianity's integration into the "unified" medieval Church.[17] Ignatius of Antioch had introduced the term *catholic* at the turn of the second century: "Wheresoever the bishop shall appear, there let the people be, even as where Jesus may be, there is the universal [Greek: *katholikos*] church."[18] The phrase "one, holy, catholic and apostolic church" was incorporated into the Nicene Creed, and ecclesiastical leaders in both Rome and Constantinople began to speak of "the Catholic Church."

15. Bede, *Ecclesiastical History*, book 3, XXV.

16. Hardinge, *The Celtic Church*, 22–23.

17. Unity was never complete, but the early Middle Ages witnessed the closest approximation ever achieved.

18. Ignatius of Antioch, *Epistle to the Smyrnaeans*, 8.

The English church preserved many Celtic traditions. The love of nature and the optimism of the Celtic spirit—albeit combined with ascetic discipline—passed into medieval English Christianity. The English church also preserved great reverence for music, art, and poetry.

Lindisfarne remained the center of Christianity in Northumbria, which at that time included northeast England and southeast Scotland. Etheldreda (c. 636–79), daughter of an Anglo-Saxon king, was given in marriage first to a Prince Tolbert and, after his death, to the king of Northumberland. But by that time Etheldreda had developed a religious vocation and, with two female attendants, fled to the Isle of Ely, in Cambridgeshire. In 673 she founded a double monastery, which eventually became Ely Cathedral.

Missionaries from Anglo-Saxon England continued to travel to continental Europe. Boniface, a Benedictine monk from Wessex, became the "Apostle of Germany." According to legend, in 723 Boniface challenged the god Thor to strike him dead if he cut down a sacred oak tree in northern Hesse. Not only did Boniface live, but an unexpected gale toppled the tree. Impressed by the power of the Christian God, the people of Hesse converted to Christianity.

The English church confronted, and surmounted, many obstacles. At the end of the eighth century Vikings began to raid England. Lindisfarne was destroyed in 793, and monks were slain or sold into slavery. The few who escaped founded a new Benedictine monastery at Durham. Initially the raids were for booty; monasteries' rich collections of artwork and liturgical regalia made them favored targets. But within a hundred years Danes had settled large areas of northern and eastern England. For a short time, the kings of Wessex managed to unify England as an Anglo-Saxon nation, and the Danes were converted to Christianity. Then in 1066 the Normans, French of Norse origin, conquered England and established a new dynasty under William I. Norman French supplanted Old English as the preferred secular language, while Latin continued to be used in the church.

The Norman invaders were Christian, and they viewed themselves as reformers of Christianity in "backward" Anglo-Saxon England. William I even had papal encouragement for his invasion. The conquerors tried, fortunately with only partial success, to eradicate Anglo-Saxon culture. Artwork and manuscripts were destroyed or sent to France. In some cases French liturgies replaced Anglo-Saxon ones. Senior ecclesiastical positions were filled by Normans; for instance, Osmund, a French noble-man, was appointed bishop of Sarum—present-day Salisbury—in 1078.

Papal authority over the English church was relatively weak throughout the Anglo-Saxon period and even into the Norman period. Following European custom, William I viewed himself as head of his kingdom's church. But in 1215 King John was forced to sign the Magna Carta, which declared that "the English Church is to be free and to have all its rights fully and its liberties entirely."[19] In actuality, the "Great Charter" simply traded royal control for papal control.

From then on, Roman domination of English Christianity steadily increased. Edmund (1175–1240), archbishop of Canterbury, led an un-successful campaign to maintain independence. In 1233 he threatened John's successor, Henry III, with excommunication if the king appointed foreigners to ecclesiastical and civil offices. Henry complied, but the pope retaliated by demanding 300 benefices for members of the papal court—who would never visit their churches but would live off the income. Powerless to end the practice; Edmund resigned and was suc-ceeded by Boniface of Savoy. The incident highlighted Rome's power to intimidate monarchs and clergy. Papal legates, who served as the pope's personal representatives, could exert enormous pressure. Roman domi-nance continued until the Reformation.

Dioceses, Cathedrals, and Parishes

Canterbury retained its primacy, but in 735 the English church was divid-ed into the Provinces of Canterbury and York, a structure that survives to the present. Each province was governed by an archbishop who, in turn supervised the diocesan bishops in his jurisdiction. Dioceses typically were centered on large towns, and each bishop had a cathedral (Latin: *cathedra*, "seat").[20] A bishop was elected by the cathedral's governing body, or *chapter*, confirmed by the monarch, and consecrated by three existing bishops. Thus consecration affirmed the apostolic succession.

Roughly one-half of the cathedrals were abbey cathedrals—a unique feature of the English church that connected it with Celtic tradition. In addition to performing their monastic duties, the monks served as celebrants, acolytes, and choristers for public worship. The ab-

19. Magna Carta, §1.

20. A chair or throne was reserved for the bishop when exercising his official duties.

bot and monks also comprised the cathedral chapter. Canterbury and Winchester Cathedrals were just two of many staffed by Benedictine monks. Benedictine abbeys were ideally suited because they were usually located in urban areas, whereas contemplative orders like the Cistercians preferred the countryside.

The remaining English cathedrals, termed *secular* or *collegiate*, were governed by a dean and canons. But even secular cathedrals, like Exeter, operated in a quasi-monastic mode in which "vicars canon" and "vicars choral" lived apart from the townspeople.

The faithful in rural areas initially were served by traveling clergy sent out by abbeys or large churches. They functioned like the circuit riders of America, ministering to people in homes or barns or at "preaching crosses" along country roads.

Parishes with resident priests first appeared in the eighth century and had spread throughout England by the tenth. They quickly became the center of village life. Most parishes came into existence when aristocratic families endowed churches for their own and tenants' use. Under the practice of *advowson* (Latin: *advocatio*, "support"), local landowners provided a "benefice," "preferment," or "living," in exchange for the right to appoint clergy. The living usually included a *glebe*, a small plot of land on which the incumbent could raise crops or livestock. In the cities, guilds often endowed churches. Needless to say, the holder of a benefice owed considerable loyalty to his benefactor and would be reluctant to criticize behavior or impose harsh penances.

Many church buildings constructed during the Celtic and Anglo-Saxon periods were destroyed by Viking raids. Churches were repaired, however, and new ones erected during a period of relative peace after 950. By the eleventh century thriving churches, abbeys, and cathedrals once again graced the English landscape. A few survive to the present, including St Laurence's, Bradford-on-Avon, Wiltshire; St Mary's, Sompting, Sussex; and All Saints', Brixworth, Northamptonshire.

The Norman Conquest of 1066 ushered in another period of destruction. Many church buildings, including York Minster, were destroyed. However, the Normans embarked on a vast building program in which hundreds of new churches and cathedrals were constructed. The Normans built in Romanesque styles, with massive pillars and rounded arches. The surviving, eleventh-century Durham Cathedral is a good example.

Romanesque architecture gave way to the Gothic style, which originated in France in the twelfth century—though the term "Gothic" was not used until four centuries later.[21] Gothic architecture spread to England as soon as experienced stonemasons could be brought in. William of Sens rebuilt the choir of Canterbury Cathedral in Gothic style, following a fire in 1174. Construction of the all-Gothic Wells Cathedral, "most poetic of English cathedrals," began in 1180 and was completed in 1239.

Both Romanesque and Gothic styles used the cruciform floor plan,[22] but the latter offered slim, soaring columns, pointed arches, and large windows. Tall windows and circular rose windows provided rich opportunities for stained-glass artistry, which reached its apogee in the late Middle Ages. Spires became popular, aptly symbolizing soaring religious aspirations. But not infrequently they collapsed under their own weight or were struck by lightning. The spire of Lincoln Cathedral, atop an already high tower, collapsed in 1548. As at Canterbury, fire posed an additional, ever-present danger.

The Gothic style developed over a period of three centuries— even while some cathedrals were under construction. For example, Ely Cathedral evolved from Romanesque, when construction began in 1083, to Gothic by the time it was completed in 1375. In many cases Gothic cathedrals were built over the foundations of Romanesque or Anglo-Saxon buildings. York Minster, consecrated in 1472, was built on the site of at least three earlier structures. But the Romanesque cathedral at Sarum was demolished and the materials used to build the new Gothic Salisbury Cathedral, two miles away.[23]

Medieval churches of all sizes included a chancel, or "sanctuary," where the main ceremonies were conducted, and the nave where ordinary people assembled. In all but the smallest buildings, chancel and nave were separated by a screen. The screen in a small church might be a simple lattice, while one in a cathedral might be a massive structure supporting the organ. Large churches incorporated a choir, or *quire*, on the chancel side of the screen, providing seating for the choristers and also for the nobility. Common people stood or walked around in the

21. The term was coined after Gothic styles had fallen into disfavor and was intended to denigrate them as rude and barbaric!

22. Some English cathedrals were built with a double, "patriarchal," cross floor plan.

23. Foundation of the cathedral and the new town of Salisbury is described in Rutherford's historical novel *Sarum*, 375–90.

nave; pews were a relatively late invention. When services were not in progress, the nave might be used for social or business purposes.

Larger churches incorporated multiple side chapels. Most common was a lady chapel. The earliest known one was in the Anglo-Saxon cathedral at Canterbury, but Winchester, Salisbury, Exeter, St Albans, Chichester, and Ely all had famous lady chapels; Westminster Abbey had two. Chapels were also dedicated to popular saints or notable civic figures; chapels often served as burial sites for important patrons. Finally, most cathedrals had chantry chapels, where endowed Masses were said for the souls of the departed. Rarely did anyone but the priest attend, but endowments might specify that a daily Mass be celebrated in perpetuity.[24]

Scholarship and the Arts

The Venerable Bede (c. 672–735) was born after the Synod of Whitby, but his *Historia Ecclesiastica*, completed in the 730s, provided a comprehensive religious history of his country, including the conflict between the Celtic and Anglo-Saxon churches.

The *Historia* recorded the establishment of the twin Benedictine monasteries of Wearmouth and Jarrow. Wearmouth Abbey, dedicated to St Peter, was endowed in 674 by King Egfrith of Northumbria. Its first abbot, Benedict Biscop (c. 628–90), made several trips to the continent to bring back stonemasons and glaziers, and later to acquire books and relics. Pope Agatho took an interest in the monastery and granted it special privileges. Jarrow, endowed eight years later, was dedicated to St Paul.[25] The latter acquired fame throughout Europe for its library of several hundred volumes. Bede spent most of his life at Jarrow, and his writings are considered among the finest of the early Middle Ages. Besides the *Historia*, he produced many other works, including a new edition of the Latin Vulgate.[26] Bede died while translating the fourth gospel into Old English.[27]

24. Chantries were abolished at the Reformation, and funds confiscated.

25. Farmer, *The Age of Bede*, 30–31.

26. The Latin Vulgate, translated by Jerome, was the standard Bible for western Christianity.

27. Aldhelm, bishop of Sherborne, may have translated the psalms into Old English a few decades earlier.

Wilfred, who led the Roman contingent at Whitby, served as abbot of Ripon, Northumbria, and bishop of York in the 670s.[28] He built several churches as well as Hexham Abbey, endowed by Queen Æthelthryth. Wilfred also commissioned works of art, including altar cloths of silk with gold threads. A gospel book, written on parchment with gold leaf lettering, was enclosed in a gold case set with gems.

The richly illustrated Lindisfarne Gospels were produced in the 710s. Dedicated to the seventh-century Cuthbert, the book was enclosed in a jewel-studied leather case, sadly lost in Viking raids. In the 950s Aldred, provost of Chester-le-Street, Northumbria, translated the four gospels into Old English, inserting the translation as a *gloss* between the lines of Latin text.[29] Aldred's is the oldest extant translation of the complete gospels into the vernacular.

Anglo-Saxon Christianity absorbed the musical tradition of the Celtic church and also introduced new genres from Europe. Gregorian chant gradually became the standard Latin chant for the monastic daily offices.[30] Abbot Biscop took advantage of the papal privilege bestowed on Wearmouth to persuade John the Precentor, of St Peter's, Rome, to come to the twin monasteries and teach the monks "the system of chanting and reading."[31]

The *proper* of the Mass, the parts that changed from day to day, was set to Gregorian and other medieval chants. Eventually the monophonic styles of Gregorian chant were enriched by harmony. Polyphonic settings of the unchanging *ordinary* of the Mass appeared in the fourteenth century. The pipe organ appeared in the West in the eighth or ninth century.[32] Organs were popular not only because of their richness of sound but because they could be heard in large cathedrals. By the fifteenth century, brass, woodwind, and stringed instruments added to the sacred musical repertory.

Monasteries and cathedral schools in the British Isles kept the flame of learning burning during the "Dark Ages." Their scholars were in great

---

28. Wilfred, who doubted the validity of the Celtic succession, was consecrated in Gaul.

29. Brown, *The Lindisfarne Gospels*, 90–92.

30. Named for the sixth-century Gregory I, the chant actually owes more to composers in eighth-century Carolingian France.

31. Bright, *Early Chapters*, 354–55.

32. Williams, P., & Owen, *The Organ*, 42–61.

demand as continental Europe awakened from its long slumber. Alcuin of York (c. 735–804) became a tutor to Charlemagne in 781. Fifteen years later he was appointed abbot of the famous monastery of St Martin at Tours, where he established a school, library, and scriptorium. Under Alcuin's leadership the scriptorium achieved the notable productivity of three complete Bibles per year. The Irish scholar John Scotus Eriugena (810–77?) was invited to the court of Charlemagne's grandson Charles the Bald.[33] The twelfth-century John of Salisbury served as bishop of Chartres, France. The cathedral school of Chartres, whose intellectual preeminence lasted 200 years, was founded by his predecessor, Bishop Fulbert.

The schools of Aachen and Chartres retained their traditional Platonic orientation, filtered through Neoplatonism and the writings of Augustine of Hippo.[34] But the Aristotelian revival that nurtured scholasticism was already beginning. Arabic versions of the works of Aristotle and other Greek writers reached Europe in the eleventh and twelfth centuries, and translation into Latin quickly followed.[35] Among the translators was Robert Grosseteste (c. 1175–1253), bishop of Lincoln. He wrote a commentary on Aristotle and is also remembered for treatises on science and aesthetics. Grosseteste's most famous student was Franciscan friar Roger Bacon. In the thirteenth century Peter of Hibernia lectured at the University of Naples and introduced the young Thomas Aquinas to Aristotle's works.[36]

BELIEFS AND PRACTICES IN THE MEDIEVAL CHURCH

Doctrine

The Celts were drawn less to theological speculation than to probing the mysteries of faith through the arts, devotion, and mysticism. But they had great reverence for scripture, particularly the Old Testament. Most widely read was the Old Latin Bible, known as the *Textus Itala*, which was also popular in Gaul and North Africa and may date from the second century.[37] Later, as we have seen, the Celts and Anglo-Saxons

33. Carabine, *John Scottus*, 18–20.

34. By that time scholastics knew little Greek and had to rely on Latin translations of Plato and Aristotle.

35. Greek manuscripts had been lost in the West, but Islamic scholars had translated them into Arabic.

36. Fox, *Sheer Joy*, 14.

37. Hardinge, *The Celtic Church*, 31. See also Jülicher, *An Introduction*.

devoted much effort to copying and illuminating the scriptures, even translating them into the vernacular.

Celtic Christianity preserved the beliefs and practices of third- and fourth-century Christendom but, because of increasing isolation, remained unaware of later developments. Patrick's teachings on the Trinity were basically Pauline, with little definition of the role of the Holy Spirit.[38] In consequence the Celtic church occasionally was accused of Arianism. A Judaic view of the afterlife seems to have been common, in which only the righteous won immortality. Celtic optimism may have rejected notions of an eternal hell. That optimism was also expressed in the embrace of the teachings of Pelagius and his Irish disciple Celleagh. Pelagianism, condemned by the Council of Ephesus in 431, questioned the force of original sin and asserted that man, by nature, was capable of moral choice.

More firmly integrated with mainstream Christianity, the Anglo-Saxon church embraced the christological and trinitarian decrees of the ecumenical councils. The later Anglo-Saxons and Normans would have been familiar with the amendment to the Nicene Creed. The original wording was: "We believe in the Holy Spirit, the Lord, the giver of life, who proceeds from the Father." Augustine of Hippo urged that it be amended to read: "proceeds from the Father and the Son" (*ex Patre, Filioque procedit*). The *filioque* clause was endorsed by the Synod of Toledo in 589, with support from Charlemagne, and finally was approved by Pope Benedict VIII in 1014. The amendment was never accepted by the Eastern churches and became a major point of contention in the East–West schism of 1054.

Scholasticism dominated western theology from the eleventh century until the Renaissance. Scholastics, or "schoolmen," were professional scholars, typically attached to major institutions of learning. Most famous of the early scholastics was the Italian-born Anselm (c. 1033–1109), archbishop of Canterbury. Robert Grosseteste and Peter of Hibernia have already been mentioned. Scholasticism reached its peak with the work of Dominican friars Albertus Magnus (c. 1198–1280) and Thomas Aquinas (1225–74). Another notable figure was the Scottish Franciscan friar John Duns Scotus (1266–1308) who lectured at the universities of Oxford, Paris, and Cologne.

The scholastics acknowledged that some mysteries lay beyond the reach of the human mind but insisted that what we accept on faith must

38. Hardinge, *The Celtic Church*, 54–55.

be reasonable and internally consistent. They built upon scripture, the decrees of the councils, and earlier writings to produce a great body of doctrine. In Aquinas's words: "We study what men have thought in order to discover the truth."[39] Proofs for the existence of God became popular, though it is doubtful whether they would convince nonbelievers. Anselm himself conceded: "I do not seek to understand so that I may believe, but believe so that I may understand." Scholasticism put many doctrines on a firm intellectual basis; but increasingly it ignored the experiential dimension of religion, producing a cold, abstract God, remote from the one to which scripture, the liturgy, and mysticism attested.

Sacramental Rites

Until the late Middle Ages, the number of sacramental rites in common use varied from two to ten.[40] Baptism, the "Lord's Supper," and holy orders were universally accepted. But the importance attached to other rites varied from one ecclesiastical jurisdiction to another. Decentralization in the Celtic church guaranteed broad pluralism.

Adult baptism, combined with confirmation, was typical of primitive Christianity and most likely was practiced in both the ancient British church and the Celtic church. The Celts favored baptism by triple immersion. Immersion recalled Christ's baptism in the Jordan as well as his death and resurrection; it also recalled ancient initiation rites of death and rebirth. A white veil or cloth, anticipating the baptismal gown of later centuries, was often placed over the catechumen's head to signify purity. Newly baptized persons were welcomed into the church by ceremonial foot-washing.[41] Foot-washing was also incorporated into a number of other Celtic sacraments—even into the Eucharist, recalling that Christ washed his disciples' feet at the Last Supper.[42] Augustine of Canterbury eliminated the practice only with difficulty in the Anglo-Saxon church.[43]

The Celtic church may have been among the last to accept infant baptism. When infant baptism became common, confirmation evolved into a separate sacrament. Anglo-Saxon practice was to confirm chil-

---

39. Pegis, *Introduction to St Thomas*, xv.
40. Ware, *The Orthodox Church*, 275.
41. Hardinge, *The Celtic Church*, 101–10.
42. Ibid., 117–19.
43. Ibid., 111–13.

dren when they reached puberty. Baptism, confirmation, and first Communion were viewed as rites of passage. Confirmation became a prerequisite for first Communion A common belief was that Christians were incapable of good works until they received the Holy Spirit. Chrismation—anointing with oil—in the confirmation rite also united the person with Christ, the Anointed One.

The three grades of clergy: deacons, priests or presbyters, and bishops, became standard throughout most of Christendom.[44] But abbots and presbyters played the major roles in the Celtic church; and in Ireland, little distinction was made between abbots and bishops. Furthermore, there is scant evidence of an Irish diaconate. By Anglo-Saxon times, the three grades were well-established in England, and episcopal ordination was the norm.

Belief that Christ was really present in the Eucharist was pervasive in the Celtic and Anglo-Saxon churches.[45] That belief set the Eucharist apart from other sacraments; Christ's power flowed through the other sacraments, but he was corporeally present in the Eucharist. How the corporeal presence was understood, however, and how many people seriously reflected on it, are not known. We do know that Holy Communion was distributed "under both kinds" in the early Middle Ages; communicants received the wine as well as the bread. Moreover the Irish *Stowe Missal* specified that water be mixed with the wine in the chalice.

By the eighth century the Latin Mass had acquired a form we would recognize today, and from the ninth century onward "Mass books," or *missals*, were in use in the larger dioceses. The *Stowe Missal* included Celtic rites, while the *Leofric Missal*, adopted by Bishop Leofric (1016–72) of Exeter, was based in part on ninth-century French rites. Most popular in the south of England was the eleventh-century *Sarum Rite*, or *Sarum Use*, developed by Bishop Osmund in the new diocese of Salisbury established after the Norman Conquest. Combining Anglo-Saxon and Gallic rites, the Sarum Rite provided a liturgy for the Mass and divine office. Other popular liturgies were developed in the dioceses of York, Hereford, Bangor, and Aberdeen.

The Celtic church offered a healing ministry involving chrismation in addition to the prescription of herbal medications; missionaries treat-

---

44. Notions of a threefold ministry resonated with the Trinity.

45. Hardinge, *The Celtic Church*, 119–20. The term "real presence" was not coined until the Reformation.

ed the sick as well as administering the sacraments and preaching the gospel. The *Stowe Missal* described sacramental healing and also some healing practices of pre-Christian origin.[46] An active healing ministry continued for a while in the Anglo-Saxon church. Two English bishops: Cuthbert of Lindisfarne and the eighth-century John of Beverly gained renown for their gifts.[47]

Confidence in the efficacy and propriety of sacramental healing declined in the West after Pope Gregory I taught that sickness should be accepted as atonement for sin.[48] Augustine, whom Gregory sent to England, no doubt brought the new attitude with him. Anointing of the sick was replaced by the last rites, or "extreme unction." Discouraged from seeking relief within the church's sacramental ministry, the sick turned to relics or folk medicine.

Early Christians treated sin as a betrayal of the Christian community's trust and demanded public confession. The more modern practice of private, or *auricular* ("whispered in the priest's ear"), confession is believed to have originated among the Celts and to have spread through Irish missionary activity.[49] In the seventh century *penitentials*: lists of sins and recommended penances, were published to guide priests hearing confessions. The penitentials provide insights into the sins heard—or imagined—by experienced confessors. Celtic penitentials listed pagan practices, such as burning grains of wheat where a person had died and even eating horse meat.[50] Later penitentials tended to focus on sins of a sexual nature.

Celtic asceticism carried over into rugged penitential practices. The Celts believed that atonement should match the seriousness of sin and that the soul must be healed by whatever means necessary. Penances included rigorous fasting, long pilgrimages, public humiliation, self-mortification, flogging, even amputation—a literal response to Matthew 5:30.[51]

In the Anglo-Saxon church and elsewhere, the harshest penances fell into disuse. But lighter penances led to fear of longer sentences in purgatory. Indulgences provided a remedy for those who planned

46. Ibid., 120–21.

47. Perry et al., *A Time to Heal*, 33.

48. Nash, J. F., "Esoteric Healing," 37–50.

49. Hardinge, *The Celtic Church*, 135–51.

50. Ibid.

51. Ibid.

ahead. Granted by papal authority, indulgences were attached to saying certain prayers, visiting certain shrines, serving on crusades, or donating money. Indulgence sales funded construction of the new basilica of St Peter's, Rome. The practice led to widespread abuse in which there was the perception of "buying forgiveness for sin."[52]

Prayers for the dead could also reduce the time in purgatory. They might even tip the balance between heaven and hell. A tenth-century offertory from the Requiem Mass pleaded: "O Lord Jesus Christ, King of Glory, deliver the souls of all the faithful departed from the pains of hell and from the deep pit; deliver them from the jaws of the lion, lest they fall into darkness and the black gulf swallows them up. But let thy standard-bearer, blessed Michael, bring them into that holy light which of old thou didst promise to Abraham and his seed."[53]

Marriage was not regarded as a sacrament until comparatively late in the Middle Ages. Boniface complained that the English people "utterly despise matrimony . . . refuse to have legitimate wives, and continue to live in lechery and adultery after the manner of neighing horses and braying asses."[54] The church had to tolerate divorce, polygamy, and concubinage at all levels of society,[55] even among the clergy. The ideal of lifelong, monogamous marriage did not win universal acceptance until the end of the first millennium. Even then marriage was seen primarily as a common-law union. Church weddings and prohibition against premarital sex were not enforced until the sixteenth century.[56]

The canon of seven sacraments: baptism, confirmation, the Eucharist, penance, extreme unction, holy orders, and matrimony, was suggested by the twelfth-century Peter Lombard and confirmed by the Council of Florence (1439). All seven were declared to have been instituted by Christ, though some of the sacraments cannot easily be traced back to scripture or apostolic usage. Other rites, like burial, exorcism, and profession of monastic vows, were demoted to the lower status of "sacramentals."

52. Indulgences never were intended to absolve sin, but unscrupulous indulgence salesmen sometimes misrepresented their products.

53. Robertson, *Requiem*, 21.

54. Taylor, G., *Sex in History*, 11.

55. Charlemagne was widowed twice but had four wives and several concubines.

56. MacCulloch, *The Reformation*, 634.

Popular Piety

Until the fifth century Celtic Christians observed the Sabbath on Saturday, beginning at sunset on Friday evening.[57] Sunday, "Lord's Day," observance eventually took root, but during a transition period many Celts observed both a day of rest and a day of worship. Devout Celts fasted, as Eastern Orthodox Christians still do, every Wednesday and Friday throughout the year as well as during Lent. Judaic proscriptions against certain type of food allegedly were observed in some places.[58]

When Christianity came to the Celtic lands it overlaid a rich tradition of folklore, storytelling, and song. It also became intertwined with druid mythology, strong links to the earth, and belief in nature spirits. The spoken or sung word had great power, and Celtic Christians became renowned for their blessings and curses.[59] The blessings that have come down to us reveal great poetic sensitivity. Sacred places were venerated, and special days were observed, like All Hallows' Eve.[60] Numerous saints—some confused unintentionally or intentionally with pagan gods and goddesses—had their festivals.[61] Saints' days also filled the liturgical calendar of the Anglo-Saxon church, and there we find the developing tradition of intercession to the saints.

Mary the mother of Jesus gained a special place in devotion and intercession. Marian devotion may have extended back to earliest times, and the ancient church at Glastonbury allegedly was dedicated to her. But its popularity increased after the Council of Ephesus declared her *Theotokos*, rendered by Cyril of Alexandria as "Mother of God."[62] Devotion gained further momentum in England after the arrival of Augustine. Twenty churches reportedly were dedicated to Mary by 800, and 2,000 by the time of the Reformation. Lincoln already had a St Mary's church, but when Remigius de Fécamp, the diocese's first bishop, ordered

---

57. Sunday observance began in Palestine around 70 CE, but it was not accepted universally until the end of the eighth century.

58. Hardinge, *The Celtic Church*, 196–98.

59. Woods, *The Spirituality*, 145–60. The Celtic saints were known to curse their enemies, but the *anathemas* issued by the ecumenical councils were curses on a much larger scale.

60. Sacred sites, where people felt particularly close to the unseen world, were referred to as "thin places." Holy days were "thin times."

61. Woods, *The Spirituality*, 144–45.

62. *Theotokos* literally means "God Bearer."

the construction of a cathedral in 1072, it too was dedicated to her. Most large churches had lady chapels as well as Marian statuary, paintings, and stained glass. Shrines proliferated, and relics were bought and sold.

Anselm dedicated three poems to Mary, one of which began: "Mary, great Mary, most blessed of all Marys, greatest among all women, great Lady, great beyond measure, I long to love you with all my heart."[63] Other fervent devotees were Edmund of Canterbury, Richard of Chichester, and Thomas Becket. Simon Stock, prior-general of the Carmelite Order, reported a vision of Mary in 1251 in which he received the brown scapular with the explanation: "This is for you and yours a privilege; the one who dies in it will be saved." The scapular became the order's traditional habit.

England proudly called itself "Mary's Dowry." Mary was seen as the compassionate intercessor between the faithful and a less accessible, or less sympathetic, Christ. Bishop Grosseteste insisted that his flock in Lincoln learn the Hail Mary as well as the Lord's Prayer. As reports of miracles accumulated, people began to pray more to Mary than to Christ, and devotion expanded to the level of adoration. In 1060 England became the first country to celebrate the feast of the assumption.

Sunday observance was well-established in Anglo-Saxon and Norman times, and attendance at Mass became obligatory. But, with increasing separation between clergy and laity, and between nobility and peasantry, the peasant laity was excluded from active participation. The Mass was celebrated behind a screen, recalling Jewish rituals in the Holy of Holies. Ordinary people, confined to the church nave, watched the clergy and social elite process into the chancel or quire. Then they stood or walked around, seeing nothing and hearing little more than the bells rung during the service. The faithful received Holy Communion only a few times a year. Sermons were rare, and singing—by choirs only—was confined to cathedrals and monasteries. Medieval congregations were bored and disorderly.

What ordinary people did see were statues, frescoes, and stained-glass windows—the "poor man's Bible"—depicting biblical and other religious stories. Crucifixes were prominently displayed, and sacred symbols were carved into stone- or woodwork. The masses of people also enjoyed the colorful processions on major feasts. Statues, relics, and sometimes the Sacrament were carried through the streets with great pageantry. Laypeople followed the clergy and chanted the litany

63. Anselm, *Third Great Prayer.*

responses: *ora pro nobis* ("pray for us"), *miserere nobis* ("have mercy on us"), and *libera nos* ("deliver us").

People also watched outdoor dramas, or "morality plays," performed on major festivals. A scene in a religious drama was called a *pagent*, from which our word "pageant" is derived. Outdoor dramas, accompanied by public entertainments and fairs, reached their peak of popularity in the thirteenth and fourteenth centuries. But efforts to suppress dramas began in the fifteenth century, after they degenerated into tasteless spectacles, often mocking the clergy.[64]

Those who had the means and could escape work responsibilities went on pilgrimages to sacred sites associated with saints or with miracles or apparitions. The motivation might be devotion, the possibility of healing, or penance; pilgrimages were especially popular during Lent and Advent. The shrine of Our Lady of Walsingham became a much-visited pilgrimage destination after Richeldis de Faverches, a devout Saxon noblewoman, had a vision of Mary there in 1061. Geoffrey Chaucer's (c. 1343–1400) *Canterbury Tales* described pilgrimages to Canterbury, where Thomas Becket was murdered in 1170.

The Religious Life

Monasteries formed the very basis of Celtic Christianity. But the Celtic church had no religious orders; each monastery was independent, and monks owed obedience only to their abbot or abbess. With Augustine's arrival, the Benedictine Order, established by Benedict of Nursia in the sixth century, spread to England and soon dominated Anglo-Saxon monasticism.

The level of asceticism in Anglo-Saxon and Norman monasteries varied greatly. Some communities emulated Celtic asceticism, while others provided comfortable retirement for wealthy patrons. Dunstan (c. 909–88), abbot of Glastonbury and later archbishop of Canterbury, campaigned against monastic laxity. The Cistercians, Carthusians, and other new orders were established in the eleventh and twelfth centuries to recover the original rigor of the Benedictine rule. Many new houses were founded after the Norman Conquest, ushering in the golden age of English monasticism. Religious orders became powerful, and monasteries accumulated extensive land holdings.

64. Schaff, *History of the Christian Church*, vol. V, ch. XVI, §134.

Some ascetics shunned the communal life in favor of complete isolation, perpetual prayer, and contemplation. But rather than retreating to remote hermitages, like the Desert Fathers, medieval anchorites lived in cells built into the walls of churches. They depended on others to supply necessities like food, while those of means employed servants to bring devotional literature and writing materials. Best known of the medieval anchorites was Julian of Norwich (c. 1342–1416) who lived in a tiny cell in the church of St Julian in Norwich, England.[65] During her long seclusion, she had sixteen visions of Christ which inspired a series of books, including *Revelations of Divine Love*. Like many mystics, she was depressed by the prospect that so many people faced eternal punishment. But Christ reassured her: "It is sooth that sin is cause of all this pain; but all shall be well, and all shall be well, and all manner of thing shall be well."[66]

The thirteenth century saw the creation of mendicant friars (Latin: *mendicus*, "beggar"). Friars led itinerant lives, relying on charitable contributions to survive. The recently founded Franciscans, or "Grey Friars," and Dominicans, or "Black Friars"—named for the color of their habits—arrived in England in the 1220s. Also, two previously cloistered orders, the Carmelites and Augustinians, were converted to mendicants, becoming respectively the "White Friars" and "Austin Friars." Related religious orders were established for women, but they were enclosed; begging was considered improper for women and the itinerant life too dangerous.

Establishment of the mendicant orders was opposed both by traditional monastic orders and by the episcopate. But the four major orders of friars gained papal approval, and the Second Council of Lyons (1274) gave them autonomy from local bishops and extensive rights to preach, say Mass, and hear confessions. The mendicants had a lasting impact on English religious history. They did not beg for long, however. Within a few decades the mendicants set up friaries, which acquired considerable wealth—though never on the scale of the monasteries.

PRELUDE TO THE REFORMATION

Decline of the Western Church

Over the course of the Middle Ages institutional Christianity built an impressive organizational structure. Sadly, moral laxity, corruption,

---

65. "Julian's" real name is not recorded.
66. Julian, *Showings*.

and pastoral ineffectiveness became pervasive. The church became self-serving and disconnected from the spiritual needs of the faithful.

The papal court was more opulent, and more decadent, than most of the royal courts of Europe. A sixty-year period in the tenth century became known as the "pornocracy." Scandals rose to a disgusting climax during the pontificate of Alexander VI, at the turn of the sixteenth century.[67] By then the political power of the papacy was in decline, after reaching its peak under Boniface VIII in 1300. From 1305 to 1378 popes were prisoners of the French king at Avignon. Then, for thirty-nine years, two and eventually three men claimed the chair of Peter. The conciliar movement of the fifteenth century pitted councils of bishops against the pope in a contest for supremacy. Despite those various problems, Roman dominance of western Christendom continued unabated.

Moral failings also occurred closer to home. In Scotland, "Bishops lived openly in concubinage and married their daughters into the ranks of the nobility."[68] When the Earl of Crawford married in 1546, his wife was identified in the marriage records as the eldest daughter of Cardinal David Beaton, archbishop of St Andrews. In the opening volleys of the Scottish Reformation, Beaton was murdered in his own castle, reportedly after spending the night with a mistress.[69] The bishop of Winchester operated brothels in the London parish of Southwark; they were finally closed because of a syphilis epidemic.[70] Denied the comfort of marriage, many priests kept "housekeepers."

Corruption was rampant in the English church. Cathedral chapters often were coerced into voting for the king's nominees for bishoprics. Political patronage became more important than saintliness or even education. The stakes were high; medieval bishops were major landowners and retained huge retinues. Lust for material rewards and power was rife, and overlap between ecclesiastical and civic offices only increased temptations for wrongdoing. As many people observed, the affluence and arrogance of the episcopate contrasted sharply with the humility and poverty of Jesus.

Lucrative positions at cathedrals, collegiate churches, and well-endowed parishes were filled from the ranks of the gentry on the basis of patronage or for a fee. Ambitious clergy accumulated multiple livings,

---

67. Nash, J. F., *Christianity*, vol. 1, 144–48.

68. Schaff. *History of the Christian Church*, vol. VI, ch. IX, §73.

69. Ibid.

70. MacCulloch, *The Reformation*, 632.

delegating parochial responsibilities to curates. Some "clergy" never visited their benefices or even bothered to take holy orders.[71] As early as the ninth century Gildas the Wise observed clergy who were "wallowing, after the fashion of swine, in their old and unhappy puddle of intolerable wickedness, after they have attained unto the seat of the priesthood or episcopal dignity (who neither have been installed, or resident on the same), for usurping only the name of priesthood, they have not received the orders or apostolical preeminence."[72]

Appointments to rural parishes were made from the peasantry, and there the main problem was ineffectiveness. Some saintly men served in the parish ministry, but many more were unsuited to their responsibilities; "vocations" might be nothing more than a desire to avoid military service. Priests were poor, uneducated, and poorly supervised by their bishops. Livings and tithes were inadequate, and the meager income had to be divided four ways, to the priest, the bishop, the poor, and upkeep of the church.[73] Clergy often were reduced to petty crime to survive.

Training for the priesthood was minimal. Clergy learned the Latin liturgy by rote, with little or no understanding of its meaning, and stumbled, or mumbled, their way through the Mass. It hardly mattered to the laity who heard little and understood less. Sermons were beyond the capability of the average priest.

Efforts to improve the situation were made in the thirteenth century. The Fourth Lateran Council in 1215 imposed penalties on clergy for intoxication, hunting, or fighting; it also sought to enforce celibacy. The establishment of orders of friars helped meet the need for preaching and teaching. But the mendicant orders' ideals became clouded, and the burden of administering properties took time and energy away from their ministries.

The failure of pastoral care became critical at times of hardship. During the Black Death of the 1340s and '50s many clergy deserted their flocks and fled. People began to question the church's legitimacy and relevance. The majority grumbled but remained within the church, others were expelled, and still others sought God elsewhere. Grassroots movements arose as people searched for spiritual comfort and for bet-

71. Moorman, *A History of the Church*, 97–98.

72. Gildas, *On the Ruin*, §66. Parenthesis in original. Gildas also depicted clergy as "deceitful raveners" and "belly beasts."

73. Moorman, *A History of the Church*, 99.

ter ways to express their religious aspirations. One such movement was spearheaded by John Wycliffe.

Ironically, the latter stages of the institutional church's decline paralleled one of the most exciting times in European history, the Renaissance. The Renaissance was multifaceted, stimulating innovations in philosophy, religion, the arts, science, and education. Beginning in Italy in the fourteenth century, it spread to the rest of Europe over the next 200 years.

Education, which had long been dedicated to training clergy, was now valued for its intrinsic and social benefits; as a result, an educated laity emerged for the first time. Scholarship, which had been pursued mainly at cathedrals and monasteries, moved to secular institutions—though, ironically, Dominicans and Franciscans soon played prominent roles. The Universities of Paris, Oxford, Cambridge, and St Andrews embraced new fields of inquiry—even fields that embarrassed the church. Doctrine was sometimes shown to rest on obscure scriptural passages or dubious translations. In 1440 the Italian humanist Lorenzo Valla demonstrated that the *Donation of Constantine*, which purportedly gave popes temporal control of the western Roman Empire, was a forgery.

Scholars undertook critical analyses of scriptural texts in Latin, Greek, and Hebrew. Dutch humanist Desiderius Erasmus (c. 1467–1536) collected ancient texts to prepare a new Greek edition of the New Testament. Known as the *Textus Receptus* ("Received Text"), it formed a basis of both Luther's German Bible and the King James Bible.

John Wycliffe

John Wycliffe (c. 1325–84), a contemporary of Julian of Norwich's, was a priest and, for a while, master of Balliol College, Oxford. Deliberately inviting controversy, Wycliffe declared that the pope was the Antichrist. He attacked clerical abuses, criticized ecclesiastical taxes, and advocated the confiscation of church property. He claimed that the Mass had no basis in scripture and denied the real present in the Eucharist.

Not surprisingly Wycliffe outraged church officials, but political support shielded him from their wrath. Relief from taxes appealed to the poor, and the prospect of sharing seized property appealed to the nobility. When Pope Gregory XI condemned him as a heretic in 1377, John of Gaunt and other powerful individuals protected him.[74] Ordinary people rallied around Wycliffe in a pietist movement known as the "Lollards," a derogatory Dutch term implying that they muttered their prayers. Wycliffe also organized the "Poor Priests" who, like the Waldensian Poor Men of Lyon, embraced lives of austerity that contrasted with episcopal opulence.[75]

Wycliffe believed that scripture was the only legitimate source of religious authority. But ordinary people could not understand the Latin Vulgate, so he spent the last several years of his life translating the New Testament into English. It appeared four years after his death, along with a translation of the Old Testament by his friend Nicholas of Hereford. Angered by the new Bible, William Courtenay, archbishop of Canterbury, denounced Wycliffe as a "pestilent wretch of damnable heresy who, as a complement of his wickedness, invented a new translation of the Scriptures into his mother tongue."[76] Distribution was limited by the laborious process of manual copying; Gutenberg's printing press was not perfected until 1450.[77] Nevertheless, Wycliffe's Bible was the only complete English translation until Tyndale's appeared in the 1520s.

Wycliffe died of natural causes, still holding his living in Leicestershire. The Poor Priests were suppressed, but the Lollards gained in both numbers and influence—ensuring their downfall. The bishops felt threatened by a powerful group advocating the democratization of religion, and the king felt threatened by the very notion of democracy. Several Lollards were burned in 1401 and more in the years to come.[78] Others went underground, hoping for a more tolerant environment. But the Reformation was more than a century away.

Wycliffe's teachings influenced the Czech reformer Jan Hus. In 1415 Hus was lured to the Council of Constance on a treacherous guarantee of safe passage, only to be burned at the stake. The same council denounced forty-five statements attributed to Wycliffe, including: "The Roman Church is the synagogue of Satan," and "God ought to obey the devil."[79] Wycliffe's and Hus's crusades were just two of several early re-

74. Walker, Williston, *A History*, 268–69.

75. Ibid., 269–70.

76. Walker, Williston, *A History*, 270. Waldensian scholars had translated portions of the Bible into French, attracting similar denunciations.

77. The Gutenberg Bible, published in the 1450s, was in Latin.

78. Walker, Williston, *A History*, 270.

79. Council of Constance, session VIII, May 4, 1415. Historians question whether

form movements. They were ahead of their time and failed to produce lasting change. But the need for reform continued. In the sixteenth century the Reformation erupted in Germany, Switzerland, and England. But for the Renaissance, it might not have been possible.

REFLECTIONS

The church of Roman Britain and the Celtic church—both of which may possibly date from apostolic times—provide a worthy beginning to our story. While the one was short-lived, the other flourished for more than 500 years, producing great saints, scholars, and artists. Celtic Christianity provided a strong foundation for the sacramental church of the Middle Ages. The Anglo-Saxon church preserved valuable Celtic traditions as well as developing its own. Remarkably, the Church in England managed to retain a distinctive character despite the ravages of the Viking raids, Danish settlement, and Norman Conquest.

Religion penetrated the whole of medieval life. England's embrace of Christianity was strong, and its religious achievements matched those of any other country. England's reputation as Mary's Dowry—along with Ireland's as the "Island of Saints"—attested to the high level of popular devotion. But the spirituality of England was captured in a special way by the monastic system that drew upon native Celtic traditions as well as on the monastic heritage of Egypt and continental Europe.

The period from the Norman Conquest onward witnessed the best and worst of medieval Christianity. The sacramental church reached the height of splendor. The magnificence of the English churches and cathedrals affirmed society's willingness to invest vast resources for the glory of God. Those cathedrals and churches profoundly fulfilled the Celtic notion of "sacred spaces" and provided worthy settings for the pageantry of the Mass. The aesthetics and drama of Christian worship spoke to the very souls of the faithful. The period saw rich developments in sacred music and liturgy, including the Sarum Rite, a masterpiece that continues to win acclaim.

On the other hand, full participation was denied to the great majority of the people. The Mass was celebrated behind a screen, and Holy Communion was offered just a few times a year. Communion was distributed under one kind only: the bread but not the cup. Popular

---

Wycliffe ever made the latter statement.

sentiment understandably soured. Wycliffe in England, and later Ulrich Zwingli in Switzerland, gave expression to that dissatisfaction; sadly, they could not separate their contempt for clerical attitudes from contempt for sacramental Christianity. The very survival of the Mass and sacraments was threatened.

The heavy hand of Roman oppression fell on England in the thirteenth century when the papacy was at the peak of its political power but in moral and spiritual decline. Oppression was naturally resented, after the English church had enjoyed a thousand years of self-sufficiency or substantial autonomy. However, Rome cannot be blamed for the corruption of the English episcopate, the ineffectiveness of parish clergy, and the stark stratification of feudal society. We must take ownership of those weaknesses and resolve that they will never recur.

The recovery of beliefs, practices, and attitudes of the pre-Reformation English church must necessarily be selective. Few people would want to recreate in their entirety the conditions in any particular century. Anglo-Catholic aspiration is to draw upon what was good, and discard what was bad, from a period of nearly 1,500 years. In very broad terms the vision is to recover the doctrine and sacramental practices of the early centuries, the art and scholarship of the Celtic and Anglo-Saxon churches (and possibly the Renaissance), the monasticism of the tenth–twelfth centuries, and the church architecture and sacred pageantry of the twelfth and thirteenth centuries.

3

The Church of England

ESCAPING FROM ROMAN DOMINATION was easier than might have been expected. Building a church that would serve England's needs in the centuries to come, while honoring the legacy of pre-Reformation English Christianity, was much more difficult. This chapter discusses the Church of the England's struggle to define itself on the spectrum from Roman Catholicism to Calvinism. The end-result was a church that was both "catholic and reformed"—and inclusive enough to provide a spiritual home for the great majority of English people.

This chapter pays special attention to the development of a distinctive liturgy that survives largely intact today, in England and throughout the Anglican Communion. It discusses the hesitant steps toward formulating a confessional statement and touches on issues of church governance and church–state relationships. The chapter ends with some comments on the rich tradition of Anglican sacred music.

THE ENGLISH REFORMATION

In April 1509, Henry VIII (1491–1547) succeeded his father, Henry VII, as king of England, lord of Ireland, and claimant to the throne of France.[1] Shortly before his coronation, Henry had married Catherine of Aragon, daughter of Ferdinand and Isabella of Spain and his older brother's widow. Henry received a papal dispensation to contract the marriage, which would otherwise have been prohibited on grounds of affinity.

---

1. The English Pope Adrian IV had granted Ireland as a Lordship to Henry II in 1155. The claim to the French throne had little credibility at that time.

The English church at that time was in full communion with Rome. While many people had issues with ecclesiastical authority, most revered the traditions of the medieval church. However, a group of scholars at Cambridge University questioned those traditions. Desiderius Erasmus had been professor of divinity for a number of years and maintained ties with the university after he left England in 1514. He continued to influence scholars like Miles Coverdale, Thomas Cranmer, William Tyndale, and Hugh Latimer, who would play important roles in the decades to come. Erasmus was critical of Rome but distanced himself from Luther—creating an apt metaphor of the English Reformation.

On October 31, 1517, Martin Luther (1483–1546), an Augustinian friar and university professor, launched the Protestant Reformation by posting his Ninety-Five Theses on the door of the Castle Church in Wittenberg, Germany. Luther's ideas found fertile ground at Cambridge. But Henry did not share them, and in 1521 he wrote *A Defence of the Seven Sacraments* and dedicated it to the pope. An appreciative Leo X gave Henry the title *Fidei Defensor* ("Defender of the Faith"). To Rome's dismay, Henry soon initiated England's secession from the Roman communion. Ironically, British monarchs, who are constitutionally barred from becoming—or even marrying—Roman Catholics continue to use the title.

The Break with Rome

The English Reformation was motivated primarily by dynastic concerns. Henry VIII needed a male heir to assure the succession. By 1526 Catherine had conceived seven times but had borne only one surviving child, Mary. The king attributed the problem to God's curse on his marriage[2] and sent an envoy to Rome to petition for annulment. The petition, however, stalled in bureaucratic wrangling.

Angered by the delays, Henry finally took matters into his own hands. In January 1533 he secretly married Anne Boleyn, whom he had been courting for seven years. Four months later, Thomas Cranmer convened an ecclesiastical court that declared Henry's previous marriage void and validated the marriage to Anne. Cranmer (1489–1556), a priest and fellow of Jesus College, Cambridge, had been nominated archbishop of Canterbury but had not yet been consecrated.[3] The pope excommu-

2. Leviticus 20:21 threatened violation of affinity laws with childlessness.

3. Cranmer had taken holy orders in 1520 and was consecrated Archbishop of Canterbury in March 1533.

nicated Henry and Cranmer in July 1533. In September Anne gave birth to a daughter, Elizabeth.

Henry had already taken steps to secure the bishops' compliance. In February 1531 he coerced the Convocation of Canterbury into acknowledging him as "supreme head of the Church in England." Then in 1534, with Cranmer presiding, the Convocation formally rejected papal authority: "[B]y the Word of God, he [the pope] could not exercise greater authority in this country than any other foreign prelate." Cranmer altered his official title from "Legate of the Apostolic See" to "Metropolitan."[4] All references to the pope were removed from the liturgy, and the faithful were ordered to pray for "our Sovereign Lord Henry VIII, being immediate, next to God, the only and supreme head of this our Catholic Church of England."[5] "Catholic" was of the greatest significance; "catholic and reformed" became the hallmark of the newly designated Church of England.

In the Act of Supremacy of 1534, parliament endorsed Henry's claim to be head of the church, adding that the monarch shall enjoy "all honours, dignities, preeminences, jurisdictions, privileges, authorities, immunities, profits, and commodities to the said dignity." The Act of Succession, passed the same year, declared that Anne Boleyn was Henry's rightful wife and that Elizabeth, and any other offspring Anne might have, were the heirs to the crown. It required all subjects, on command, to swear an oath acknowledging the King's supremacy and recognizing the marriage. Lord Chancellor Thomas More and John Fisher, bishop of Rochester, declined to do so and were executed.

Anne Boleyn did not give Henry VIII the male heir he so desperately wanted, and in 1536 he had her beheaded on charges of adultery. Henry went on to marry four more times: to Jane Seymour, Anne of Cleves, Catherine Howard, and Catherine Parr. Jane gave him his only son, the future Edward VI.

Religious Volatility

Aside from the break with Rome, Henry's most significant church reform was suppression of the monasteries and friaries. With the help of his chief minister Thomas Cromwell (c. 1485–1540), Henry abolished

4. Lathbury, *A History of the Convocation*, 127.
5. Hook, *An Ecclesiastical Biography*, 257.

the religious orders in England and seized their property. Some abbey churches were converted to secular churches, while others were left in ruins. Otherwise, much of the church's pre-Reformation character was preserved, including the liturgy.

Henry had a good grasp of theological issues and sought to mold the new church to his own religious vision. His views fluctuated over time, occasionally leaning toward Lutheranism. But four years before his death, he published *A Necessary Doctrine and Erudition for Any Christian Man*. The "King's Book" showed that he had returned almost entirely to his beliefs before the break with Rome.

Henry's death in 1547 and accession of the boy-monarch Edward VI gave Cranmer his long-awaited opportunity to implement further reforms. In 1549 Cranmer published the *Book of Common Prayer*, the first complete English vernacular liturgy. The same year he invited the Calvinist-leaning Martin Bucer and Peter Martyr Vermigli to England and gave them university appointments. Cranmer's revised Prayer Book of 1552, published just three years after its predecessor, reflected their influence. A proposed doctrinal statement, the Forty-Two Articles, issued by Cranmer in June 1553, also had a Calvinist flavor. The reformist heyday ended the following month, when the young king died.

Edward's half sister, Mary I, who succeeded him, sought to avenge Henry's divorce of her mother and return England to Roman Catholicism. She recalled the capable Cardinal Reginald Pole from Rome and appointed him archbishop of Canterbury. Mary pressured parliament into revoking the Act of Supremacy, banned the Prayer Book, and reinstated medieval heresy laws. Under those laws Cranmer; Latimer, bishop of Worcester; Nicholas Ridley, bishop of London; and 277 others were burned at the stake.[6] Mary, who had married the much-younger King Philip II of Spain, died childless in 1558, and her romanization campaign came to an abrupt end. She was succeeded by Edward's other half-sister, Elizabeth, who had been raised protestant.

Nascent Churchmanship

Roman Catholic loyalists like Moore and Fisher opposed the break with Rome, but most English people either supported it or were indifferent. On the other hand, people did not move in lockstep from pre-Refor-

---

6. Cranmer, Latimer, and Ridley (bishop of Rochester), executed at Oxford in 1555–56, are known as the Oxford martyrs.

mation practices and beliefs to those of the new Church of England. Tension arose between traditionalists and reformists as the emerging church straddled the sacramental–evangelical divide.

Traditionalists—customarily considered the right-wing party in Anglican politics—were representative of "sacramental Christianity," as the term was defined in chapter 1. They supported an independent Church of England but valued the sacraments, existing forms of worship, and the episcopate. Henry himself certainly was a traditionalist, as were Stephen Gardiner (c. 1497–1555), bishop of Winchester, and Cuthbert Tunstall, bishop of Durham. Traditionalists eventually became known as *orthodox*, or *high-church*.

Reformists—the left-wing party—wanted to embrace protestant beliefs, emphasize the Bible, and simplify the liturgy; their support for the episcopate was at best weak. Along with their mentors on the continent of Europe, the English reformists represented "evangelical Christianity."

Cranmer developed close contacts with Lutherans in Germany. He also familiarized himself with the teachings of Ulrich Zwingli and John Calvin. Zwingli (1484–1531), pastor of the Grossmünster Church in Zürich, Switzerland, argued for a return to the "apostolic church," free from all later perversions—a category into which he placed ceremonial ritual and the real presence in the Eucharist. Calvin (1509–64), a French lawyer who had left the Roman church some years earlier, took up residence in Geneva in 1541 and promoted the "Reformed Church," or Presbyterianism. Calvin rejected the episcopate, downplayed the sacraments, promoted simple liturgical forms, and preached the doctrine of predestination.

Calvin had the most influence in England, but the reformists embraced the various aspects of Calvinism to different degrees. Some, like Cranmer and Latimer, bishop of Worcester, were moderate reformists. They were influenced by Calvinist theology but supported the episcopate and a scripted liturgy. Others were largely indifferent to theological issues but embraced ideals of democratic church governance and simple forms of worship. Prominent among the latter were the Puritans, who were more extreme reformists. Like many religious descriptors, "Puritan" was first applied by others; it referred to their dour, austere lifestyles—perhaps a throwback to Celtic asceticism. Puritans themselves preferred "the Godly."

Mary I's accession disrupted the churchmanship patterns. Traditionalists remained to the right of the reformists but found themselves to the left of Roman Catholics like Pole. A few, like Tunstall, managed to find accommodation in the new regime. Others, like Ridley, were executed along with reformists who had not fled the country. Traditionalist–reformist partisanship returned after Elizabeth came to the throne.

THE MATURE CHURCH OF ENGLAND

The Elizabethan Period

Elizabeth I (1533–1603) had the wisdom and diplomacy her predecessor lacked. A few months after her accession, parliament passed a new Act of Supremacy recognizing her as "supreme governor" of the Church of England—a rewording to accommodate her gender.[7] Elizabeth unified her country and helped heal the sharp religious differences by recreating the Edwardian church, without its Calvinist extremism. Another version of the Prayer Book was published in 1559, and four years later the Convocation of Canterbury adopted the Thirty-Nine Articles—the Church of England's only official confessional statement. The Prayer Book and Thirty-Nine Articles will be discussed in due course.

Ambiguity in Elizabeth's own religious convictions enabled her to remain aloof from partisan strife and create an environment of stability in which the Church of England could work out its destiny. The major religious achievements of the reign were the "Elizabethan Settlement" and the doctrine of the *via media*. The former recognized and accepted a degree of pluralism broad enough that the majority of English people could find a home in the Church of England. Remaining outside were the more extreme reformists and a smaller group of Roman Catholic loyalists. Pope Pius V excommunicated Elizabeth in 1570, the eleventh year of her reign, and forbade Roman Catholics from worshiping in Anglican churches.[8]

The *via media*, or "middle path," sought to transcend the differences between Roman Catholicism and continental Protestantism. Its principal exponent was Richard Hooker (1554–1600), the most important theologian of the Elizabethan era. Although Anglicanism did not have a

---

7. The style "Supreme Governor" survives to the present.

8. Pius V, *Regnans*. His action was prompted by the imprisonment of Mary Queen of Scots.

founder, like a Luther or a Calvin, Hooker did more than anyone else to mold its beliefs. He was three years old when Elizabeth came to the throne and died three years before her death. Hooker served at various times as a parish priest, master of the Temple Church in London, and subdean of Salisbury Cathedral. His best-known work was the monumental *Laws of Ecclesiastical Polity*, a collection of eight books published from 1594 onward.[9] Book V, from which we quote liberally, defended the Prayer Book against puritan assault. Hooker acknowledged the primacy of scripture, but he argued for reason, tolerance, and respect for tradition—which became known as the "three-legged stool" of Anglicanism.

The Stuart and Hanoverian Periods

Elizabeth had no children, and upon her death in 1603 she was succeeded by James I (1566–1625), who already reigned as James VI of Scotland.[10] Two years later James narrowly escaped assassination when the Roman Catholic Guy Fawkes tried to blow up the Houses of Parliament during the state opening of parliament. The plot was discovered, and Fawkes and his co-conspirators were executed; all they achieved was to intensify anti-Roman sentiment.

James's policy toward the Church of England remained essentially the same as his predecessor's, and the Elizabethan Settlement and the via media continued to be guiding principles. His greatest contribution was to commission the Authorized Version of the Bible, published in 1611.

During James's reign and that of his son, Charles I, Puritans gained strength and came to control parliament, setting the stage for confrontation with crown and church. To make matters worse, unwise policies by Charles and William Laud, archbishop of Canterbury, antagonized parliament. During four short years, from January 1645 to January 1649, Laud was executed, the episcopate abolished, the church reorganized on presbyterian lines, England wracked by civil war, and finally the king himself beheaded. The monarchy was abolished and England declared a "commonwealth." Military leader Oliver Cromwell took the title "Lord Protector of England" and ruled as a dictator. Harsh religious laws were imposed: use of the Prayer Book and the Communion Service were

---

9. The first four books were published in 1593 and the fifth in 1597. The last three books, whose authorship is disputed, were published posthumously.

10. The two kingdoms remained separate until 1707.

prohibited, Sabbath observance was strictly enforced, and Christmas festivities were banned.

Republican sentiment eventually ran its course, and the monarchy was restored after Cromwell's death. The late king's son, Charles II, ascended the throne in May 1660. The period between the father's execution and the son's accession is referred to as the *Interregnum* ("gap in the monarchy"). Under Charles II, the Church of England was reestablished with its traditional episcopate. Some pre-Civil War bishops fortuitously survived the Interregnum to preserve the succession. The seventy-eight-year-old William Juxon, former bishop of London, was appointed archbishop of Canterbury.[11]

Charles II, the "merry monarch," fathered an estimated sixteen children but produced no legitimate heir, and upon his death he was succeeded by his brother James II. James had two daughters by his late wife: Mary and Anne, both protestant and both future queens of England. But by the time he came to the throne he had remarried and converted to Roman Catholicism. James's second wife gave birth to a son, promising, or threatening, a Roman Catholic succession. The result in 1689 was England's last revolution and invasion, fortunately almost bloodless. The protestant William of Orange was allowed to land with an army in England, and James fled the country. William was the husband of James's daughter Mary, and the two ruled jointly as William III and Mary II.

Three months after their accession, parliament passed the Act of Toleration (1689), permitting certain groups of religious dissidents, who took oaths of allegiance to the crown, to appoint their own ministers and establish their own places of worship. Dissidents had held clandestine worship services since Elizabethan times. Eligible groups were now permitted to compete openly with the Church of England. The Act of Toleration referred to them as "Nonconformists." In addition to the declining numbers of Puritans, they included Presbyterians, Congregationalists, and Baptists. Methodists would join them later. Expressly excluded were Roman Catholics and Unitarians.[12]

Nonconformists left the Church of England. But other Evangelicals of the period, like their forebears, the moderate reformists of the sixteenth century, preferred to remain within the church and try to bend it to their vision of Christianity. By contrast with "high-church," evangelical

---

11. Juxon administered the last rites to Charles I before his execution.

12. Comprehensive religious emancipation had to await the nineteenth century.

Anglicans became known as "low-church." Bishop Proudie—and Mrs. Proudie—of Anthony Trollope's *Barchester* novels provide an amusing caricature of the episcopate in low-church hands

The accession of William and Mary led to a schism in the Church of England and Church of Scotland. Nine English bishops, one Irish bishop,[13] all the Scottish bishops, and about 400 priests declined to swear allegiance to the new monarchs and forfeited their appointments. Referred to as the "Non-Abjurors" or "Nonjurors," they felt unable in good conscience to *abjure* the oaths they had taken to James II and "his heirs and lawful successors."[14] The Nonjurors' ranks were swelled in 1714 when George I came to the throne. Parliament had ruled in 1701 that, upon the death of Queen Anne, James II's other protestant daughter, the crown should pass to the Hanoverian line to prevent a Jacobite succession. Some clergy, who had been willing to swear loyalty to William and Mary and to Anne, refused to take the oath to George, who was in no way James's heir.

Most of the English Nonjurors retired to private life. However, a few nonjuring bishops exercised their episcopal functions in defiance of the Church of England. For example, in 1694, three Nonjurors consecrated George Hickes, bishop of Thetford, and Thomas Wagstaffe, bishop of Ipswich.[15] Nineteen years later Hickes and two Scottish bishops consecrated Jeremy Collier, Samuel Hawes, and Nathaniel Spinckes. The schismatic English groups posed little threat to the Church of England. By contrast, the new Scottish Episcopal Church formed by the nonjuring Scottish bishops had great impact on the future of Anglicanism. It will be discussed in the next chapter.

The eighteenth century was a period of relative political stability, but the Church of England went into spiritual decline. Bishops became lax in their attention to the sacraments, doctrine, and church discipline. Some clergymen acquired multiple livings, in the style of their medieval forebears, leaving parish duties to poorly paid—and often unenthusiastic—curates. The Church of England increasingly was viewed as the religion of the upper classes. Many others felt marginalized and were attracted to nonconformist denominations. The evangelical revival of the

13. Bishop William Sheridan of Kilmore.

14. Nonjuring bishops claimed that the schisms began not when they refused to take the oath of loyalty but when others were appointed to their sees.

15. Overton, *The Nonjurors*, 29.

mid-1700s, led by John and Charles Wesley, temporarily reinvigorated the church, but the "Methodist Societies" eventually seceded to form their own denomination.

The intelligentsia was influenced by the Scientific Revolution and the Enlightenment. Rationalist philosophers argued that many facets of religion were relics of primitive superstition. A supreme being might be needed to account for phenomena not yet ~~been~~ explained by science—but, with each new discovery, the "god of the gaps" shrank in importance. Intellectuals who still felt a religious impulse were drawn to deism. Deism spoke of a completely transcendent God who created the world and then left it to its own devices. It offered an optimistic view of human progress and acknowledged moral imperatives, but it rejected organized religion and attached little importance to Christ. By the 1830s deism had run its course and no longer posed a threat, but other forms of rationalism played a role in the emerging broad church.

Church Organization

By the fifteenth century the provinces of Canterbury and York had their own bicameral convocations. The archbishop and bishops formed the upper house; abbots, priors, cathedral deans, archdeacons, and other clergy sat in the lower house. Archdeacons were senior clergy appointed by bishops to help administer their dioceses. The convocations served as the governing bodies of their provinces. But their autonomy was short-lived; they came under royal control in the 1530s. And in the early eighteenth century they ceased to function altogether. George 1 dissolved the convocations in 1717, and, except for a few meetings in the 1740s, they were not convened again until 1854.

Since the Church of England was the established church,[16] it was subject to both royal and parliamentary oversight. Over time, political power in England shifted increasingly to parliament. Episcopal appointments, theoretically a royal prerogative, came to be made by the prime minister. Under the provisions of the Magna Carta, a number of bishops, including the archbishops of Canterbury and York, sat in the House of Lords as "lords spiritual."[17] When the bishops voted as a block they could influence legislation, but on a number of occasions—notoriously in

16. The Church of England is the only legally established church in the Anglican Communion.

17. At the time of writing, twenty-six bishops sit in the Lords.

1830 and 1927/8—parliament passed measures strongly opposed by the church. Those incidents will be discussed in later chapters. Furthermore, the Privy Council served in the monarch's name as the ultimate court of appeal in church-related matters—even matters of doctrine and liturgy. Its judicial authority was used, to the church's great detriment, in the late nineteenth century.

By the nineteenth century, several former British colonies had attained self-government, and the United States had become an independent nation. Their Anglican churches were autonomous religious entities, with their own primates and governing bodies. Fears were expressed that the churches could lose contact with their common roots in the Church of England and with one another. In response, Archbishop Charles Longley of Canterbury convened the first Lambeth Conference in 1867. The objective was to provide a forum where bishops from the various Anglican provinces could discuss issues of mutual concern. Similar meetings have been held ever since, at intervals of about ten years. Resolutions of the Lambeth Conference are not binding, but they exert strong influence on members' governing bodies. The Lambeth Conference gives meaning to the concept of the Anglican Communion.

"Province" is used in two ways in the Anglican vocabulary. It may denote an ecclesiastical province, like Canterbury or York. Alternatively it can denote a national church, like the Episcopal Church in the United States, which may itself include multiple ecclesiastical provinces. The primates of the national provinces meet annually under the presidency of the archbishop of Canterbury, who is regarded as "first among equals."

An important development in the mid-nineteenth century was the establishment of theological seminaries. Their purpose was to provide more focused and practical training than did traditional divinity programs. Not surprisingly, seminaries acquired either high- or low-church orientations. Cuddesdon Theological College, Oxford, was founded in 1854 to serve high-church interests, and other high-church seminaries were created at Chichester, Wells, Leeds, and Ely. Ridley Hall, Wycliffe Hall, and St Peter's Hall, Oxford, were established to serve low-church interests.

ANGLICAN WORSHIP

The Latin Mass, using the eleventh-century Sarum Rite or one of the other medieval forms, remained the norm throughout the reign of

Henry VIII.[18] Canticles like the *Te Deum, Magnificat,* and *Nunc Dimittis*
in the Daily Offices continued to be recited or sung in Latin. But sentiment was already moving toward vernacular worship. In 1536 Thomas
Cromwell ordered that the Creed, Lord's Prayer, Hail Mary, and Ten
Commandments be recited in English.[19] And Cranmer composed an
English litany in 1544. Few opportunities arose for further liturgical
innovation, but Cranmer quietly worked on a whole new vernacular
liturgy. By the time Edward VI ascended the throne in 1547 the work
was well in hand.

The Prayer Book

Cranmer was the chief architect of the *Book of Common Prayer* (*BCP*),
authorized by parliament in March 1549 and implemented at Pentecost
of that year. Its purpose was to unify liturgical practices throughout
the kingdom and to bring the faithful into more active participation.
"Common prayer" was to be in the ordinary language of the people.
The *BCP* provided a comprehensive liturgy for services and sacramental
rites, replacing the several pre-Reformation missals, breviaries, ordinals,
and manuals. It combined translations from Latin liturgies, scriptural
passages, adaptations of Lutheran works, doctrinal notes, and rubrics
governing how worship should be conducted.

Cranmer's genius soon became evident. His challenge was to replace the long-established and familiar Latin liturgy with a vernacular
liturgy of comparable value and beauty. Whereas some earlier attempts
had produced clumsy translations and poor compositions, the 1549 *BCP*
offered fine prose and poetry—"directness, simplicity and harmony."[20]
Much of what Cranmer wrote has survived to the present, through the
many revisions to the Prayer Book.

The second and third collects from Evening Prayer recalled the poetic sensitivity of Celtic blessings: "O God, from whom all holy desires,
all good counsels, and all just works do proceed; Give unto thy servants
that peace which the world cannot give; that both our hearts may be set
to obey thy commandments, and also that by thee we, being defended

18. Wriothesley, *A Chronicle*, vol. I, 83. Evidently the Mass occasionally was said in
English.

19. Ibid., 55.

20. Pfatteicher, "The Prayer Book," 222. See also Stanwood, "The Prayer Book,"
140–49.

from the fear of our enemies, may pass our time in rest and quietness." And: "Lighten our darkness we beseech thee, O Lord, and by thy great mercy defend us from all perils and dangers of this night, for the love of thy only son, our saviour Jesus Christ. Amen."[21]

Cranmer was also a master of ambiguity, and he employed that strategy to secure broad consensus for the new liturgy. In the words of one commentator: "The temper of compromise . . . is visible in the sacramental offices of the Prayer Book, which left so much out to satisfy the Protestants, and left so much in to satisfy the Catholics."[22] To quote another: "At times his [Cranmer's] language resembles a kind of verbal incense that offers an attractive religious haze but no clarity of meaning."[23] Ambiguity of language has facilitated Anglican cohesion throughout the centuries.

It was impossible to please everyone, and rebellion broke out in Cornwall in the summer of 1549. Joined by sympathizers from neighboring counties, a ragtag army of Roman Catholic loyalists besieged the city of Exeter. Insurrection also erupted elsewhere: rebels burned the city of Norwich, in eastern England, and martial law was declared in London. The rebels sought restoration of the Latin Mass and "other ceremonies of the Pope's law."[24] The rebellions were crushed, and a royal decree in 1550 mandated use of the *BCP* throughout the realm.[25]

Soon after they arrived in England Bucer and Vermigli pressed for more radical reform of public worship. They noted that some churches preserved pre-Reformation ceremony and criticized what they considered overly-elaborate chancels, altars, and liturgical regalia.[26] The visitors' criticisms were promptly acted upon. Their influence, as well as Cranmer's own shift toward Calvinism, were also reflected in revisions to the Prayer Book. Compared with its predecessor of only three years earlier, the 1552 *BCP* was farther removed in content and format from the pre-Reformation liturgy. But its immediate impact was minimal; Edward VI died the following year and England returned to Roman Catholicism.

21. *BCP* 1549, "Order for Evensong."

22. Church, *The Oxford Movement*, 248.

23. Jeanes, "Cranmer," 28.

24. Wriothesley, *A Chronicle*, vol. 11, 15–18. See also Wood, *The 1549 Rebellions*.

25. *Act for Uniformity of Service and Administration of the Sacraments throughout the Realm*, January 21, 1549.

26. Maltby, "The Prayer Book," 80.

The 1559 *BCP*, published when Elizabeth I ascended the throne, was based primarily on the 1552 version but made concessions to high-church sentiment. Clergy were urged to use "such ornaments in the church, as were in use by authority of parliament in the second year of the reign of king Edward the VI"—that is, according to the 1549 Prayer Book. Precisely what "ornaments" meant—candles, sacred images, clerical vestments, or more—would be debated for centuries. Several saints' days were returned to the liturgical calendar, while a verse in the litany praying for deliverance "from the tyranny of the Bishop of Rome and all his detestable enormities" was deleted. Minor revisions to the Prayer Book were also made in 1604, after James I came to the throne.

Restoration of the monarchy in 1660 created an opportunity for more extensive revision. Polarization within the church was acute at that time, and Charles II carefully selected a group of twelve Anglican bishops and twelve representatives of puritan and presbyterian interests to review the 1559 and 1604 versions of the *BCP* and recommend changes. Accepted Frewen, archbishop of York, was appointed chairman of the "Savoy Conference," named for the London palace where meetings were held. The bishops resisted pressure from the Puritans and Presbyterians to make radical alterations, and in the end the proposed changes were relatively minor. Nevertheless, the new 1662 *Book of Common Prayer* was considered a worthwhile improvement over earlier versions and soon won wide acclaim.

Continued revision was anticipated: "[I]t is but reasonable, that upon weighty and important considerations, according to the various exigency of times and occasions, such changes and alterations should be made therein, as to those that are in place of Authority should from time to time seem either necessary or expedient."[27] Notwithstanding, the 1662 *BCP* became the standard for three centuries and is still the only legally authorized liturgy in England. It also became a model for liturgies created by Anglican provinces outside England. The authors noted that it "may be always useful for the baptizing of Natives in our Plantations, and others converted to the Faith."

The several versions of the *Book of Common Prayer* shared a similar structure of five major sections: the Daily Offices, the Litany, the Communion Service, the Pastoral Offices, and the Ordinals. Morning Prayer replaced the pre-Reformation offices of Matins, Lauds, and Prime,

27. *BCP* 1662, Preface.

while Evening Prayer combined Vespers and Compline. Readings from scripture were selected according to an annual calendar, except for the psalms, which were to be recited in their entirety each month.

Although the Prayer Book simplified the pre-Reformation liturgical calendar it retained a strong sense of rhythm, with its seasonal, monthly, and daily cycles. Clergy recited Morning and Evening Prayer every day and offered them in church on Sundays. The Prayer Book required that people receive Holy Communion at their parish churches at Easter and on at least two other Sundays per year. Despite occasional attempts to encourage more frequent Communion, the response was poor, and few clergy offered the full Communion Service even monthly.

The Litany was to be sung during procession into the church on Sundays. Litanies had been popular in medieval times, often at times of national emergency. Significantly, Cranmer published his English litany of 1544 when England was at war with Scotland and France.[28] The Pastoral Offices included baptism, confirmation, the marriage ceremony, the churching of women, visitation to the sick, and the burial service.

Sacramental Rites

Like their Lutheran counterparts the English Reformers attached greatest importance to the "dominical" sacraments of baptism and Holy Communion, the two whose institution by Christ had strong scriptural support. Even so, Cranmer had less trust in the efficacy of the sacraments than did his medieval predecessors. He conceded that sacraments were "signs of holy things." Betraying Calvinist influence, however, he insisted that their power was not universal; only the elect could expect to receive grace.[29]

Sacramental rites evolved during the Edwardian reign, as Cranmer and others struggled to develop a new understanding of the sacraments. In several instances the 1549 BCP offered transitional forms, intermediate between pre-Reformation forms and those in the 1552 and subsequent versions of the Prayer Book. Liturgical development continued into the Elizabethan era and beyond, as reformists and traditionalists gained or lost influence. Debate ended with the Savoy Conference, after which the English liturgy attained its stable and enduring form.

28. Alexander, "The Shape," 65.

29. Jeanes, "Cranmer," 30.

The 1549 baptismal rite expressed a shift of emphasis away from remitting original sin to welcoming the child into the church. Also, baptism was to be public, performed on Sunday or a major feast when people were assembled for Morning or Evening Prayer.

The 1549 rite, however, retained traditional ceremony and symbolism that dated back to Celtic times. The baptismal party assembled at the church door, symbolizing entry into the *church*. After naming the child, the priest made the sign of the cross over the child's head and heart, saying: "Receive ye the sign of the holy Cross . . . in token that thou shalt not be ashamed to confess thy faith in Christ crucified, and manfully to fight under his banner against sin, the world, and the devil."[30] After the party processed to the font, the priest dipped the child's face in the water three times and pronounced: "I baptize thee in the name of the father, and of the son, and of the holy ghost."[31] The priest and godparents laid their hands on the child, and the priest vested the child in a white baptismal gown and anointed him or her with oil. Invocation of the Holy Spirit and chrismation recalled practices in the early church where baptism and confirmation were combined.

The ceremony and symbolism came under assault as protestant influence increased. In the 1552 and later versions the whole rite took place at the font, and the vesting, laying-on of hands, and anointing were eliminated. The priest began with the formal pronouncement of baptism. Then, making the sign of the cross over the child's forehead only, he proclaimed: "We receive this child into the congregation of Christ's flock, and so sign him with the sign of the cross, in token that hereafter he shall not be ashamed to confess the faith of Christ crucified."[32] Even that stripped-down rite failed to please the Puritans, and criticism continued well into Elizabethan times. Puritans objected to the sign of the cross, claiming that it was merely a human invention. But signation was defended by both traditionalists and moderates, including Richard Hooker.[33] In that and many other matters Hooker was the voice of restraint, defending what became mainstream Anglican practice and belief.

---

30. *BCP* 1549, "Administration of Public Baptism."

31. Provision was made to pour the water if the child's health did not permit dipping.

32. *BCP* 1552, "Ministration of Baptism."

33. Hooker, *Of the Laws*, §LXV.1–3, 317–19.

Confirmation was transformed from an initiatory sacrament into a gateway to first Communion. The Prayer Book provided a catechism for clergy to examine candidates in the essentials of their faith. Children recited the Apostle's Creed and Ten Commandments and acknowledged duties to God and neighbor. Anointing with oil was eliminated, but the laying-on of hands was retained, as was the tradition of episcopal confirmation.[34]

The English Reformers resisted puritan pressure to eliminate the church hierarchy and preserved the three-level ministry of bishops, priests, and deacons. When initially published, the 1549 *BCP* did not contain an ordination rite. The Ordinal—for "making deacons," ordaining priests, and consecrating bishops—was inserted the following year after receiving parliamentary approval. Several decades later, Hooker defended the sacred nature of ordination: "The ministry of things divine is a function which as God himself did institute, so neither may men undertake the same but by authority and power given them in lawful manner."[35] Clerical celibacy rules were abolished for all three levels of the ministry.[36]

The formal consecration of bishops was important to maintain the apostolic succession. According to the 1662 *BCP* the officiating bishop gave the candidate the charge: "Receive the Holy Ghost for the Office and Work of a Bishop in the Church of God, now committed unto thee by the Imposition of our hands; In the Name of the Father, and of the Son, and of the Holy Ghost. Amen."[37] The Ordinal did not define "the work of a bishop," and that lack of specificity prompted a nineteenth-century pope to declare that Anglican orders were invalid and the succession broken.

The ordination rite for priests included the words: "Whose sins thou dost forgive, they are forgiven; and whose sins thou dost retain, they are retained." Prior to the Reformation those words were interpreted as giving priests the power to dispense absolution in the sacrament of penance—that is, in auricular confession. But the Reformers abolished private confession, except as an optional rite in the visitation to the sick.

In the Anglican liturgy, confession became public but nonspecific, and absolution was incorporated into the Communion Service. The 1552 and later versions of the *BCP* required priest and people to recite

---

34. Jeanes, "Cranmer," 35–36.

35. Hooker, *Of the Laws*, §LXXVII.1, 455.

36. Cranmer secretly married in 1532, before his appointment as archbishop of Canterbury.

37. *BCP* 1662, "Form of Ordaining."

the rather self-incriminating confession: "We acknowledge and bewail our manifold sins and wickedness, Which we, from time to time, most grievously have committed, By thought, word, and deed . . . provoking most justly thy wrath and indignation against us: we do earnestly repent, and be heartily sorry for these our misdoings." The priest then pronounced absolution: "Almighty God, our heavenly Father, who of his great mercy hath promised forgiveness of sins to all them that with hearty repentance and true faith turn unto him; Have mercy upon you; pardon and deliver you from all your sins; confirm and strengthen you in all goodness; and bring you to everlasting life."[38]

The pre-Reformation burial rite focused on intercession for the soul in purgatory, and the 1549 rite retained a prayer for the deceased. But the prayer was eliminated from 1552 onward. Without a purgatory, or some other intermediate state, the soul was either in heaven or hell, beyond the reach of intercession. Medieval abuse of indulgences and chantries left a bad taste in the Reformers' mouths. Instead of focusing on the deceased, the burial service instead comforted survivors or warned of the inevitability of death: "Man that is born of a woman hath but a short time to live, and is full of misery. He cometh up, and is cut down, like a flower; he fleeth as it were a shadow."[39]

Holy Communion

The Fourth Lateran Council in 1215 proclaimed the Roman doctrine of transubstantiation: that the eucharistic elements were transformed—not in their "accidents," or outer appearance, but in "substance"—into the body and blood of Christ.[40] The real presence was corporeally invested in the elements as soon as the priest uttered the words of consecration. The elements, no longer bread and wine, were elevated for adoration, and the Sacrament could be reserved for future use. Communicants received the body and blood of Christ, worthily or sacrilegiously according to their state of grace.

The Reformers rejected the doctrine of transubstantiation and sought to understand the Eucharist in other ways. Zwingli, like Wycliffe before

38. *BCP* 1662, "Order for the Administration of the Lord's Supper."

39. *BCP* 1662, "Order for the Burial of the Dead."

40. The concept of transubstantiation was suggested by Radbertus Paschasius in the ninth century, but the Aristotelian revival subsequently provided the philosophical categories of substance and accidents.

him, took the extreme view of denying the real presence altogether: the Eucharist was purely commemorative, the elements were not transformed, and communicants received nothing but ordinary bread and wine.

The English Reformers were more cautious. They regarded the real presence as a mystery that could not, and should not, be reduced to a simplistic formula.[41] Hooker endorsed that caution in the famous confession: "[W]hat these elements are in themselves it skilleth not, it is enough that to me which take them they are the body and blood of Christ, his promise in witness hereof sufficeth, his word he knoweth which way to accomplish; why should any cogitation possess the mind of a faithful communicant but this 'O my God thou art true, O my soul thou art happy!'"[42]

Devotion did not require an intellectual understanding of the Eucharist. Nevertheless, to the extent that Anglicans acquired one, it lay somewhere between the Zwinglian and Roman extremes. Plenty of room remained for belief in the real presence without subscribing to transubstantiation.

The evolution of the Communion Service shows how eucharistic understanding developed over time. Again the 1549 form was transitional. It was based largely on the Sarum Rite, even bearing the subtitle: "commonly called the Mass." Later versions made no mention of the Mass and bore less resemblance to the Latin rite. Also, accompanying rubrics were changed to eliminate ritual gestures that implied blessing and adoration.

Table 3.1 shows how the institution narrative—the part of the Communion Service that recalls Christ's institution of the Eucharist at the Last Supper—evolved from the Sarum Rite,[43] through the 1549 form, to the mature form in the 1552 and 1662 Prayer Books. The words of consecration—or what the English Reformers preferred to call "words of institution"—remained the same. They were taken almost verbatim from 1 Corinthians 11:24–25. "Take, eat, this is my body . . . drink ye all of this, for this is my blood of the new Testament."

41. The Eastern Orthodox Churches take a similar position.

42. Hooker, Of the Laws, §LXVII.12, 362.

43. Ordinary and Canon, 12–13.

TABLE 3.1. EVOLUTION OF THE INSTITUTION NARRATIVE IN THE EUCHARIST

Sarum Rite (English translation)	1549 BCP	1552–1662 BCP
We therefore beseech Thee, O Lord, graciously to accept this oblation of our service . . . . Which oblation do Thou, O Almighty God, we beseech thee, vouchsafe to render in all respects, bles✝sed, app✝roved, effec✝tual, reasonable, and acceptable, that is may be made unto us the Bo✝dy and Blo✝od of our Lord Jesus Christ. Who, the day before He suffered, took Bread. . . gave thanks and bles✝sed and broke, and gave to His disciples saying: Take and eat ye all of this; For this is My Body. Likewise after that He had supped, taking also this pre-eminent Chalice . . . , He blessed and gave to His disciples saying: Take and drink ye all of this; For this is the Cup of My Blood, of the New and eternal Testament, the mystery of faith; which shall be shed for you and for many, for the remission of sins. As often as ye shall do these things, ye shall do them in remembrance of Me.	Hear us (o merciful father) we beseech thee; and with thy holy spirit and word, vouchsafe to bl✝ess and sanc✝tify these thy gifts, and creatures of bread and wine, that they may be unto us the body and blood of thy most dearly beloved son Jesus Christ. Who in the same night that he was betrayed: took bread, and when he had blessed, and given thanks, he brake it, and gave it to his disciples, saying: Take, eat, this is my body which is given for you, do this in remembrance of me. Likewise after supper he took the cup, and when he had given thanks, he gave it to them, saying: drink ye all of this, for this is my blood of the new Testament, which is shed for you and for many, for the remission of sins: do this, as oft as ye shall drink it, in remembrance of me.	Hear us (o merciful father) we (most humbly) beseech thee; and grant that we, receiving these thy creatures of bread and wine, according to thy son our Saviour Jesus Christ's holy institution, in remembrance of his death and passion, may be partakers of his most blessed body and blood: who in the same night that he was betrayed, took Bread; and, when he had given thanks, he brake it, and gave it to his disciples, saying, Take, eat, this is my Body which is given for you: Do this in remembrance of me. Likewise after supper he took the Cup; and, when he had given thanks, he gave it to them, saying, Drink ye all of this; for this is my Blood of the New Testament, which is shed for you and for many for the remission of sins: Do this, as oft as ye shall drink it, in remembrance of me. *Amen.*

The prayer immediately preceding the words of institution changed significantly, however. The Sarum Rite and the 1549 *BCP* sought God's blessing on the eucharistic elements, and the priest made the sign of the cross ☩ over the elements. The 1549 prayer asked God the Father "*with thy holy spirit and word, vouchsafe to bless and sanctify these thy gifts*" (emphasis added). Invocation of the Holy Spirit gave the prayer the quality of an *epiclesis*, which, as will be seen later in the book, became a significant indicator of high-church eucharistic understanding. Both the Sarum Rite and the 1549 *BCP* asked that the bread and wine "may be unto us the body and blood of . . . Christ," expressing anticipation that the elements would be transformed, at least for communicants.

The 1552 and later versions offered no blessing of the elements, either by God or by the priest. The prayer asked only that "we . . . may be *partakers* of his [Christ's] most blessed body and blood" (emphasis added). Also, a note in the 1552 *BCP* played down expectations of trans-formation: "the natural Body and Blood of our Saviour Christ are in Heaven, and not here; it being against the truth of Christ's natural Body to be at one time in more places than one." [44]

The belief that ~~that~~ the bread and wine remain unchanged, but wor-thy communicants receive the body and blood of Christ in their souls, is referred to as *receptionism*.[45] It became the mainstream Anglican interpretation of the real presence. Hooker's "skilleth not" confession was ambiguous but suggested that he was a receptionist. Other inter-pretations offered at various times affirmed that Christ is in some sense present on the altar, in his sacramental body and blood, as well as being received by communicants. One interpretation, *objectivism*, asserts that the real presence is localized in the eucharistic elements. The various interpretations of the real presence will be discussed in later chapters.

The 1552 and subsequent versions specified that the priest and faithful receive Holy Communion immediately after the words of insti-tution. Since nothing significant happened to the bread and wine, noth-ing more needed to be said, and the eucharistic elements required no special attention. The 1552 and 1559 versions even stated: "*[I]f any of the bread or wine remain, the Curate shall have it to his own use.*" (Rubrics conventionally were italicized and also printed in red.)

44. *BCP* 1552, "Order for the Administration."
45. See for example Crockett, "Holy Communion," 309.

The words of administration—the prayer addressed to each communicant—evolved, even within the parameters of receptionism. The 1549 *BCP* affirmed the real presence: "The body of our Lord Jesus Christ which was given for thee, preserve thy body and soul unto everlasting life. The blood of our Lord Jesus Christ which was shed for thee, preserve thy body and soul unto everlasting life." The 1552 form, which Zwingli would have endorsed, was: "Take and eat this, in remembrance that Christ died for thee, and feed on him in thy heart by faith, with thanksgiving. Drink this in remembrance that Christ's blood was shed for thee, and be thankful." The 1559 and 1662 Prayer Books combined the two forms, giving Zwinglians, receptionists, and even objectivists language to which they could relate.

The Reformers soon eliminated adoration of the eucharistic elements. From 1552 onward, neither the elevation of the host and chalice nor reservation of the Sacrament was permitted; moreover, the communion table was not to be decorated. Puritans objected to kneeling to receive Communion, complaining that it implied adoration. In response, the "Black Rubric"—so called because it was printed in black, instead of the conventional red—was inserted into the 1552 Prayer Book and retained in the 1662 version; it instructed communicants to "*receive the same kneeling; (which order is well meant, for a signification of our humble and grateful acknowledgment of the benefits of Christ therein given to all worthy Receivers, and for the avoiding of such profanation and disorder in the holy Communion, as might otherwise ensue.*" But a note reassured communicants that "no adoration is intended, or ought to be done, either unto the Sacramental Bread or Wine there bodily received, or unto any Corporal Presence of Christ's natural Flesh and Blood."[46]

Another important change concerned the sacrificial nature of the Eucharist. The Sarum Rite clearly stated that the Eucharist was a sacrifice, or oblation, offered to God on the people's behalf (Table 3.1). The Reformers felt strongly that Christ's sacrifice on the Cross was complete and no human act could add to it. Furthermore, to offer up the eucharistic elements might suggest that good works had merit. All versions of the *BCP*, from 1549 through 1662, included the statement: "O God heavenly father, which of thy tender mercy didst give thine only son Jesus Christ to suffer death upon the cross for our redemption, who made there (by his oblation once offered) a full, perfect, and sufficient sacrifice, oblation,

46. *BCP* 1552, 1562, "Order for the Administration."

and satisfaction, for the sins of the whole world." Even self-oblation was discouraged. The 1549 liturgy affirmed "we offer and present unto thee (O Lord) our selves, our souls, and bodies to be a reasonable, holy, and lively sacrifice unto thee." The prayer was eliminated from 1552 onward.

Denial of the eucharistic sacrifice was a major factor leading to removal of stone altars, with their sacrificial associations. At Bucer's and Vermigli's insistence, "all altars in every parish through London were taken away," a chronicler reported in 1550.[47] All versions of the Prayer Book, from 1552 onward, instructed priests to provide a simple communion table: "*The Table at the Communion time having a fair white linen cloth upon it, shall stand in the body of the Church, or in the Chancel . . . . And the Priest [shall stand] at the north side of the Table where Morning prayer and Evening prayer are appointed to be said.*[48] Perhaps the notion of gathering around a communion table recalled the eucharistic meals of the early church and improved lay participation. But any favorable effect was muted by the infrequency with which Holy Communion was offered.

Every version of the Prayer Book provided guidance on who could receive Holy Communion. The 1549 version denied Communion to an "open and notorious evil liver," but offered it to any man who "openly declared himself to have truly repented, and amended his former naughty life."[49] That instruction was omitted from the 1552 Prayer Book, reinstated in 1559, and omitted again in 1662. How the penitent should declare repentance was not spelled out, but presumably the congregation would be aware of his or her improved behavior.

ANGLICAN DOCTRINE

The Church of England never fully endorsed Luther's principle of *sola scriptura* ("by scripture alone"), but it affirmed the primacy of scriptural authority. Doctrinal formulations should be nothing more than an elucidation of Christ's teachings, as recorded in the New Testament. Moreover, as Wycliffe had urged a century earlier, everyone should study the Bible. That ideal that was becoming more feasible because of the availability of English translations and improving literacy rates.

47. Wriothesley, *A Chronicle*, vol. 11, 41. Wriothesley noted on p. 47 that adjustments were made to the position of the table in St Paul's.

48. *BCP* 1662, "Order for the Administration."

49. *BCP* 1549, "Supper of the Lord."

The Bible

Henry VIII had no inclination to change the Latin liturgy, but he believed that scripture should be read—and read aloud—in the vernacular. Only two English translations were currently available: the Wycliffe–Hereford Bible of the late fourteenth century and a more recent version by William Tyndale (c. 1484–1536), which had been published abroad and smuggled into England.[50] Neither was considered adequate, and pressure developed for a new translation. The work fell to Myles Coverdale, and the result was the "Great Bible," so called because of its physical size. In 1538 Thomas Cromwell ordered every parish in the land to place a copy "in some convenient place . . . whereas your parishioners may most commodiously resort to the same and read it." Coverdale's Psalter is counted among the world's most beautiful sacred texts.

A more ambitious project was undertaken when Elizabeth I ascended the throne. A group of English bishops prepared a new translation, under the direction of Matthew Parker (1504–75), archbishop of Canterbury. The "Bishop's Bible" was an improvement on the Great Bible because the Old Testament was based on Hebrew, Aramaic, and Greek texts instead of the Latin Vulgate. It also helped meet competition from the Geneva Bible, which was acknowledged to be a good translation but whose margin notes were Calvinist in tone.

The translation commissioned by James I was even more ambitious. The work was entrusted to forty-seven scholars, under the general direction of Lancelot Andrewes (1555–1626), dean of Westminster and master of Pembroke College, Cambridge.[51] Work began in 1604, and the project was completed seven years later. The new translation drew liberally on the Coverdale and Bishops' Bibles but also reflected new scholarship. The "Authorized Version," or "King James Version," soon became the standard text for the English-speaking world. It is still considered a masterpiece of biblical scholarship, for its time, and a masterpiece of English literature.

No further official translation was attempted until the late nineteenth century. Work on the "Revised Version," involving more than fifty scholars, began in 1870. The New Testament was published in 1881 and

---

50. Tyndale was executed in Antwerp even though, by then, he would have been welcomed back to England.

51. Andrewes went on to serve successively as bishop of Chichester, Ely, and Winchester.

the Old Testament in 1885. The Revised Version incorporated the results of more recent scriptural research but was intended to retain seventeenth-century language and idiom. Not everyone shared the desire for a new translation or liked the finished product. The present archbishop of Canterbury, Rowan Williams, offered as one explanation "the conviction. . . that the 1611 text was the supreme gift of God to Reformed Christianity in the supremely favoured Protestant nation."[52] Since the 1880s many new translations have appeared, but the King James Bible is still revered.

Doctrinal Development

The early sixteenth century was awash with theological discussion. The English Reformers had grown up with pre-Reformation teachings. Erasmus had shared his insights at Cambridge. Henry VIII shared his own insights, and the works of Luther, Zwingli, and Calvin were widely read. From that potent mix Cranmer, his contemporaries, and successive generations of churchmen tried to sort out their ideas and decide what the Church of England's doctrinal position should be. Ideas developed over time—and are still developing today. Church leaders also had, and have, to decide how best to disseminate doctrine and encourage acceptance.

Cranmer was a pastor rather than an academic theologian, and his main concern was to guide the beliefs of ordinary people. Accordingly, his main vehicle of dissemination became the Prayer Book. The two Edwardian versions provided a wealth of doctrinal teachings. The notion of communicating doctrine through the liturgy, and allowing it to evolve through the liturgy, was embodied in one of Anglicanism's favorite maxims: *lex orandi lex credendi*: "the law of prayer is the law of belief," or "as people pray, so they believe."[53] In a real sense, Anglicans first worshipped together and then reflected on their shared beliefs.

Until Elizabethan times, the Church of England had no official doctrinal statement, comparable with the Augsburg Confession of 1530 or the Westminster Confession of 1646. The volatility of the times and reformist–traditionalist tension within the church certainly contributed to the hesitation. But another important factor was the pragmatic tem-

52. Williams, R., *Anglican Identities*, 75.
53. Stevenson, W. T., "Lex Orandi," 187–202.

perament of the English people.[54] Anglicans tended to shun doctrinaire attitudes in favor of an untidy but successful pluralism.

That said, groundwork was being laid for an official statement. As early as 1536 Cranmer issued the Ten Articles, which documented his and Henry VIII's moderate protestant leanings. But they were never endorsed by the bishops or parliament. Six years later, when Henry had retreated from a protestant outlook but the archbishop had moved closer, Cranmer and others began writing a series of homilies. The ostensible purpose was pastoral: to help clergy meet the new challenge of weekly preaching, though the scholarly language would have been too much for the average priest and congregation. The first *Book of Homilies* was published in 1547, the year of Henry's death. It contained twelve homilies; Cranmer wrote at least five and edited them all.

The first six homilies presented conventional protestant theology, such as the authority and sufficiency of scripture, the inherent sinfulness of man, and justification by faith. The second homily: "Of the Misery of All Mankind," reminded the faithful that "we have no goodness, help nor salvation, but contrariwise, sin, damnation, and death everlasting." But it retreated somewhat from Calvinist pessimism to end on the hopeful note: "If we thus humbly submit our selves in the sight of God, we may be sure that in the time of his visitation, he will lift us up unto the kingdom of his dearly beloved son Christ Jesus our Lord."[55]

Despite insistence on justification by faith, the fourth homily: "Of the True and Lively Faith," affirmed that "a true faith can not be kept secret, but when occasion is offered, it will break out, and show itself by good works."[56] The tenth homily: "An Exhortation to Obedience," urged obedience to the civil authorities in the interest of preserving divine order. Fortunately, England was blessed that "God hath sent us his high gift, our most dear Sovereign Lord King Edward, with a godly, wise, and honorable Counsel, with other superiors and inferiors, in a beautiful order, and godly."

The *Book of Homilies* was revoked by Mary I but restored and republished by Elizabeth.[57] The second set of twenty-one homilies was written between 1562 and 1571. John Jewell (1522–71), bishop of Salisbury,

54. Ibid., 192–93.
55. Homily II.
56. Homily IV.
57. *Certain Sermons.*

wrote all but two. The homilies in the second set were more practical and devotional. The introduction to the second book exhorted clergy:

> For that the Lord doth require of his servant, whom he hath set over his household, to show both faithfulness and prudence in his office: it shall be necessary that ye above all other do behave your-selves most faithfully and diligently in your so high a function: that is, aptly, plainly, and distinctly to read the sacred Scriptures, diligently to instruct the youth in their Catechism, gravely and reverently to minister his most holy Sacraments, prudently also to choose out such Homilies as bemost meet for the time, and for the more agreeable instruction of the people committed to your charge.[58]

Jewell and his protégé, Richard Hooker, wrote many other works that contributed to Anglican doctrinal understanding. Jewell's *Apology of the Church of England* (1562) defended the break with Rome. Secession, he emphasized, was not approached "disorderly or wickedly, but quietly and soberly," and "we have done nothing herein against the doctrine either of Christ or of His Apostles." We have not departed, he continued, from "the primitive Church, from the Apostles, and from Christ."[59] The Anglican church had returned to the faith of the early church and escaped from Roman perversions. It was necessary to sever relations with "that Church, whose errors were proved and made manifest to the world, which Church also had already evidently departed from God's word."[60]

Hooker's sermon: *A Learned Discourse of Justification* (1585), offered a good illustration of the *via media* and also expressed qualities of tolerance and inclusiveness rare in the sixteenth century. He affirmed the doctrine of justification through faith and criticized the Church of Rome for "teaching justification by inherent grace."[61] But Hooker conceded that Rome had remained faithful to most of the fundamental doctrines of Christianity. Needless to say, reformists were displeased by his comments. His *Laws of Ecclesiastical Polity* (1594–97) eventually provided a comprehensive presentation of Anglican theology and ecclesiology as it evolved, largely under his influence, during the latter years of the Elizabethan reign.

58. "An Admonition."
59. Jewell, J., *The Apology*, 93–94, 132.
60. Ibid., 94.
61. Hooker, *A Learned Discourse*.

Articles of Faith

The Thirty-Nine Articles of Religion were formulated under the direction of Archbishop Parker and published in 1563. Based in part on Cranmer's Forty-Two Articles of ten years earlier, they provided Anglicanism's most authoritative and enduring confessional statement.

The Thirty-Nine Articles reaffirmed some pre-Reformation doctrines but rejected others.[62] The first five would have been perfectly acceptable to Roman Catholics or Eastern Orthodox Christians. They accepted the christological decrees of the ecumenical councils: that Christ was begotten by the Father before all ages and that he was one person with two natures. They affirmed Jesus's virgin birth. The Articles affirmed that Christ and the Holy Spirit were co-equal with God the Father. They did not question the *filioque* interpolation in the Nicene Creed. They did not revisit the condemnation of Pelagianism; indeed Calvinist emphasis on human depravity would not have allowed them do so.

Many of the articles reaffirmed characteristically protestant beliefs. Article VI affirmed the sufficiency of scripture: "Holy Scripture containeth all things necessary to salvation: so that whatsoever is not read therein, nor may be proved thereby, is not to be required of any man, that it should be believed as an article of the Faith, or be thought requisite or necessary to salvation." Was it *permissible* to believe doctrines that were not in scripture? The answer was a guarded "yes." But Article XXII warned that belief in "Purgatory, Pardons, Worshipping and Adoration, as well of Images as of Relics, and also Invocation of Saints, is a fond thing, vainly invented, and grounded upon no warranty of Scripture, but rather repugnant to the Word of God."

Three articles addressed justification through faith. Article XI made the standard Lutheran assertion: "We are accounted righteous before God, only for the merit of our Lord and Saviour Jesus Christ by Faith, and not for our own works or deservings." The doctrine of justification was based primarily on three passages in Romans, notably: "[B]eing justified by faith, we have peace with God through our Lord Jesus Christ" (Rom 5:1).[63] Belief in justification by faith had to confront the passage in the Epistle of James asserting that "faith without works is dead" (Jas

62. Thirty-Nine Articles.

63. In his German translation Luther appended "alone" to "justified by faith" to strengthen his argument.

2:20). Luther's response was to question the canonicity of James and relegate it to an appendix to his Bible.

While Luther rejected the notion that good works could secure salvation, he conceded that they were the "fruits of faith" and that we should "offer up ourselves for our neighbors' benefit and for the honor of God."[64] Articles XII supported that view, allowing for belief in the merit of good works performed after justification and inspired by the grace it afforded. Good works, it proclaimed, "are the fruits of Faith, and follow after Justification . . . . [They are] pleasing and acceptable to God in Christ, and do spring out necessarily of a true and lively Faith." On the other hand, Article XIII warned that "Works done before the grace of Christ, and the Inspiration of his Spirit, are not pleasant to God." And Article XIV reminded preachers that "Voluntary Works besides, over and above, God's Commandments . . . cannot be taught without arrogancy and impiety."

Predestination never became a conspicuous feature of Anglican teachings. Nevertheless, Article XVII testified to Calvinist influence: "Predestination to Life is the everlasting purpose of God, whereby (before the foundations of the world were laid) he hath constantly decreed by his counsel secret to us, to deliver from curse and damnation those whom he hath chosen in Christ out of mankind, and to bring them by Christ to everlasting salvation." However, "curious and carnal persons, lacking the Spirit of Christ, [should] have continually before their eyes the sentence of God's Predestination . . . a most dangerous downfall, whereby the Devil doth thrust them either into desperation, or into wretchlessness of most unclean living, no less perilous than desperation." The simultaneous affirmation of predestination in Article XVII and good works in Articles XII and XIII created an uneasy compromise between competing philosophical positions; but it was understandable in the spirit of Anglican ambiguity.

Article XXV affirmed the efficacy of the sacraments: "Sacraments ordained of Christ be not only badges or tokens of Christian men's profession, but rather they be certain sure witnesses, and effectual signs of grace, and God's good will towards us, by the which he doth work invisibly in us, and doth not only quicken, but also strengthen and confirm our Faith in him." It went on to distinguish the dominical sacraments from the other five in the Roman canon:

64. Luther, "The Fruits of Faith."

> There are two Sacraments ordained of Christ our Lord in the
> Gospel, that is to say, Baptism, and the Supper of the Lord. Those
> five commonly called Sacraments, that is to say, Confirmation,
> Penance, Orders, Matrimony, and Extreme Unction, are not to be
> counted for Sacraments of the Gospel, being such as have grown
> partly of the corrupt following of the Apostles, partly are states
> of life allowed in the Scriptures, but yet have not like nature of
> Sacraments with Baptism, and the Lord's Supper, for that they
> have not any visible sign or ceremony ordained of God.

Article XXVI reaffirmed the Roman doctrine that sacramental efficacy was not undermined by a priest's unworthiness; the sacraments were performed in Christ's name, not his. Interestingly, both Wycliffe and Cranmer had questioned that doctrine.

Article XXVII asserted the regenerative power of baptism and its efficacy in forgiving sin:

> Baptism is not only a sign of profession, and mark of difference,
> whereby Christian men are discerned from others that be not
> christened, but it is also a sign of Regeneration or New-Birth,
> whereby, as by an instrument, they that receive Baptism rightly
> are grafted into the Church; the promises of the forgiveness of
> sin, and of our adoption to be the sons of God by the Holy Ghost,
> are visibly signed and sealed, Faith is confirmed, and Grace increased by virtue of prayer unto God..

Article XXX insisted on the distribution of Communion under both kinds: the cup as well as the bread. And Article XXVIII reaffirmed the Cranmerian understanding of the Eucharist, already enshrined in the Prayer Book:

> The Supper of the Lord is not only a sign of the love that
> Christians ought to have among themselves one to another, but
> rather it is a Sacrament of our Redemption by Christ's death:
> insomuch that to such as rightly, worthily, and with faith, receive
> the same, the Bread which we break is a partaking of the Body
> of Christ; and likewise the Cup of Blessing is a partaking of the
> Blood of Christ.
>
> Transubstantiation (or the change of the substance of
> Bread and Wine) in the Supper of the Lord, cannot be proved
> by Holy Writ; but is repugnant to the plain words of Scripture,
> overthroweth the nature of a Sacrament, and hath given occasion
> to many superstitions.

> The Body of Christ is given, taken, and eaten, in the Supper, only after an heavenly and spiritual manner. And the mean whereby the Body of Christ is received and eaten in the Supper, is Faith.

The belief that the eucharistic elements were not corporeally transformed was also supported by Article XXIX, which denied that unworthy communicants receive the body and blood of Christ.

Article XXXI rejected notions of eucharistic sacrifice: "The Offering of Christ once made is that perfect redemption, propitiation, and satisfaction, for all the sins of the whole world, both original and actual; and there is none other satisfaction for sin, but that alone."

Articles XXV warned that "The Sacraments were not ordained of Christ to be gazed upon, or to be carried about"; and Article XXVIII ended with "The Sacrament of the Lord's Supper was not by Christ's ordinance reserved, carried about, lifted up, or worshipped." The latter statement targeted elevation of the eucharistic elements during the Communion service. The two Articles also targeted devotions like Benediction of the Blessed Sacrament and processions involving the Sacrament.

Cranmer had sought to standardize Anglican worship. But Article XXXIV provided flexibility for future changes: "It is not necessary that Traditions and Ceremonies be in all places one, or utterly like; for at all times they have been divers, and may be changed according to the diversity of countries, times, and men's manners." That article provided support for the creation of liturgies for Anglican provinces outside England—and possibly for the optional forms provided in most modern liturgies.

Article XXXV retroactively gave the homilies canonical status: "The Second Book of Homilies, the several titles whereof we have joined under this Article, doth contain a godly and wholesome Doctrine, and necessary for these times, as doth the former Book of Homilies, which were set forth in the time of Edward the Sixth; and therefore we judge them to be read in Churches by the Ministers, diligently and distinctly, that they may be understood of the people."

Parliament decreed in 1571 that clergy and university faculty subscribe to the Thirty-Nine Articles. The Articles were included in that year's printing of the *Book of Common Prayer*, together with a royal declaration stating: "no man hereafter shall either print or preach, to draw the Article aside any way, but shall submit to it in the plain and Full meaning thereof: and shall not put his own sense or comment to be the meaning of the Article, but shall take it in the literal and grammatical sense." They were also included in the 1662 *BCP*. The Test Act of 1672, which was not repealed until 1824, made subscription to the Articles a prerequisite for holding civil office. Otherwise, the laity were not examined on their theological views, beyond subscribing to the Creed. Unless a layperson publicly denied a principle in the Creed, he or she could not be charged with heresy.

Whether the Thirty-Nine Articles were intended as statements of eternal truth, or as provisional statements expressing current understanding, is unclear. In any event, in the spirit of the Elizabethan Settlement, they were phrased loosely enough to permit a range of interpretations, and—notwithstanding the 1571 warning—debate continued on what the Articles truly meant. In the seventeenth century. John Bramhall, archbishop of Armagh, noted that some of the Articles repeated truths already covered by the Creeds, while others were of a practical rather than a doctrinal nature. He also declared that "some of them are pious opinions or inferior truths, which are proposed by the Church of England to all her sons, as not to be opposed; not as essentials of Faith necessary to be believed by all Christians . . . under pain of damnation."[65] Objections to the Articles became more strident with the growth of liberalism in the nineteenth and twentieth centuries.

The Thirty-Nine Articles remained the Anglican Communion's principal confessional statement for four centuries. But in 1968 the Lambeth Conference passed a resolution "suggesting" that member churches no longer require ordinands to subscribe to the Articles, or at least that subscription "be required, and given, only in the context of a statement which gives the full range of our inheritance of faith and sets the Articles in their historical context."[66] The Articles were to be treated as historical artifacts.

ANGLICAN SACRED MUSIC

Sacred music was one of the great strengths of pre-Reformation Christianity. But it faced serious challenges at the Reformation. While

---

65. Bramhall, "Schism Guarded," 476.
66. Anglican Communion, *Lambeth Conference*, 1968, §43a–c.

Luther was a strong supporter, Calvin was hostile, and Zwingli banned all church music on the grounds that it distracted from preaching.

The English Reformers recognized the importance of music in public worship, taking heed of the scriptural verse: "[Speak] to yourselves in psalms and hymns and spiritual songs, singing and making melody in your heart to the Lord" (Eph 5:19). Henry VIII abolished the religious orders, which had been the primary sources of sacred music in medieval times. But he was a renowned music lover. Eight monastic cathedrals, including Canterbury, and six abbeys were converted into secular cathedrals staffed by non-monastic clergy and lay choirs. The Church of England preserved sacred music's traditional roles of proclaiming the glory of God and raising spiritual consciousness.

Cranmer commissioned John Merbecke (c. 1510–c. 1585), organist of St George's Chapel, Windsor, to create new chants for the vernacular liturgy: "And (to the end the people may the better hear) in such places where they do sing, there shall the lessons be sung in a plain tune after the manner of distinct reading."[67] The result was the 1549 *Book of Common Prayer Noted*, published a few months after the *BCP* itself.[68] Fitting English words to the melodies of medieval chant, in which one syllable often extended over multiple notes, was difficult; it also conflicted with the ideal of a liturgy accessible to ordinary people. But Merbecke managed to adapt passages from Ambrosian and Gregorian chant in addition to composing new melodies. No corresponding musical companion to the 1552 Prayer Book was composed, and his compositions fell into disuse.[69]

Anglican chant, as we know it, dates from Elizabethan times. Its objective was to create simple musical forms for the psalms, canticles, and other biblical texts—forms that would be suitable for choir or congregational use. Again, the goal was to capture the sense of reading aloud. Each verse or half-verse, however long, was chanted on a single recitative tone, with a short metrical ending. Anglican chant is a unique style whose beauty and reverence have stood the test of time. Numerous composers have offered settings, often in four-part harmony. Anglican chant was ideal for responsive use; part of the verse could be sung by a cantor and the remainder by the choir or congregation. Alternatively, double choirs could sing alternate verses or half-verses antiphonally.

67. *BCP* 1549, "An Order for Matins." Parenthesis in original.

68. Leaver, "The Prayer Book Noted," 39–43.

69. Merbecke's chants were revived in the nineteenth century.

In the Anglican liturgy, spoken and chanted, the custom was to end all psalms and some canticles with the doxology: "Glory be to the Father, and to the Son, and to the Holy Ghost. Amen."[70]

Richard Hooker recognized the sacramental dimension of music, proclaiming that "so pleasing effects it hath in that very part of man which is most divine, that some have been thereby induced to think that the soul itself by nature is or hath in it harmony." Music, he continued, fills "the mind with an heavenly joy and for the time in a manner [severs] it from the body."[71]

Despite political and religious tumult, the Tudor and early Stuart periods—including the reign of Mary I—represented a golden age of English sacred music. John Taverner, Thomas Tallis, Christopher Tye, William Byrd, and Orlando Gibbons were just a few of the composers whose names are as familiar today as in their own time. They served the musical needs of the great cathedrals and college chapels: Taverner was master of the choristers at Christ Church, Oxford; Tye choirmaster of Ely Cathedral; and Byrd organist and choirmaster at Lincoln Cathedral. In 1567 Archbishop Parker published a Psalter containing nine harmonized melodies by Tallis.[72]

Musicians' religious orientations and musical tastes sometimes conflicted with their monarchs'. Taverner's Lutheranism clashed with Henry VIII's Catholicism. Tye's Protestantism offended the Roman Catholic Mary I. Latin compositions were discouraged by Edward VI, but found favor again with Mary, and also by Elizabeth.[73] Elizabeth was willing to overlook Tallis's and Byrd's Roman Catholicism because of their musical genius.

The Chapel Royal enjoyed its greatest prominence under Elizabeth, but its musical excellence continued, and later "gentlemen of the chapel" included John Blow and Henry Purcell in the seventeenth century and Jeremiah Clarke, William Croft, and George Frideric Handel in the eighteenth. Their work was also performed in large churches and cathedrals and eventually in concert halls. Polyphonic choral and instrumental music provided opportunities for composers and performers to strive

70. The *Lesser Doxology*, cited here, and the *Greater Doxology* ("Glory to God in the highest . . .") both date from the fourth century. The latter is based on Luke 2:14.

71. Hooker, *Of the Laws*, §XXXVIII, 159–60.

72. Caldwell, *The Oxford History*, vol. 1, 285.

73. Ibid., 293.

for new heights of creativity. The five choral sections of the ordinary of the Mass: the *Kyrie, Gloria, Credo, Sanctus,* and *Agnus Dei/Benedictus,* inspired innumerable compositions with organ or orchestral accompaniment. Requiem Masses offered opportunities to explore emotions ranging from the depths of despair to the heights of expectant joy.

Only the largest churches had organs and trained choirs, and opportunities to incorporate music into the liturgy of most parish churches were limited. Independent groups of professional singers traveled around England, offering occasional sung services, but the singers were often unruly and sometimes intoxicated.[74] When congregational singing was encouraged at all, it was to sing metrical psalms. Simple psalm-tone settings of the canticles and parts of the Communion service were occasionally used. Congregational hymn singing eventually blossomed with the work of Charles Wesley in the eighteenth century. However Anglicans distanced themselves from the "street-corner" hymn singing, often based on secular tunes and accompanied by town bands, that became popular among Nonconformists.[75]

REFLECTIONS

To ask whether the break with Rome was a religious or a political decision is almost meaningless, so closely allied were religious and civil institutions in sixteenth-century England. That the break came because of Henry VIII's personal and dynastic desires stained the church's record. Yet the king was a stabilizing influence, stemming a precipitous slide toward continental Protestantism and promoting Anglicanism's "catholic and reformed" identity. Good outcomes clearly can come from questionable beginnings.

The English Reformers' greatest contribution was the *Book of Common Prayer.* It came to define the church; a good argument can be made that 1549, rather than 1534, was the year when the Church of England became truly *Anglican.* The church's cohesion—remarkable, considering the turmoil of the post-Reformation period and the tensions of later times—was achieved not through confessional conformity

---

74. Rosman, *The Evolution,* 238–39.

75. William Booth, whose Salvation Army organized its own bands, would retort: "Why should the Devil have all the best tunes?"

or ecclesiastical discipline but through common worship. *Lex orandi lex credendi* was, and remains, a powerful concept.

By the time Elizabeth ascended the throne England had swung, in less than a quarter-century, from Roman Catholic, to independent Catholic, to Calvinist, back to Roman Catholic, and finally to the enduring and distinctive Anglicanism. The Elizabethan Settlement set the church on its inclusive, pluralistic course, providing welcome relief from the strife of the previous quarter-century; few people went to the stake after Elizabeth ascended the throne. Those who stressed "catholic," in the catholic-and-reformed formula, and those who stressed "reformed," were all able to find a place in the church. The high-church party and, what became known as the low-church party—consisting at different times of reformists, Puritans, and Evangelicals—have managed to coexist for nearly five centuries.

The via media, the other great achievement of Elizabeth's reign, has sometimes been dismissed as an expedient compromise. But the intention was to build a church that could enjoy the strengths of the Roman and protestant traditions while avoiding their respective weaknesses. Hooker, the via media's principal exponent, is honored on November 3 in the modern calendar of saints. The collect for the day pays due tribute: "O God of truth and peace, who didst raise up thy servant Richard Hooker in a day of bitter controversy to defend with sound reasoning and great charity the catholic and reformed religion: Grant that we may maintain that middle way, not as a compromise for the sake of peace, but as a comprehension for the sake of the truth."[76] We can all affirm "Amen."

During the Civil War and Commonwealth periods the Church of England came under extreme stress, threatening its very survival. But when the episcopate was restored the church returned to the form that developed under Elizabeth I. From then on it faced few external challenges until the nineteenth century.

The Prayer Book, the Elizabethan Settlement, and the via media combined to keep apparently incompatible positions in creative tension in the hope of eventual resolution into a larger synthesis. The distinctive response to controversy has been extraordinarily successful,[77] and our prayer is that it be given a chance as the church faces the challenges of the twenty-first century.

76. Source: Standing Commission on Liturgy and Music, ECUSA.

77. See the discussion in Avis, "What is 'Anglicanism'?" 469.

Few Anglicans would question England's right to escape from Roman jurisdiction that was both oppressive and of questionable legitimacy. The break with Rome fulfilled a heartfelt yearning for independence. But that realization does not prevent us from seeing the Reformation as an overreaction to medieval Christianity's problems.

Had the wisdom and will been there, the problems could have been addressed without destroying centuries of tradition. The episcopate was preserved, and many church buildings survived. But the monasteries, the spiritual centers of medieval English Christianity, were destroyed, along with the ascetic, scholarly, artistic, and service ideals they embodied. The poor and sick, who relied on monastery-based welfare, were left without help at the very time when the assault on "good works" diminished society's concern for the needy. Government Poor Law programs never compensated for the loss.

Most serious was the attack on sacramental mystery. The process of demystification, which began with scholasticism but was greatly intensified by the Reformation, not only hurt the emerging Anglican consciousness but led inexorably to the modern polarities of liberalism and fundamentalism. Fortunately, a high-church tradition emerged to ensure that the mystical heritage of the English church was not entirely lost.

4

The Anglican Church in Scotland and North America

EXPANSION BEYOND ENGLAND OPENED up vast new opportunities for growth but also exposed Anglican traditions to stresses very different from those in the home country. The daughter churches in Scotland and North America encountered crises that very nearly caused their demise. But they survived and went on to make unique contributions to worldwide Anglicanism, while retaining essential traditions of the mother church.

The Scottish Episcopal Church remained small but offered an Anglican alternative to the Presbyterianism of John Knox and preserved a sacramental liturgy seriously impaired in England. The Episcopal Church in the United States inherited the Scottish liturgy. It also showed how Anglicanism could flourish in a new nation committed to democratic government and church–state separation. Anglicanism in British North America—which eventually became Canada—was molded by political and cultural ties with Great Britain but became much more than a missionary outpost of the Church of England.

THE CHURCH IN SCOTLAND

Christianity may have reached Scotland as early as the fifth century, and the famous monastery on the island of Iona was founded in 563 (see Figure 2.1). Celtic Christianity flourished for centuries, despite the ravages of Viking attacks. In the eleventh century the saintly Queen Margaret revitalized the Scottish church, albeit at the expense of destroying what remained of its Celtic tradition. Among much else she founded Dunfermline Abbey, north of Edinburgh.[1] Her son, David I, converted Dunfermline into a Benedictine abbey and installed an abbot and twelve monks from Canterbury. The Scottish church was brought firmly into the Roman orbit.

The fifteenth century was important for Scotland. The diocese of St Andrews, founded in 906, was raised to an archdiocese in 1465. Education was strengthened by establishment of the Universities of St Andrews (1413), Glasgow (1450), and Aberdeen (1495), whose scholars played important roles in the Reformation. Meanwhile Scotland acquired new territory. When King James III married Margaret of Denmark in 1468 he received the Orkney and Shetland Islands as dowry. Twenty years later the Scottish king brought the Western Isles, previously ruled by chieftains of Celtic–Norse ancestry, under royal control.

Scotland and England had a long history of mutual hostility, which from time to time erupted into outright war. Scotland was militarily weaker but leveraged its position through the "Auld Alliance" with France.

The Scottish Reformation

The Scottish monarchy was weak and corrupt in the first half of the sixteenth century. The Roman Catholic Mary Stuart succeeded her father, James V, in 1542, when she was only six days old. The resulting power vacuum was filled by equally corrupt nobles and churchmen, including the archbishop of St Andrews, Cardinal David Beaton.

Reformist ideas circulated in Scotland despite the authorities' attempts to suppress them. Among the men brave enough to speak out was John Knox (c. 1513–72), former priest and lecturer at St Andrews University. Exiled after Beaton's murder in 1546, he served as chaplain to King Edward VI in England and then spent time in Geneva with Calvin. By the time Knox returned to Scotland in 1559, he was a committed Calvinist, and the country was eager to hear his message. Appointed minister of St. Giles' Cathedral, Edinburgh, his fiery preaching attracted a large following.

The next year the "Reformation Parliament" passed a series of measures rejecting papal jurisdiction, banning celebration of the Mass, and endorsing the Confession of Faith: a twenty-five-chapter statement

---

1. Margaret's remains were buried at Dunfermline, and she was canonized in 1250.

of Calvinist beliefs written by Knox and five others. An accompanying *Book of Discipline* outlined a new governance structure for the Church of Scotland, the *Kirk*. The episcopate was abolished and governance entrusted to a General Assembly composed of ministers and elders—the latter chiefly representing the nobility and gentry. In place of consecrated bishops, parliament was to appoint district supervisors; they should not, the book warned, "live idle, as the bishops had done heretofore."[2]

Royal assent to the parliamentary measures was impossible while Mary was on the throne. She was deposed in 1567 in favor of her infant son who became King James VI.[3] But the standoff between reformers and court continued. A compromise agreement was finally negotiated in 1572 by then-regent Lord Morton. The Concordat of Leith endorsed the statutes of 1560, except for the proposed system of district superintendents.[4] Bishops were to be appointed by the crown and would have seats in parliament. Instruments of royal policy, they were bishops in name only. No provision was made for valid consecration, and in ecclesiastical matters they would be answerable to the General Assembly.

After he became king of both England and Scotland, James pressed the General Assembly to restore an ecclesiastically relevant episcopate. In 1610 three of the titular bishops were consecrated in London: John Spottiswood of Glasgow, Andrew Lamb of Brechin, and Gavin Hamilton of Galloway.[5] Even then, the Kirk was in no sense Anglican. It embraced Calvinist beliefs. And worship followed Knox's *Book of Common Order*, which provided an outline for public worship and administration of the sacraments but made liberal allowance for extemporaneous prayer.

In due course James sought to bring the Scottish church into liturgical conformity with the Church of England. In 1618 the General Assembly approved episcopal confirmation, administration of the Eucharist to the sick, and observance of holy days. It also required the faithful to kneel to receive Holy Communion.

Charles I, continued his father's anglicization policy, and a new Prayer Book for Scotland—the so-called "Laud's Book"—was published in 1637. Many Scots perceived it as further English interference. Calvinist

2. Tytler, *History of Scotland*, 210–18.

3. Mary Queen of Scots took refuge in England where she was imprisoned and finally executed by Elizabeth I.

4. MacCulloch, *The Reformation*, 381. Leith is close to Edinburgh.

5. Goldie, *A Short History*, 4–5.

clergy exploited public anger both to reject the Prayer Book and to re-establish presbyterian governance. The General Assembly met in 1638, in defiance of a royal order of dissolution, and ordered that all fourteen Scottish bishops be deposed; eight were excommunicated.[6]

By then Charles was unpopular in both kingdoms, and the situation deteriorated rapidly, leading to Laud's and Charles's execution, abolition of the English episcopate, and Civil War. English parliamentarians shared many of the Scottish Calvinists' religious ideals, and in 1646 they jointly formulated the Westminster Confession, which became an official statement of presbyterian doctrine. Yet when Oliver Cromwell appealed to the Kirk for support he was rebuffed. In retaliation he invaded and occupied the lowlands of Scotland. Charles II, who had been crowned king of Scotland in 1649, fled to France.

After Charles II was restored to the thrones of England and Scotland in 1660, he created a Scottish episcopate once again. Of the bishops who had been in office in 1638 only Thomas Sydserf of Galloway survived, so four new bishops were consecrated in England to fill vacancies. The restored episcopate enjoyed official support for nearly thirty years. Its succession flowed solely through the Church of England; no link remained with the pre-Reformation Scottish episcopate.

The Nonjuring Church

James VII (II of England), Charles's brother, was deposed in 1689, and William and Mary came to the thrones of the two kingdoms. Having taken oaths of allegiance to James, the Scottish bishops refused to recognize the new monarchs and, like their English nonjuring counterparts, were dismissed from their sees. William disestablished the Church of Scotland, which at once made the presbyterian system permanent. The Nonjurors initially claimed that they represented the rightful Church of Scotland, but they lacked legal status. Eventually it became clear that they represented a separate religious entity, and they accepted the name "Scottish Episcopal Church" (SEC).

The bishops performed all the normal episcopal duties, ordaining priests and appointing them to parishes whose patrons supported the nonjuring cause. In due course they consecrated new bishops to preserve the succession. Appointing diocesan bishops was considered a royal

---

6. "A Brief History," §4. See also Rankin, *A Handbook*, 189–90.

prerogative, so in the king's absence most new bishops were designated bishops-at-large, or *collegial* bishops.

In 1712, after the Acts of Union united England and Scotland into Great Britain, parliament in Westminster created a "qualified" Scottish Episcopal Church. It had no bishops of its own but was served by priests ordained by English or Irish bishops. Functioning as a missionary outpost of the Church of England, it used the 1662 *Book of Common Prayer*. Not unexpectedly the Nonjurors refused to recognize the qualified church. The outcome was that four denominations competed for the hearts and minds of the Scottish people: the presbyterian Church of Scotland, with greatest support in the lowlands; the qualified church, influential in the border counties; the nonjuring SEC; and Roman Catholicism in the highlands.

An estimated one-third of the population initially supported the nonjuring SEC. But support dwindled over time,[7] until its strength lay only in the adjacent dioceses of Brechin and Aberdeen in the Northeast. Despite its small size and paucity of resources, the nonjuring Scottish church had a disproportionate influence on the future of Anglicanism. In 1747 the bishops instituted a system of governance very different from that of the Church of England. Presbyters—"priest" never became common in Scotland—elected bishops, and the bishops elected a *primus*.[8] The latter title originated from the Latin *primus inter pares* ("first among equals"). No provision was made for archbishops. With some interaction with English Nonjurors, the bishops developed a distinctive liturgy, notably the 1764 Communion Service, which will be discussed later.

The Scottish Nonjurors' cause always overlapped with Jacobite claims to the throne, and harsh penal laws were imposed after the failed rebellions of 1715 and 1745.[9] A law enacted in 1748 prohibited public worship; bishops and clergy were imprisoned, and mobs burned Episcopal churches. The church was virtually destroyed in the western highlands, which had been the hotbed of insurrection.[10] By the time George II died in 1760, the SEC was, in the words of Walter Scott,

---

7. Hefling, "Scotland," 168, 174.

8. Stevick, *Canon Law*, 222.

9. Gaskoin, "Nonjurors," 394–96.

10. Goldie, *A Short History*, 104.

"a shadow of a shade."[11] Only four bishops remained in the whole of Scotland.[12]

The situation changed with the accession of George III and then with the death of the last credible pretender to the throne. In 1788 John Skinner (1744–1816), bishop of Aberdeen and recently elected primus, convened a synod at which the Nonjurors affirmed their allegiance to King George.[13] Four years later, royal assent was given to a parliamentary measure ending the penal laws and recognizing the nonjuring church as the legitimate Scottish Episcopal Church. The qualified church gradually faded away.

The Modern Scottish Episcopal Church

The ancient church buildings were all in the hands of the Church of Scotland. When the penal laws were lifted and the SEC was allowed to worship publicly, new churches needed to be built. The first was St Andrew's Chapel, Aberdeen, constructed in 1792 next to Bishop Skinner's residence. The present building, destined to become St Andrew's Cathedral, was constructed in 1817. Cathedral construction in Scotland and elsewhere will be discussed in chapters 5 and 7.

The power center of the SEC moved from Aberdeen to Edinburgh. Aberdeen became famous for the longevity of its bishops, however; during the 120 years from 1786 to 1906, the diocese was served by only four bishops, including Skinner and his son William.

Official recognition opened the way for integration of qualified congregations into the SEC. William Drummond (1719–1806), consecrated bishop of Edinburgh in 1787, worked tirelessly to that end. A major step in the reconciliation process was agreement by the Scottish bishops to embrace the Thirty-Nine Articles. Another was the election of Daniel Sandford to succeed Drummond as bishop of Edinburgh. Sandford had been the presbyter of a qualified congregation and was an Englishman—the first ever elected to the Scottish episcopate.[14] One congregation reconciled with the SEC during Sandford's tenure was St

11. Scott, W., *Guy Mannering*, vol.1, 60.

12. Goldie, *A Short History*, 72.

13. Ibid., 70–71.

14. Ibid., 111–12. Sandford was born in Ireland of English parents.

George's Chapel, Edinburgh, where Walter Scott had worshipped. Full unity was achieved by 1820.

The training of clergy in the nonjuring Scottish church had been based on a system of internships. Bishops Skinner and Arthur Petrie (d.1787) of Ross and Moray both trained men personally, and the latter organized a small school in his home at Meiklefolla, Aberdeenshire.[15] From those small beginnings came the Theological Institute of the SEC. The seminary's headquarters is in Edinburgh, but branches are now located in all seven Scottish dioceses.

The Scottish Episcopal Church grew steadily during the nineteenth century. For example, ten new congregations were created within the Brechin diocese between 1840 and 1875, most of them during the tenure of the Anglo-Catholic Bishop Alexander Forbes.[16] From 1876 to 1900 the number of communicants in the SEC increased from 9,000 to 46,000, and the total number of members to over 100,000.[17]

Bishops, who had been excluded from the General Assembly of the Kirk, initially exercised sole control of the SEC; but presbyters were brought into the governance system in 1811 and laypeople in 1863.[18] The SEC, an autonomous member of the Anglican Communion, is now governed by a tricameral General Synod, consisting of the Houses of Bishops, Clergy, and Laity. The primus, elected by the bishops, remains a diocesan bishop. Scotland has had no metropolitan diocese since Bishop Arthur Rose of St Andrews died in 1704.

An order of deaconesses in the SEC was approved in 1929. The General Synod of 1993–4 approved the ordination of women to the priesthood, and the first ordinations took place in December 1994. The consecration of women bishops was approved by the Synod of 2002, though none has yet been elected. Debate continues over inclusiveness with respect to persons in same-sex relationships.

ENGLISH SETTLEMENT OF NORTH AMERICA

King Henry VII of England sponsored the voyage that brought the Venetian explorer John Cabot to Newfoundland. Cabot's party landed

15. Ibid., 69.
16. "A History of the Diocese."
17. Goldie, *A Short History*, 124.
18. Hefling, "Scotland," 223.

FIGURE 4.1: EARLY CENTERS OF ANGLICAN CHRISTIANITY IN NORTH AMERICA

on June 24, 1497, the feast of John the Baptist. The city of St John's was named in commemoration. (Figure 4.1 shows St John's and other locations of interest in the settlement of North America.) Thirty-six years later the king's son, Henry VIII, broke with Rome and the Church of England became an independent religious entity.

The rival maritime powers of Europe were all exploring North America in the sixteenth and seventeenth centuries. Territorial claims often were contested, and land changed hands as wars—some fought far away—were won or lost. Settlements and colonies were established, but conditions were harsh, and only a few succeeded. Colonial development was often outsourced to the private sector.[19] Companies, like the Dutch East India Company and the London Company, were charged with establishing a presence, developing agriculture and trade, providing for the educational and spiritual needs of settlers, and generating a satisfactory return to stockholders. Various forms of Christianity were introduced: Roman Catholicism by Spain and France, Lutheranism by Sweden, Calvinism by the Netherlands, and Anglicanism by England.

English exploration accelerated in the late sixteenth century. Martin Frobisher landed on Baffin Island in 1578, and his chaplain, Robert Wolfall, conducted the first Anglican service on North American soil.[20] Frobisher Bay is named in the explorer's honor. Five years later Humphrey Gilbert claimed the island of Newfoundland and attempted to found a settlement there—England's first in North America—but it failed. Also in the 1580s Walter Raleigh tried to establish a colony on Roanoke Island in present-day North Carolina. It failed too, but Virginia Dare was born on the island in 1587, the first child to English parents in the Americas. Also a native man reportedly was baptized there.

The first successful English settlement in North America was Jamestown, Virginia, named in honor of King James I (VI of Scotland). It was founded by Christopher Newport and John Smith in May 1607, one year before the French founded Quebec City. The Colony of Virginia was chartered to the London Company, renamed the Virginia Company two years later.[21]

New England was the responsibility of the Plymouth Company. A colony in present-day Maine failed, but in 1620 the Pilgrims—congregationalist dissidents originally from England, many via the Netherlands—arrived on the *Mayflower* and established Plymouth Colony. The first known settler in what is now Boston was William Blaxton, an Anglican clergyman who built a cabin on Beacon Hill in 1625. He left when settlers of the Massachusetts Bay Company arrived five years later. In 1643 the Plymouth and Massachusetts colonies were absorbed into the New England Confederation, a political and military

19. Roman Catholic Spain and France never employed that strategy. Some historians have suggested that large corporations were products of the Reformation.

20. The Canadian *Book of Common Prayer* commemorates the event on September 3.

21. James I revoked the company's charter in 1724 and made Virginia a crown colony.

alliance to resolve inter-colony disputes and defend against Native American attacks.[22]

The Province of Carolina, which included land between present-day Virginia and Georgia, was founded by sugar planters from Barbados.[23] It was subsequently divided by royal charter into North and South Carolina. The penal colony of Georgia soon followed. New Hampshire, Maryland, Rhode Island, and Pennsylvania were also established by royal charter. New York, Connecticut, New Jersey, and Delaware were seized from the Dutch in the 1660s.[24] The thirteen colonies eventually formed the United States.

Great Britain, created by the union of England and Scotland in 1707, gained additional territory through victories in a series of wars with France. In 1713 Britain acquired Acadia and subsequently divided it into the colonies of Nova Scotia ("New Scotland"), Prince Edward Island, New Brunswick, and Maine.[25] It acquired Quebec in 1763. Initially the British treated the Québécois badly, but their use of the French language, Roman Catholic faith, and French civil law were restored in 1774.[26] Spain ceded Florida to Britain in 1763 in exchange for Havana, Cuba.

By 1770 Britain controlled the whole eastern seaboard of North America, as well as Bermuda and numerous islands in the West Indies. Within a decade, however, it had lost much of its North American empire in the American Revolutionary War. Under the Treaty of Paris (1783) Britain surrendered the thirteen colonies, recognized the sovereignty of the United States, and returned Florida to Spanish rule.[27] What remained in British hands after the Revolutionary War, the area that eventually became Canada, was termed British North America (BNA), a belated attempt to view—but still not to administer—the colonies as an integrated whole.

---

22. Connecticut and New Haven also joined the confederation.

23. The *Fundamental Constitutions of Carolina*, attributed in part to political philosopher John Locke, were adopted in 1669.

24. Dutch forces had seized Delaware from Swedish settlers in 1655.

25. As many as 10,000 Acadians were deported. Many settled in Louisiana.

26. The Quebec Act of 1774, which also extended the borders of Quebec to the Great Lakes and Ohio Valley, was intended to dissuade the Québécois from joining the American Revolution.

27. Maine's status was contested by Britain and the United States until the War of 1812. Disputes over its status in the U.S. continued until it attained statehood in 1820.

During and after the Revolutionary War tens of thousands of loyalists fled the thirteen colonies. Many returned to the mother country, but the British government offered grants of land in BNA to encourage immigration. Settlers were reluctant to move to Quebec because of its French language and culture and the dominance of Roman Catholicism. So the Canada Act of 1791 divided the colony into Lower and Upper Canada. Francophone Lower Canada eventually recovered the name Quebec, while English-speaking Upper Canada became Ontario.[28] The two Canadas were temporarily reunited in 1841 to create the United Province but separated again when the Dominion of Canada was created in 1867.

Until the mid-eighteenth century, people of European descent were concentrated in the coastal regions of North America and along a few major rivers, like the St Lawrence and the Mississippi. The Arctic regions and much of the interior remained thinly populated by indigenous tribes but unexplored by Europeans. The United States subsequently made huge territorial gains from the Louisiana Purchase (1803), acquisition of Florida (1822), annexation of Texas (1845), and purchase of Alaska (1867). Meanwhile BNA/Canada expanded northward and westward. The separate colonies of Newfoundland and Labrador were united with the Dominion of Canada in 1949.[29]

THE CHURCH IN THE UNITED STATES

Anglicanism in the American Colonies

The Church of England acquired a strong presence in North America in the early seventeenth century, rivaled only by the Congregationalists of New England. The Virginia Company took the spiritual needs of its settlers seriously. It appointed Robert Hunt, chaplain on the initial voyage and a graduate of Magdalen College, Oxford, to serve the new parish of Jamestown. For his services he was paid £500 per year, a considerable sum for the time.

Worship facilities were primitive: "When the English first settled at Jamestown, their place of worship consisted of an awning, or old sail, suspended between three or four trees, to protect them from the sun.

28. "Upper Canada" referred to its location, farther up the St Lawrence River.

29. Canada did not achieve full independence within the British Commonwealth until 1982.

[T]he seats were unhewed trees, till plank was cut; the pulpit was a wooden crosspiece nailed to two neighboring trees. In inclement weather an old decayed tent served for the place of worship."[30] Later, "a homely structure like a barn was erected."[31] Despite the primitive facilities, "the service was read daily, morning and evening, and on Sunday two sermons were preached, and the communion celebrated every three months, till the Rev. Mr. Hunt died."[32] Construction of a brick church began in 1639, after the "homely structure" and a second wooden building both burned.

The Anglican church was dominant in Virginia. In 1699 the capital of colonial Virginia was moved from Jamestown to nearby Williamsburg, and Bruton Parish Church became the "court" church.[33] Pews were reserved for the governor and other dignitaries. George Washington, Thomas Jefferson, and Patrick Henry worshipped there when the legislature was in session.

When the Virginia House of Burgesses was created in 1619, the Church of England was legally established in the colony, ensuring public funding. Clergy were given *glebes*, or plots of land, as they had in medieval England, and stipends were paid, normally in tobacco, which could be sold at market prices. On the other hand the laity took control of church affairs. Parish vestries, created in 1662, were given broad powers, and most were soon controlled by wealthy plantation owners. Vestries established schools, cared for the poor, maintained local roads, and even adjudicated minor legal matters.[34] They also hired and fired clergy. Many priests were kept on renewable, one-year contracts, and concerns over job security made them hesitant to criticize parishioners' behavior.

Scarcity provided some bargaining power—and also prevented the colony from mandating Sunday church attendance. Ordination was possible only in England, and an estimated one in five men perished from shipwreck, disease, or piracy on the round-trip voyage. Also about

---

30. Campbell, *History of the Colony*, 52.

31. Whether the Jamestown church was the first Anglican house of worship in the New World is disputed; St George's, Bermuda, founded in 1612, also claims that distinction.

32. Campbell, *History of the Colony*, 52.

33. The capital of the new state of Virginia was moved to Richmond in 1780.

34. Hein & Shattuck, *The Episcopalians*, 11.

two-thirds of the clergy in pre-1660 Virginia died within five years of arrival.[35]

In 1693 the Church of England became the established church in the southern portion of New York, closest to New York City. Over the next several decades it was also legally established in Maryland (1702), South Carolina (1706), North Carolina (1730), and Georgia (1758). The robust agricultural structure of South Carolina supported a strong Anglican presence, particularly in the Charleston area.[36] But North Carolina and Georgia were poor, and by the time Anglicanism was legally established there, other denominations had gained a strong foothold.

Anglicanism remained a minority denomination in the mid-Atlantic colonies but still exerted considerable influence. Christ Church, Philadelphia, was founded in 1695 as a condition in William Penn's charter for the colony of Pennsylvania. It soon attracted former Quakers, including some of Penn's heirs.[37] When the First Continental Congress met at Carpenters' Hall in September 1774, Jacob Duché, rector of Christ Church, led the opening prayers. Fifteen signatories of the Declaration of Independence worshipped at Christ Church, and five, including Benjamin Franklin, are buried there. Anglicans were influential in founding the College of Philadelphia, which eventually became the University of Pennsylvania.

For a century every governor of New York was Anglican. In 1696 Governor Benjamin Fletcher approved the purchase of land in Lower Manhattan to build Trinity Church, Wall Street. The parish received its charter from William III the following May, and the church opened in 1698. Trinity, one of the best-known churches in the colonies, benefited greatly from royal patronage. With financial assistance from Queen Anne, the parish increased its land holdings and founded a charity school. In 1754 George II chartered King's College, now Columbia University. Trinity's parishioners included several colonial governors as well as George Washington. Alexander Hamilton is buried in the churchyard.

Congregationalism was the established religion in New England from the time the Pilgrims landed at Plymouth Rock. Under Governor John Winthrop and his successors, the colony of Massachusetts operated

35. Ibid., 12, 21.
36. Holmes, *A Brief History*, 34–35.
37. Ibid., 31.

as a theocracy. Remembering their ancestors' treatment in Elizabethan and Stuart England, the Congregationalists disliked the Anglican church as much as they disliked imperial rule. Until the Anglican King's Chapel, Boston, was organized in 1686, Congregationalists had a monopoly on worship in Massachusetts. The Act of Toleration ensured greater legal protection, but until 1727 Anglicans had to pay taxes to support the Congregational Church.[38]

Congregationalism was legally established in Connecticut and New Hampshire, and remained the official religion until the 1830s. Nevertheless, Anglican churches were built there and elsewhere in New England during the eighteenth century. Connecticut would eventually have more churches than Massachusetts, and it became the focus of Anglican activity after the Revolution.

The fact that some of the richest and most powerful people in the American colonies were Anglican made the church influential. The downside was that Anglicanism was perceived, as in England, as the religion of a wealthy elite. In the southern states some large-scale slave owners were Anglicans. Poorer and less educated people gravitated toward the less threatening Methodist Societies, which eventually broke away, or they joined other denominations that never bore the class stigma.

Support for the Colonial Churches

Clergy and parishes in the American colonies nominally fell under the jurisdiction of the bishop of London, but without a local episcopate they lacked effective ecclesiastical support. While we may speak of "the church" in Virginia or Connecticut, parishes operated more like independent congregations. Archbishop William Laud had considered appointing a bishop to Massachusetts in the 1630s, but he was executed in the approach to the Civil War, and the English episcopate was abolished. After the Restoration English bishops were preoccupied with rebuilding their own dioceses. The church in the colonies was largely forgotten until Henry Compton (1632–1713) became bishop of London. He created the system of commissaries. In addition to serving as parish rectors, commissaries had colony-wide responsibilities, functioning—albeit with considerably less power—like the papal legates in European countries.

---

38. Ibid., 28–29.

The first commissary, James Blair (1656–1743), was appointed in 1689 and served Virginia for fifty-seven years. One of his greatest accomplishments was to secure the charter for the College of William and Mary in Williamsburg, the first Anglican institute of higher education in America. Its mission included training men for the ministry, though they still had to go to England for ordination. The second commissary, Thomas Bray (1658–1730), was appointed to Maryland in 1695.

By the 1740s commissaries were working in nine colonies.[39] They brought a degree of order to the church, but in the supervision of clergy they competed with parish vestries. Colonial governors sometimes exercised a kind of lay-episcopal role, and they had the necessary political clout. Queen Anne gave the governor of New York strict instructions on how to run the church in his colony.[40] The same principle that enabled a monarch to serve as supreme governor of the church gave royal governors local ecclesiastical authority.

Bray spent only three months in Maryland, but after returning to England he collected religious books and pamphlets for poor parishes. Out of that initiative grew the Society for Promoting Christian Knowledge (SPCK), which supplied parishes on both sides of the Atlantic. Blair was also a charter member of the Society for the Propagation of the Gospel in Foreign Parts (SPG), founded in 1701. Its charge was to make such "provisions as may be necessary for propagation of the Gospel [in] the plantations, colonies, and factories of Great Britain beyond the seas."[41]

SPG money supported an estimated 300 clergy in the American colonies,[42] as well as missionaries in Nova Scotia and the Caribbean. The SPG also performed missionary work among immigrants from other European countries and among Native Americans and African slaves. Its reach extended from New England to Georgia, but its impact was greatest in the middle and northern colonies, where the church lacked public funding. High-quality training and the dedication of its people made the SPG an effective force. Two of its missionaries conducted the first Anglican service in Connecticut in 1702. Another was John Wesley.

Under SPG influence, seven clergymen in New Haven, Connecticut—all associated with the congregationalist bastion of Yale University—

39. Prichard, *A History*, 27–28.
40. Holmes, *A Brief History*, 41.
41. Pascoe, *Classified Digest*, 7.
42. Holmes, *A Brief History*, 45.

converted to Anglicanism.[43] They included the university's rector Timothy Cutler, tutor Daniel Browne, former tutor Samuel Johnson, and Samuel Seabury, father of America's first bishop. September 13, 1722, when the "Yale apostates" announced their conversion, became known in Congregational circles as Black Tuesday.

In 1660, the clergy of Virginia petitioned the bishop of London for the appointment of a bishop for the colony, and in due course other colonies made similar requests. High-church clergy strongly supported the creation of an American episcopate, but their efforts were opposed by an odd coalition of forces. In the South powerful vestries feared curtailment of their power. New England legislatures were unwilling to endorse any measure that would benefit Anglican interests. Throughout the colonies, suspicions arose that that bishops—who might perhaps sit in the House of Lords—would increase royal control. Even the creation of resident *suffragan*, or assistant, bishops was opposed. Despite resistance in the colonies, British clergyman William Jones blamed his government's failure to create a colonial episcopate for the American Revolution.[44]

A National Anglican Church

When the Revolutionary War broke out, 400 Anglican parishes operated in the thirteen colonies, ninety-eight in Virginia alone. Clergy, most now born in the colonies, found themselves in much the same position as the Nonjurors. They had sworn allegiance to the British crown and could not easily support the revolution. Their forebears had remained loyal to the monarchy during the English Civil War and Interregnum. Moreover, clergy were obligated to use the *Book of Common Prayer* which contained prayers for the monarch and parliament.

In the northern colonies, where SPG provided broad financial support, most clergy—an estimated eighty percent in New England—supported the loyalist cause. Unwilling to break their ordination oaths, many priests either closed their churches or delegated parish responsibilities to laypeople. In the South clergy had taken oaths to the legislatures as well as to the crown. Not incidentally, they were also employed by vestries dominated by landowners who supported the revolution. In consequence, about three-quarters of southern clergy sided with the pa-

---

43. Hein & Shattuck, *The Episcopalians*, 18.
44. Wilde, "Hutchinsonianism," 10.

triots. Nonetheless, the church in the South ultimately fared worse than it did elsewhere.

During and after the war 80,000 people left the colonies. Some 30,000 sought refuge in Nova Scotia, doubling the population; among them was Charles Inglis, rector of Trinity Church, New York City, who became the colony's first bishop.[45] Another 10,000 emigrated to Quebec.[46] John Stuart, a missionary to Mohawk Indians in the colony of New York, led his family and a few African slaves to Upper Canada and became a founder of the Anglican church of Ontario.[47]

By the end of the war the Anglican church was weakened to the point where its very survival was in doubt. Roughly one-half of the clergy had fled, along with a large proportion of its strongest lay supporters. Clergy who remained faced economic hardship as well as persecution from the authorities and people at large. The church had no bishops and consequently no mechanism for ordination. It had no institutional structure; convocations in the various colonies had not met on a regular basis. The bishop of London, whose nominal oversight had been a unifying force, no longer exercised authority. And the SPG, whose regional meetings provided the closest approximation to a framework for inter-colony contacts, had withdrawn.

Notwithstanding, efforts soon began to reorganize the Anglican church under the new political reality. One initiative began in New England. In March 1783 a convocation of clergy in Connecticut elected Samuel Seabury (1729–96) its first bishop. Seabury, son of a "Yale apostate," had been an SPG missionary and an outspoken loyalist but subsequently had declared his allegiance to the United States. Four months after his election, with the support of clergy in Connecticut and Massachusetts, Seabury sailed for London, seeking consecration.

Peace between Britain and the United States was secured by the Treaty of Paris. But there was still no provision for clerical ordinations without the oath of allegiance to the monarch; the archbishop of Canterbury expressed sympathy for Seabury's plight but was unable to help. Seabury declined an offer of consecration by a Lutheran bishop in Denmark.

---

45. Trinity Church was destroyed by fire in 1776.

46. Hayes, *Anglicans*, 52–53.

47. DeMille, *The Catholic Movement*, 11.

Instead Seabury approached the nonjuring Scottish Episcopal Church, and on November 14, 1784, was consecrated in Aberdeen.[48] Penal laws prohibited services in public, so the consecration took place in a private residence.[49] Seabury signed a concordat with his hosts affirming a "bond of union between the Catholic remainder of the ancient Church of Scotland, and the now rising Church in Connecticut."[50] It also urged the latter to adopt the Scottish eucharistic rite, and affirmed that the parties involved "had nothing in view but the Glory of God and the good of His Church."

Upon his return to America Seabury ordained four men to the diaconate and one, Colin Ferguson, to the priesthood. Ferguson, the first Anglican priest ordained in the United States, was charged with performing "the office of a Priest in the Church of Christ, particularly in St Paul's Parish, in the State of Maryland."[51] Seabury, currently the only bishop in the nation, styled himself "bishop of all America."[52] In 1790 he took diocesan responsibility for Rhode Island in addition to Connecticut.

A separate initiative was underway in the mid-Atlantic states. In 1780 a conference of clergy and laity at Chestertown, Maryland, resolved that "the Church formerly known in the Province as the Church of England should now be called the Protestant Episcopal Church." William White (1748–1836), rector of St Peter's and Christ Church, Philadelphia, published a pamphlet in 1782 calling for the creation of a new national church. "Episcopalians on this continent," he wrote, should "institute among themselves an Episcopal government, as soon as it shall appear practicable, and that this government will not be attended with the danger of tyranny, either temporal or spiritual."[53] White defended episcopal ordination but proposed that new clergy be "conditionally

48. Stephen, *History of the Church*, 400. That was not Seabury's first visit to Scotland; he had studied medicine in Edinburgh in the 1750s.

49. Goldie, *A Short History*, 66–69. Claims that Seabury was consecrated in St Andrew's Chapel clearly are mistaken; the chapel was built eight years later.

50. *Concordat*, preamble. "Church of Scotland" was legally assigned to the Presbyterian Church at that time.

51. Sprague, *Annals*, 342–43. Ferguson later became principal of Washington College, Maryland.

52. Prichard, *A History*, 89.

53. Quoted in Armentrout & Slocum, *Documents*, 2–14. White may have been the first person to use the term "Episcopalian."

ordained" in the expectation that a bishop would formalize their ordinations later.[54] The proposal was never implemented.

While Seabury was en route to Britain, Maryland clergy voted to create a diocese,[55] which was duly recognized by the legislature. William Smith (1727–1803), chaplain to the Continental Congress, organized the first state convention of the Protestant Episcopal Church. The convention created positions of "presiding clergy" to serve in supervisory roles until bishops could be appointed. Dioceses were also created in Virginia, Pennsylvania, New York, New Jersey, Delaware, and South Carolina.

At a meeting in New York in 1784 delegates from those states agreed that there should be a General Convention to serve as the church's governing body. The convention met in 1785 and twice the following year, creating a framework for a new national church. A "Proposed Book" was compiled to replace the English *BCP*. And a petition was sent to the archbishop of Canterbury requesting consecration of three bishops to serve the United States.

The English bishops had reservations about the new church's petition, not least because of the proposed changes to the liturgy. Parliamentary approval was finally given in 1786, after the General Convention agreed to eliminate offending parts of the Proposed Book—and after the archbishop of Canterbury was persuaded that greater damage would be done if the United States were served solely by bishops of the nonjuring lineage. In place of the traditional oath of allegiance, American bishops would declare: "I do solemnly engage to conform to the doctrine and worship of the Protestant Episcopal Church."[56] In February 1787, William White of Pennsylvania and Samuel Provoost of New York were consecrated by the archbishops of Canterbury and York and two other bishops.[57] Three years later James Madison, president of William and Mary College, was consecrated in England and became the first bishop of Virginia.[58]

For a while it seemed possible that the New England Episcopal Church and the Protestant Episcopal Church of the mid-Atlantic and southern states would remain separate. Serious issues divided the two

54. Ibid.

55. The date of the meeting is recorded as August 13, 1783.

56. *Bishops' Statement*, §III.

57. Strong, J., *Cyclopedia of Biblical*, vol. VIII, 675.

58. This James Madison is not to be confused with his second cousin, the fourth president of the United States.

bodies. One was clergy's earlier sympathies in the Revolutionary War. Another was the difference in episcopal succession. A third was the nature and composition of state conventions; New England wanted episcopal control of state conventions; the southern and mid-Atlantic states wanted lay control. A fourth issue concerned the liturgy and emphasis given to the sacraments.

Creation of a national church was on the agenda of the General Convention meeting in Philadelphia in July 1789. Bishop White presided, but no representatives came from New England. Seabury boycotted the meeting because of questions concerning the legitimacy of his consecration. When it became obvious that unity was essential, the meeting adjourned until September "for the purpose of settling articles of union, discipline, uniformity of worship, and general government among all the churches in the United States."[59]

The meeting reconvened with both White and Seabury present, and on October 16, 1789, agreement was reached on a broad range of issues. Approval was given for a national church to be known as the Protestant Episcopal Church in the United States of America (PECUSA). A new *Book of Common Prayer* was also approved. The agreement, a compromise in the best traditions of Anglicanism, avoided radical reforms and secured broad consensus, just as the Elizabethan Settlement had done in the 1560s and the Savoy Conference in 1661.

The new church's constitution expressed ideals of federalism, separation of powers, and democracy similar to those embodied in the United States Constitution. It envisioned the national body as a federation of state churches—the document referred to "states" rather than dioceses.[60] Bishops would be elected, as they were in Scotland. The General Convention would be bicameral, with a House of Bishops and a House of Delegates, the latter to include clergy and laity. Each house would have specified voting protocols. On the basis of seniority Seabury became the first presiding bishop—though the position was not yet recognized as primate.[61]

Episcopal lineage remained contentious, but in 1792 the two successions merged when Seabury, Madison, and a reluctant Provoost

59. Chorley, *The New American*, ch. 4.

60. *The Constitution*, 24–26.

61. The presidency was determined by seniority until 1926. William White served as presiding bishop for forty years (1795–1836).

consecrated Thomas John Claggett (1783–1816) bishop of Maryland. Claggett was the first bishop consecrated in the United States.

While work was in progress on a new Anglican church, the Methodist Societies formed their own denomination. The new Methodist Church faced the familiar shortage of personnel but solved it in a different way. The societies already had a system of regional superintendents, and in 1784 the decision was made to give superintendents the power to ordain clergy. Three years later, the further step was taken to call them bishops, without regard for historical lineage.[62]

The Episcopal Church

The PECUSA came into existence in 1789 and within three years had five bishops. But further consecrations, creation of state conventions, and representation at General Conventions proceeded slowly. Connecticut, Pennsylvania, New York, Maryland and Massachusetts all had diocesan bishops by 1800. But North Carolina acquired its first bishop in 1817, Delaware and Georgia in 1841, and New Hampshire in 1844.[63]

The great tragedy of the Revolution era was the damage done to Anglicanism in the South. After the war the "Church of England" was disestablished throughout the southern states, traditional privileges ended, and public funding was discontinued. In Virginia, where Anglicanism won its first foothold and achieved its greatest early success, the church virtually collapsed. Parish glebe land was seized, and many clergy were left penniless. Madison's parish of Jamestown ceased to offer services in 1802, and he was forced to seek secular employment to support himself. Two years elapsed after his death in 1812 before another bishop was appointed. By then only forty parishes remained. Church buildings were abandoned, torn down, or converted to alternative use, and a broad migration took place to other denominations.[64]

The church in North Carolina was described in 1806 as being "at a very low ebb," and ten years later not a single Anglican priest resided in the state.[65] The church in the South remained in a depressed state for

---

62. Methodists in Britain experimented with an episcopate but soon rejected the concept.

63. Prichard, *A History*, 124–125.

64. Holmes, *A Brief History*, 23–28.

65. Wright, L., "Anglo-Catholicism," 44–71.

decades. The primary centers of Anglican activity moved to the mid-Atlantic states and New England.

A pressing problem for the PECUSA was training clergy. In 1817 the General Convention resolved to "establish a General Theological Seminary which may have the united support of the whole Church in the United States and be under the superintendence and control of the General Convention." The wisdom of locating the institution in New York City became apparent when wealthy parishioners of Trinity Church provided financial support. The seminary's founders included Bishop White; John Henry Hobart, bishop of New York; and Theodore Dehon, bishop of South Carolina. Hobart (1775–1830) served as first dean.

The nation's westward expansion presented the church with new opportunities and challenges. Missionary activity on the frontier was hard, and only the most idealistic clergy were willing to forego the comforts of the East to go there. Despite the challenges, dedicated individuals and groups created parishes, and built churches, schools and hospitals. Organization of the Domestic and Foreign Missionary Society in 1820 reinforced missionary efforts, but budgets remained low, and Episcopalian missionaries were at a disadvantage relative to better-funded Methodist, Presbyterian, and Lutheran competitors.

When territories attained statehood, they were expected to become self-supporting dioceses with their own conventions and bishops. But in several states, including Tennessee, Kentucky, and Vermont, Episcopalian populations were small and resources inadequate. A few missionary bishops were supported from denominational funds. The first, Jackson Kemper, was appointed in 1835 to serve Indiana and Missouri.[66] One missionary bishop's jurisdiction covered a million square miles; another converted a railroad car into his "cathedral" and toured his diocese one rail stop at a time.[67] At the other end of the spectrum, some affluent states with large populations were divided into two or more dioceses, enabling bishops to maintain closer contacts with parishes.

The Civil War split the PECUSA. When the southern states seceded in 1861, eleven dioceses withdrew to form the Protestant Episcopal Church in the Confederate States (PECCS). Each branch of the Episcopal Church supported and supplied chaplains to its respective army. Robert E. Lee and Jefferson Davis were both Episcopalians.

66. Indiana and Missouri had attained statehood in 1816 and 1821, respectively.

67. Holmes, *A Brief History*, 65, 68.

Bishop Leonidas Polk of Louisiana, who owned several hundred slaves, took a leave of absence to serve in the Confederate army; he attained the rank of general but died in action in the Battle of Atlanta. The PECCS held its own conventions and adapted the 1789 Prayer Book, making appropriate changes in wording to the prayer for the president and congress. Richard Hooker Wilmer, a strong supporter of the southern cause, was consecrated bishop of Alabama in 1862. When the war ended and Alabama was placed under military rule, Wilmer closed churches rather than obey an order to pray for the president of the United States.[68] But as soon as civil rule was restored clergy fell into line. During the war the General Convention of the PECUSA simply listed the southern states' delegations as "absent," considering the split temporary. After the war delegates from the South took their seats as before.[69] Reunification was facilitated because John Henry Hopkins (1792–1868), presiding bishop, was a northerner with Confederate sympathies. The reunited convention overwhelmingly recognized Wilmer's consecration.

Hopkins wrote to the archbishop of Canterbury in 1851 suggesting a meeting of all Anglican provinces. Nothing came of the suggestion. But a similar request from Canada in 1865 resulted in the first Lambeth Conference.

After the Spanish-American War of 1898 the United States took possession of the Philippines, Puerto Rico, Cuba, Haiti, and other former Spanish colonies. It had already annexed Hawaii and would soon occupy the Panama Canal Zone. The expansion of American rule beyond the continental United States presented vast new opportunities for the Episcopal Church. Missionary bishops were appointed, and eventually offshore dioceses were created.

Efforts, with strong churchmanship implications, began in the mid-nineteenth century to delete the word "Protestant" from Protestant Episcopal Church. At the Confederate Convention in 1861, Richard Hines, a Tennessee priest, proposed that "Reformed Catholic" be substituted for "Protestant Episcopal." His motion was defeated despite three bishops' support.[70] After more than a century, the 1979 General Convention approved "The Episcopal Church" but allowed "Protestant

68. Hunt, "Story."

69. By contrast, the northern and southern branches of most other denominations remained separate for a further century.

70. Cheshire, *The Church*, ch. 2.

Episcopal Church in the United States of America" to remain a legal name. The Episcopal Church can be abbreviated by TEC, but the more common—if inaccurate—acronym is ECUSA.[71] The "ECUSA" comprises 110 dioceses in the United States and fifteen other nations.

Like its Scottish counterpart, the Episcopal Church has no archbishops. Instead, the House of Bishops elects a presiding bishop—comparable with the Scottish primus—who, under present regulations, serves a nine-year term. One consequence of this arrangement is that dioceses enjoy greater autonomy than their counterparts do in England. Designation of the presiding bishop as primate and metropolitan dates only from 1925.

For many years women had served in parish work and as missionaries, and the 1871 General Convention created the Women's Auxiliary as a part of the Board of Missions. The Auxiliary was re-chartered in 1985 as the freestanding Episcopal Church Women, charged with assisting "the women of the church in carrying out Christ's work of reconciliation in the world and to take their place as leaders in the life, governance and worship in the Episcopal Church." In 1974 and 1975 fifteen women priests were ordained without denominational authorization. The 1976 General Convention retroactively endorsed their ordinations and declared that the priesthood and the episcopate were both open to women. Barbara Clementine Harris, an African American priest from Philadelphia, was consecrated bishop in 1989. When the 2006 Convention elected Katharine Jefferts Schori as presiding bishop, she became the first woman primate in the Anglican Communion.

The 1976 General Convention of the Episcopal Church declared that gays and lesbians are "children of God" deserving full civil rights. And between 2000 and 2009 it approved the ordination of participants in same-sex unions to the priesthood and their consecration as bishops.

THE CHURCH IN CANADA

The first Anglican house of worship in what is now Canada was the garrison chapel of St John's Fort, Newfoundland. In 1698 the townspeople of St John's petitioned Bishop Compton of London to establish an Anglican parish. The petition was granted, and the next year John Jackson, a Navy chaplain, became resident clergyman. The SPCK provided moral sup-

71. ECUSA will be used here since the focus is on the United States.

port but no money, and the parish struggled to survive. When Jacob Rice succeeded Jackson in 1709 he wrote to Compton requesting funds to repair the church and to acquire communion vessels, a pulpit cloth, surplices and glass for the windows.

In 1710 a military chaplain, John Harrison, held an Anglican service in the garrison chapel at Annapolis Royal, Nova Scotia. Its purpose was to offer thanksgiving for the garrison's capture from French forces. Harrison continued to serve the chapel after the war ended in 1713. In 1749 King George II issued a proclamation ordering the construction of a church in Halifax. The foundation stone of St Paul's Church was laid in June 1750, and services began three months later. An SPG missionary, William Tutty, preached the first sermon. St Paul's, Halifax, is the oldest surviving Anglican church in Canada.

The Quebec Act of 1774 gave the Roman Catholic Church the right to hold land and collect tithes in Lower Canada. However, the Church of England was established in Nova Scotia, New Brunswick, and Prince Edward Island, with similar rights. The colonial assembly of Nova Scotia extended religious tolerance to Calvinists, Lutherans, Quakers, and other Protestants in 1758. But it stipulated that "every popish person, exercising any ecclesiastical jurisdiction, and every popish priest or person exercising the function of a popish priest, shall depart out of this province on or before the twenty-fifth day of March 1759."[72] Such was the hostility toward the Acadian minority and toward the neighboring Québécois.

Impact of the American Revolution

The big influx of Anglican loyalists into British North America, at the end of the American Revolutionary War, increased Anglican influence, relative to the Roman Catholicism of Lower Canada. But funding was needed to support the necessary clergy and build churches and schools. In some cases funds were raised locally. For example, in 1804 the people of Montreal built a "fine church with a lofty spire and bell [which] continued for many years the principal place of worship for the Anglican Church."[73] Charles Stewart (1775–1837), son of the Earl of Galloway

72. *Act for the Establishment*, §I–III.
73. Borthwick, *History of the Diocese*, 7. The church burned down in 1856.

and future bishop of Quebec, used his fortune to build and maintain a church as well as to assist the poor.[74]

Under the terms of the Canada Act of 1791, the Church of England was given generous land endowments. They included rectory freeholds; glebes, most common in the maritime provinces; and "clergy reserves," common in the Canadas. Clergy reserves, covering more than two million acres in Upper Canada and 628,000 acres in Lower Canada, were intended to generate revenue from leases or crop sales.[75] Initially they only benefited the Anglican church, but privileges were later extended to the Church of Scotland. Funding also came from the SPG, which had diverted its missionary activity to BNA. From 1814 onward the SPG received direct grants from the British parliament. The grants were abruptly cut off in 1832 by the Whig government of Lord Grey but were partially restored to alleviate hardship among Canadian clergy.[76]

The need for a local episcopate in British North America was recognized after the American Revolution. Charles Inglis (1734–1816) traveled to England and was consecrated bishop of Nova Scotia in August 1787, six months after the consecration of White and Provoost. He was the first bishop of a British colonial diocese. Inglis was given jurisdiction over the whole of BNA, an enormous task, considering the vast territory and hazards of travel.

The diocese of Quebec, created in 1793 by letters patent of King George III, helped alleviate the problems. Jacob Mountain (1749–1825) was appointed its first bishop and given jurisdiction over British territory west of New Brunswick. Formerly chaplain to the bishop of Lincoln, Mountain had never left England prior to the appointment.[77] He insisted that as a "lord spiritual" he could sit in the legislative councils of both Upper and Lower Canada. He never exercised his right in the latter but played a role in civil affairs in Upper Canada. Among much else Mountain obtained the charter for McGill University, Montreal.

The diocese of Toronto was created in 1839, and Montreal in 1850. Additional dioceses were created as the nation expanded to the North and West. Sixteen of the present thirty dioceses were in place by 1900.

74. Ibid., 3.

75. Hayes, *Anglicans*, 60.

76. Ibid., 15.

77. Mountain came to Canada with twelve relatives. The family was called the "Thirteen Mountains."

The first Anglican seminary in BNA was King's College, Fredericton, New Brunswick, founded by royal charter in 1828. Bishop's College, later Bishop's University, in Lennoxville, Quebec, was founded in 1843 by Bishop George Mountain, Jacob's son. Trinity College, Toronto, was founded nine years later.

The Church of England's privileged status became increasingly unpopular as the nineteenth century progressed. By the 1850s bishops' rights to sit in legislative councils were abolished. Clergy reserves in the United Province were terminated in 1854 and revenues transferred to the provincial government, though existing beneficiaries were "grandfathered in" during their lifetimes. Nova Scotia and New Brunswick disestablished the church in the 1850s and Prince Edward Island in 1879.[78] The transition from public to internally generated funding was difficult. Competing denominations, by contrast, had been self-supporting for years and in many cases were better organized and more active.

Path to Independence

Until the mid-nineteenth century the several provinces of BNA were crown colonies, and the church was an integral part of the Church of England. That structure permitted micromanagement of church affairs from the mother country. All bishops were appointed by the crown, and even the appointment of archdeacons and rectors had to be cleared with London. Provincial governors' nominees sometimes took preference over local bishops'. Efforts to gain greater self-governance for the church paralleled growing aspirations for political independence.

The establishment of synods was a major step. Toronto established a diocesan synod in 1853, and other dioceses gradually followed suit. In 1856 the legislature of the United Province approved the creation of a provincial synod encompassing the dioceses of Quebec, Montreal, and Toronto. Queen Victoria issued letters patent in 1860 naming Bishop Francis Fulford of Montreal (1803–68) provincial metropolitan.[79] The way was now open for a locally elected episcopate. Bishop James Williams of Quebec, consecrated in 1863, was the first to take office other than by royal appointment.

78. Hayes, *Anglicans*, 66.
79. Fulford, "Address of Metropolitan."

Canadian bishops had always believed that the English monarch was their supreme governor. But the Privy Council ruled in 1863 that the monarch did not exercise ecclesiastical authority in self-governing colonies.[80] The bishops were concerned about the validity of their appointments. They were also concerned that, in the absence of the unifying supremacy of the monarch, notions of worldwide Anglicanism might have little meaning. The Episcopal Church in the United States already lay beyond the reach of royal supremacy. Accordingly, the Provincial Synod of Canada petitioned the archbishop of Canterbury to call a worldwide meeting to "comfort the souls of the faithful and reassure the minds of the wavering members of the Church."[81] In response Archbishop Charles Thomas Longley, convened the first Lambeth Conference in 1867. Seventy-six bishops attended, including six from Canada, sixteen from the United States, and seven from Scotland.

Political independence came in 1867 when the United Province, New Brunswick, and a reluctant Nova Scotia were integrated into the Dominion of Canada. But the name "Church of England in Canada" was retained, and a General Synod did not emerge for another quarter-century. One reason for the delay was difficulty of travel. Completion of the Canadian Pacific Railway in 1885 greatly facilitated the process, and the first General Synod met eight years later. Robert Machray (1831–1904), a graduate of the Universities of Aberdeen and Cambridge and bishop of Rupert's Land, was elected first "primate of all Canada."

At the same meeting the General Synod passed a declaration affirming the church's relationship to the mother church and Christianity as a whole:

> We declare this Church to be, and desire that it shall continue, in full communion with the Church of England throughout the world, as an integral portion of the One Body of Christ composed of the Churches which, united under the One Divine Head and in fellowship of the One Holy Catholic and Apostolic Church, hold the One Faith revealed in Holy Writ, and defined in the Creeds as maintained by the undivided primitive Church in the undisputed Ecumenical Councils; receive the same Canonical Scriptures of the Old and New Testaments, as containing all things necessary to salvation; teach the same Word of God; partake of the same Divinely ordained Sacraments, through the ministry of the same

80. *Long vs. Bishop of Cape Town*, 149, 162–65.
81. Provincial Synod of Canada, Address.

Apostolic Orders; and worship One God and Father through the same Lord Jesus Christ, by the same Holy and Divine Spirit who is given to them that believe to guide them into all truth.[82]

The declaration reflected more than just ecclesiastical courtesy. Well into the twentieth century Canadians retained strong affection for the mother country and the mother church.

The Anglican Church of Canada

The church finally changed its name in 1955 to the Anglican Church of Canada (ACC), or l'Église Anglicane du Canada. The church, like Canada itself, is bilingual, and francophone Anglicans make up a small but significant constituency. The General Synod continues to exercise legislative authority, though the growth of standing committees and other bureaucratic structures has diminished its influence. Elevation of the primate to a full-time position in 1967 further increased the power of the executive branch at the expense of synodical authority.

The ACC is divided into four ecclesiastical provinces: "Canada" (the 1860 Province of Canada, less Ontario), Ontario, Rupert's Land, and British Columbia and Yukon. Each is headed by an archbishop, and each diocese and province has its own synod. The General Synod elects the primate. Following English tradition—but contrasting with Scottish and American custom—the primate of Canada receives the title of archbishop; thus Canada has five archbishops, contrasting with England's two (Canterbury and York). The ACC's primate is not linked to a province or diocese and has no cathedral.

Women missionaries did valuable work in Canada, particularly in the far-flung settlements of the Northwest, which always experienced a chronic shortage of clergy. In 1886 the General Synod authorized the creation of orders of deaconesses and sisterhoods. However a training program for deaconesses was not created for another seven years; recruits had to seek training in the United States or Britain. Sisterhoods, whose members take vows, will be discussed in chapter 6.

The General Synod approved the ordination of women in 1976, but another eighteen years elapsed before Victoria Matthews became the first female bishop in the Anglican Church of Canada.[83] After serving as

---

82. *BCP* ACC 1962.

83. The previous year, 1993, Canada elected its first female prime minister.

suffragan bishop of Toronto, Matthews was elected diocesan bishop of Edmonton in 1997.[84] With respect to other issues of inclusiveness, the ACC has generally taken a more conservative approach than the ECUSA has. How those issues play out in Canada and elsewhere in the Anglican Communion remains to be seen.

CHURCH PARTIES

Churchmanship in Scotland

The Church of Scotland had reformist and traditionalist parties in the sixteenth and early seventeenth centuries, just as England did. But reformists took complete control after 1689. As a result, the traditionalists—who by then included the nonjuring bishops—were forced into the separate Scottish Episcopal Church. The circumstances of the SEC's origins, together with the ongoing need to distance itself from the powerful Calvinist Kirk, ensured a strong high-church orientation.

Scotland provided a good example of the emergence of geographical patterns of churchmanship in strongly polarized environments. To quote historian John Overton: "When a small body, holding one set of opinions, is settled in the midst of a larger body, holding a different set, there is always a tendency for the smaller to emphasize the differences from the larger."[85] The Church in Wales, which confronted a nonconformist majority and developed a high-church orientation, provided another example. The Anglican church in Ireland, by contrast, took on a low-church orientation in reaction to the country's dominant Roman Catholicism. Many of those low-church Irish Anglicans emigrated to Canada.

Churchmanship in the American Colonies

The situation in colonial America was more complex. Conflicting factors ensured weaker patterns of churchmanship as well as significant shifts over time. An important element was the attitude toward England and its institutions. Some settlers retained strong emotional ties with the mother country, held Tory political views, supported imperial rule, and identified with high-church Anglicanism. Others, like the Congregationalists of New England—but also including appreciable numbers of people in

---

84. Matthews resigned in 2007 to become bishop of Christchurch in the Anglican Church in Aotearoa, New Zealand, and Polynesia.

85. Overton, *The Nonjurors*, 419.

other colonies—had emigrated to *escape* those institutions and associations; to them Anglican traditions were anathema. As the public mood in the colonies turned against George III, it also turned against high-church Anglicans. Then there were Native Americans, black slaves, and immigrants from other European countries with no ties to Britain, the Church of England, or English culture.

The circumstances of the Anglican church in the colonies automatically gave it low-church characteristics. Notions of "an episcopal" church" were strained by the absence of local bishops. Because there were no bishops, confirmation was not available; children were examined by clergy in the basic areas of faith in preparation for first Communion.[86] Because of a shortage of clergy, Daily Offices were often conducted by laypeople. As in England, Holy Communion was offered infrequently.

Anglicanism was affected by the religious and philosophical movements of the times. The First Great Awakening began in the 1730s and swept America for three decades. Congregationalist Jonathan Edwards and dissident Anglican clergyman George Whitefield popularized the passionate "hellfire" style of preaching. They offered emotional forms of worship, Calvinist theology, and the promise of the conversion experience. Emphasis on the stark choice between right and wrong, heaven and hell, spoke to people's anxieties and need for religious certainty.

Anglican clergy who adhered to traditional styles of worship and preaching found themselves at a disadvantage, and some low-church Anglican clergy began to embrace evangelistic styles in the hope of replicating competitors' success. They downplayed the liturgy, sacraments, and priesthood while emphasizing religious "enthusiasm" and individual conversion. Anglican churches began to take on the character of congregational meeting houses, with no chancel but with large, three-tier pulpits.

Not everyone liked the Great Awakening, however. When a backlash developed the Anglican church won converts even—or in some cases particularly—in congregationalist New England. In yet another example of Overton's principle, when Anglicanism gained a foothold in New England, it was high-church. By presenting a viable alternative, the SPG and SPCK attracted many people, including the seven Yale "apostates."

86. Hein & Shattuck, *The Episcopalians*, 20. The administration of confirmation was lax in England at that time, too.

The Great Awakening appealed mostly to uneducated, rural people. Among the educated elite, Anglicanism faced competition from deism, to an even greater extent than in England. Thomas Jefferson, Benjamin Franklin, James Madison (the president), and John Adams all came under deist influence. Particularly strong in Virginia, deism added to the church's problems after the Revolution.

Churchmanship in the United States and Canada

Creation of the episcopate strengthened the high-church parties in the United States and British North America. Powerful high-church bishops emerged during the first part of the nineteenth century. In turn their dioceses, like New York, Connecticut, North Carolina, Nova Scotia, and Toronto, took on a high-church orientation, which became self-perpetuating as high-church conventions ensured the election of high-church bishops. By contrast, Virginia was served by low-church bishops, during its recovery in the 1820s and '30s, and took on an enduring low-church character. Ohio became another low-church state later in the century. In BNA the diocese of Huron, formed when the Toronto diocese was subdivided in 1857, emerged as a low-church stronghold.[87]

Over the course of the nineteenth century the Episcopal Church's center of gravity moved progressively to the right. Secession of the low-church Methodist Societies harmed the church's numerical strength but increased high-church influence. Under Hobart's leadership the General Theological Seminary took on a distinctly high-church orientation, and its graduates filled parishes and bishoprics throughout the nation. The Confederacy was not uniformly low-church; for example, Wilmer was a high churchman. Low-church Virginia played a major role in the Civil War, however, and the Confederacy's defeat further eroded low-church influence.

Partisanship in the Episcopal Church was already strong in the early nineteenth century, but it was exacerbated by the Catholic Revival, sometimes to the point where bishops of one party refused to ordain clergy of the other. Partisan tensions led to the emergence of competing seminaries. Berkeley Divinity School in Connecticut and Seabury Divinity School in Illinois acquired a high-church orientation, reinforc-

87. Magocsi, *Encyclopedia*, 776–77.

ing the influence of the General Theological Seminary. In 1842 three graduates of General Seminary: James Lloyd Breck, William Adams, and John Henry Hobart, Jr., founded Nashotah House in Wisconsin, which became a leading center of Anglo-Catholicism. The low-church party sought to level the playing field by establishing the Philadelphia Divinity School and the Episcopal Divinity School in Massachusetts.

In contrast to the situation in the Episcopal Church, the Anglican Church in BNA moved to the left. Its churchmanship balance was altered significantly by immigration. More than one million Irish immigrants arrived between 1830 and 1850, most to escape the potato famine. Whereas Roman Catholics dominated Irish immigration to the United States, the majority entering BNA were evangelical Anglicans.[88] The immigrants' attitudes were colored by a history of close—and often uncongenial—contacts with Roman Catholicism in their home country. Many immigrant clergy had been trained at Trinity College, Dublin, noted for its Calvinist-leaning curriculum.[89]

The issue of who should make diocesan and parish appointments was settled by the PECUSA at its 1789 Convention. But it remained contentious in BNA for another sixty years. The high-church view was that bishops should be appointed by the crown, and parish rectors by bishops. The low-church view was that all appointments should be made by lay synods or vestries. When John Inglis, Charles's son, was appointed rector of St Paul's, Halifax, in 1825 the vestry objected and sought to appoint its own nominee. Faced with a costly legal battle, the vestry backed down, but prominent members left to found a Baptist congregation.[90] Bishops were appointed by the crown until the 1860s.

The creation of bicameral diocesan and provincial synods in the 1850s and '60s, and creation of the General Synod in 1893, gave the low-church party an advantage in its campaign for greater lay control over episcopal and parish appointments. Synods elected bishops, took responsibility for appointments and disciplinary actions, and controlled budgets, fund-raising, and church construction.

The low-church party could scarcely claim victory, however. Citing the Prayer Book, bishops, who comprised the upper house, insisted on

88. Hayes, *Anglicans*, 6. In the mid-nineteenth century Irish made up the largest ethnic group in English-speaking Canada.

89. Magocsi, *Encyclopedia*, 777.

90. Hayes, *Anglicans*, 118.

sole authority in matters of doctrine and liturgy. They also enjoyed a number of other advantages. Bishops had permanent seats on the synods, while other clergy and laity served limited terms.[91] They also set the agenda and held veto power. The latter was rarely used, but in a few cases the bishops announced positions in advance and threatened to veto opposing resolutions from the lower house. Delegates to the lower house began to question the purpose of attending meetings when decisions had already been made.

Competing theological schools emerged in Canada, as they had in the United States. Bishop's University in Quebec maintained a high-church orientation,[92] whereas King's College, New Brunswick, was low-church. Montreal Diocesan College, Huron College, and Latimer College, Vancouver, added to the list of low-church seminaries. Rival schools sometimes operated in the same city. Wycliffe College, Toronto, was established in 1876 to counter the influence of the neighboring, high-church Trinity College. When Wycliffe College opened, the high-church Archbishop John Travers Lewis of Ontario objected to its textbooks and its teachings on the historic episcopate and refused to ordain its graduates.[93]

NEW LITURGIES
The Scottish Liturgies

Protestant refugees from Mary I's England brought Cranmer's second *Book of Common Prayer* to Scotland in the 1550s. But when Knox returned to Scotland he brought with him a liturgy created for English exiles in Geneva. It was subsequently published as the *Book of Common Order* (1564) and served Scottish Presbyterians for eighty years.

The first Anglican liturgy developed specifically for use in Scotland was the proposed Prayer Book of 1637. It was developed by Scottish bishops led by James Wedderburn, bishop of Dumblane, but it earned the popular name of "Laud's Book" because of the archbishop's support. Based primarily on the 1549 *BCP*, it conformed more closely to pre-Reformation liturgies than did the 1604 English *BCP*. Circumstances prevented its widespread use at the time, but the need for a Scottish

91. Ibid., 96, 120–21.

92. Ibid., 128.

93. Ibid., 271–73.

Prayer Book intensified after 1689, when the Nonjurors were banished from the Church of Scotland.

By then copies of Laud's Book were scarce, and impoverished clergy and parishes could not afford them. But the 1662 *BCP* was widely available and was pressed into use, supplemented by inserts, or "wee bookies," providing alternative eucharistic rites. The first wee bookie, published in 1722, contained the Communion Service from Laud's Book. Further bookies were issued over the next several decades, reflecting ongoing liturgical research and incorporating part of a Communion Service developed in 1718 by English and Scottish Nonjurors.[94]

The Nonjurors were among the first to study early Christian eucharistic rites, like those described in the *Didache* and the *Apostolic Constitutions*.[95] They also studied Eastern Orthodox liturgies.[96] Their work culminated in publication of the Communion Service of 1764, which attained broad acceptance and served the Scottish Church for nearly 150 years. The 1764 Communion Service became a model of high-church eucharistic worship, directly influencing the eucharistic liturgy of the Episcopal Church in the United States. It will be examined in more detail in the next chapter.

In the mid-nineteenth century anglophile Scots lobbied for closer ties to the Church of England. They pressed for use of the 1662 English Communion Service in place of the Scottish liturgy, and the General Synod of 1863 gave parishes the option to do so.[97] The 1764 Communion Service was retained as the official liturgy, however, and it was revised in 1912.

A completely new Scottish *BCP* was published in 1929, and further revisions were made in 1970 and 1982, preserving the traditional high-church orientation. An Irish Gaelic version of the 1662 English *BCP* had previously been available, but a Scottish Gaelic translation: *Leabhar na h'Urnuigh Choitchionn*, appeared in 1794. Translations of more recent Scottish liturgies have also appeared. Worship services in Gaelic have

94. The 1718 Communion Service will be discussed in chapter 5.

95. The *Didache*, conventionally dated to the late first century, was a manual of liturgical practice. The *Apostolic Constitutions* is thought to date from the fourth century. Both texts have served as important sources in liturgical revision.

96. Rowell et al., *Loves Redeeming Work,* 269.

97. Goldie, *A Short History,* 95–96.

increased in popularity in recent years with the growth of national consciousness.

Liturgies in the United States

Worship at Jamestown probably used the new 1604 *BCP* or possibly the 1559 version. In due course the 1662 version became standard throughout the American colonies. Independence from Britain subsequently necessitated the creation of a new liturgy for the fledgling Anglican church.

The first attempt was the "Proposed Book" of 1785, drafted by the mid-Atlantic Protestant Episcopal Church.[98] The prayer for the king was replaced by one for "all in authority, legislative, executive and judicial in these United States," and the prayer for the parliament by one for congressional delegates. A service was provided to celebrate the Fourth of July, a day of thanksgiving "for the inestimable blessings of civil and religious liberty."[99]

Other changes were more radical, reflecting the low-church orientation of its principal authors: William Smith of Maryland and the future Bishop White. The *Benedicite* was eliminated from Morning Prayer and "He descended into Hell" from the Apostles' Creed; the Nicene and Athanasian Creeds were deleted; and the sign of the cross in the baptismal rite was made optional. The Thirty-Nine Articles were edited down to twenty, and new psalms were created from selected verses in the canonical Psalter.[100] The Proposed Book was "to be used in this Church for ever." But it was rejected by the General Convention as well as by the English bishops.

The 1789 *Book of Common Prayer* was approved at the General Convention meeting in Philadelphia. The preface noted the circumstances of its creation: "[W]hen in the course of Divine Providence, these American States became independent with respect to civil government, their ecclesiastical independence was necessarily included; and the different religious denominations of Christians in these States were left at full and equal liberty to model and organize their respective churches, and forms of worship."[101] The authors hastened to reassure readers that

---

98. *Book of Common Prayer and Administration*, PECUSA 1785.

99. Chorley, *The New American*, ch. 3.

100. Ibid.

101. *BCP* PECUSA 1789, the preface.

the PECUSA was "far from intending to depart from the Church of England in any essential point of doctrine, discipline, or worship; or further than local circumstances require."[102]

The 1789 *BCP* was based primarily on the 1662 English Prayer Book, with the state prayers and a few other items from the Proposed Book of 1785. However, the concordat Seabury had signed with the Scottish bishops included the following provision:

> As the celebration of the Holy Eucharist, or the administration of the Sacrament of the Body and Blood of Christ, is the principal bond of union among Christians, as well as the most solemn act of worship in the Christian Church, the bishops [hoped] that Bishop Seabury would endeavor all he can . . . to make the celebration of this venerable mystery conformable to the most primitive doctrine and practice . . . which is the pattern of the Church of Scotland [sic]."[103]

On Seabury's insistence, the Communion Service in the new *BCP* incorporated language from Laud's Book and the SEC's 1764 Communion Service.

The 1789 Communion Service, which will be discussed in more detail in the next chapter, had a distinctly high-church flavor. Significantly, it referred to "words of consecration" rather than "words of institution." The service ended with the *Gloria* ("Glory to God in the highest"). The *Gloria*, or *Greater Doxology*, was located near the beginning of the service in the Sarum Rite and in the 1549 *BCP* but was eliminated in later English versions.

The low-church party insisted on eliminating the Athanasian Creed, the "ornaments rubric," and the *Magnificat*. Moreover, a 1792 amendment to the ordination rite provided an alternative to the conventional "Receive the Holy Ghost . . . ." Bishops were permitted to say simply: "Take thou Authority to execute the Office of a Priest in the Church of God, now committed to thee by the Imposition of our hands. And be thou a faithful Dispenser of the Word of God, and of his holy Sacraments."[104] As always, Anglicanism sought to accommodate pluralism.

The 1789 *BCP* served the American church for a century. The first revision appeared in 1892, at the urging of William Reed Huntington, a

102. Ibid.

103. Quoted in Armentrout & Slocum, *Documents*, 16.

104. *BCP* PECUSA 1789, "Form and Manner of Ordering Priests."

prominent member of the House of Deputies. Further revisions to the Prayer Book were made in 1928 and 1979. The revisions of 1892 and 1928 were relatively minor, though the latter was significant in restoring prayers for the dead. The 1979 *BCP* involved more comprehensive changes. It was the first in which "Episcopal Church" replaced "Protestant Episcopal Church" on its title page. The awkward "O Lord, save the State" was deleted from Evening Prayer.[105] The 1979 version used contemporary language and provided alternative forms of the Communion Service. Those forms will be discussed in chapter 8.

Liturgies in British North America and Canada

The worship service at Frobisher Bay used the 1559 *BCP*. But the 1662 version became the standard in British North America and remained so, throughout the evolution of Canada, until the early twentieth century. Retention of the 1662 Prayer Book hurt high-church Anglicanism in Canada because of its constraints on sacramental worship. It also reflected the relative weakness of the high-church party in the latter part of the nineteenth century; proposals for a new liturgy were continually thwarted by arguments that revision would be "divisive."

When the General Synod finally developed its own Prayer Book in 1918, its primary purpose was to incorporate national festivals; otherwise it made only minor revisions. The most recent version, published in 1962, still uses traditional language. A French translation, *Le Recueil des Prières de la Communauté Chrétienne*, was published in 1967.[106] *Le Recueil*, along with the Gaelic *Leabhar na h'Urnuigh Choitchionn*, remind us that the Anglican family is not limited to persons of English cultural heritage.

REFLECTIONS

Anglicanism took root in Scotland and North America during the reign of James I (VI of Scotland). An episcopate was imposed on Scotland, against the wishes of a vocal majority of the clergy, whereas the failure to create an episcopate in America, whose clergy repeatedly petitioned for

---

105. That invocation was a republican adaptation of "O Lord, save the King/Queen" in the English *BCP*.

106. The 1918 Canadian Prayer Book was translated into several languages, including Ukrainian, but never into French.

one, not only weakened the nascent church but may even have contributed to loss of the colonies. Support for the church hierarchy correlated with political perspective. All monarchs from Henry VIII to James II were strong supporters of the episcopate, whereas English and Scottish parliaments and colonial assemblies pressed for more "democratic" church governance.

James I's and Charles I's attempts to anglicize worship in Scotland faced generations of entrenched Calvinism as well as being perceived as English interference—even though both monarchs were Scots by birth. Notwithstanding, Anglicanism appealed to a substantial portion of the Scottish population. The episcopate re-established after the Interregnum continues today.

The Scottish Episcopal Church, created by the nonjuring bishops after the revolution of 1689, established its own "via media" between Roman Catholicism and the oppressive Calvinism of the Kirk. Despite chronic lack of resources and difficult relationships with successive monarchs, it made a disproportionately large impact on Anglicanism. Freed from the constraints of church–state entanglement, the Scots developed a distinctive liturgy inspired by the 1549 Prayer Book. The SEC was the first "foreign" Anglican church, and it directly influenced another: the Episcopal Church in the United States. Creation of those foreign Anglican churches gave meaning to notions of a multinational Anglican Communion—though that term was not coined until much later, and the Lambeth Conference eventually resulted from a Canadian initiative.

The New World had neither an infrastructure of civil administration nor a millennium-long Christian heritage. It presented a degree of religious pluralism not yet found in England. The vast continent also offered missionary opportunities on an unprecedented scale and had the potential to support strong national churches. The Anglican churches of North America looked to the Church of England as their source of inspiration. But they had to adapt English traditions to political independence, in the one case through revolution, in the other through gradual evolution.

The American Revolution forced the church to build ecclesiastical systems and a liturgy appropriate to the new republic. The Episcopal Church in the United States adopted an episcopal structure similar to Scotland's and based its eucharistic liturgy on Scottish precedents. Bishop Seabury's link with the Scottish Episcopal Church was pivotal. The collect for November 14, when he is honored in the calendar of saints, gives thanks "for [God's] goodness in bestowing upon this Church the gift of the episcopate, which we celebrate in this remembrance of the consecration of Samuel Seabury." It adds: "we pray that, joined together in unity with our bishops, and nourished by your holy Sacraments, we may proclaim the Gospel of redemption with apostolic zeal."

The Anglican church in British North America remained an integral part of the Church of England. During the long campaign for political independence, issues of church-state entanglement played out long after similar issues had been settled in the United States. The Canadian church's path was necessarily a cautious one. As a seminary professor commented in a sermon in 1858: "Our work . . . is not to found a new Church, but to adapt to the requirements of a Colony the rules and the spirit of our Mother Church of England and Ireland. The sphere of our action is therefore greatly limited—and there is a call not so much for invention and experiment, as for the less brilliant but safer qualities of caution, research and common sense."[107] The ecclesiastical structure and liturgy that eventually emerged were intermediate in style between those of the United States and England.

The religious history of England, Scotland, and North America reveal multiple occasions when Anglicanism's survival was in serious doubt. The Church of England was abolished in the 1550s and dismantled in 1646. But for the longevity of a handful of bishops, the episcopal succession would have been lost by the time the church was reorganized in 1660. The Scottish episcopate was restored, with English help, in 1610 after its links with the ancient Scottish church were broken. It could easily have been extinguished again in 1638 or in the 1780s. The Anglican church in the American colonies came close to extinction after the American Revolution. Seabury's consecration in Scotland was secured at a time when the SEC itself seemed to be in its death throes. Canada might never have acquired a significant Anglican presence if Britain had not defeated France in the wars of the eighteenth century. Anglicanism's ability to surmount formidable obstacles, regroup, and flourish should help put current crises in perspective.

107. Thompson, "The Conditions," 12.

5

High-Church Anglicanism

A RELATIVELY SMALL NUMBER of high-church Anglicans resisted the pressure of reformists, Puritans, Presbyterians, and Evangelicals to make Anglicanism just another protestant denomination. They kept the flame of sacramental Christianity burning through the Reformation and the centuries that followed. This chapter discusses high-church Anglicanism in England, Scotland, and North America from the sixteenth through the early nineteenth century. It explores the divergence of high-church Anglican beliefs and practices from the baseline established in chapter 3. The high church's crowning achievement was to preserve a liturgy—crafted in Scotland and then embraced in the United States—that affirmed the objective real presence and sacrificial intent of the Eucharist.

The chapter describes the lives, ideals, and struggles of the principal characters and summarizes their collective accomplishments. The present focus is on *orthodox* high-church Anglicans—as distinct from the Tractarians and ritualists who built upon their work to create modern Anglo-Catholicism.

HIGH-CHURCH ANGLICANS IN ENGLAND AND SCOTLAND

The Early Traditionalists

Henry VIII, Stephen Gardiner, Cuthbert Tunstall, and even Nicholas Ridley were traditionalists. Bishop Gardiner tried to counter Bucer's and Vermigli's influence on Cranmer during the Edwardian reign and for his pains spent five years in the Tower of London. Tunstall managed to hold the bishopric of Durham during the turbulent reigns of Henry VIII,

Edward VI, and even Mary I. He died in prison after refusing to take the oath to Elizabeth I and declining to participate in the consecration of Matthew Parker, whom he considered too protestant. Ridley, bishop of London, was not a strong partisan, but he took a traditionalist position in the vestment controversy to be discussed in its turn.

The strongest Anglican traditionalist during much of Elizabeth I's reign may have been the queen herself. Although she maintained a public face of ambiguity, she demonstrated a traditionalist orientation in her personal religious style. Most importantly she supported the episcopate against puritan pressure, recognizing commonality of purpose between it and the monarchy.

The prominent churchmen of the period: Matthew Parker, John Jewell, and Richard Hooker, were no more than moderate traditionalists. Parker, archbishop of Canterbury, resisted pressure to make the Thirty-Nine Articles more Calvinist than they were. Jewell initially had Calvinist sympathies but moved to the right before writing his *Apology of the Church of England* (1562). While fiercely critical of Rome, he affirmed the Church of England's spiritual continuity with the catholic church of the early Middle Ages. He also affirmed the real presence in the Eucharist.

Hooker came to Elizabeth's notice in 1585 and published Book V of his *Laws of Ecclesiastical Polity* twelve years later (and six years before the queen's death). His churchmanship is still debated, partly because his works were balanced in tone and partly because his writing style defies easy analysis.[1] Yet his strong defense of the Prayer Book and sacraments identify him as a high churchman—farther to the right than Parker and Jewell. Surprising for his time, he was willing to acknowledge what was good in Roman Catholicism, for example: "Where Rome keepeth that which is ancienter and better . . . we had rather follow the perfections of them whom we like not, than in defects resemble them whom we love."[2] Hooker's balanced position between Roman Catholics and "them whom we love" provided a good example of the via media. Pope Clement VIII, who presumably represented "them whom we like not," conceded that Hooker's work "had in it such seeds of eternity that it would abide until the last fire shall consume all learning."

1. Hooker acknowledged that his *Laws of Ecclesiastical Polity* was "perhaps tedious, perhaps obscure, dark, and intricate"; but he explained that it was "in [readers'] own hands to spare that labour which they are not willing to endure."

2. Hooker, *Of the Laws*, §XXVIII, 127.

The Caroline Divines

By the end of the Elizabethan reign stronger traditionalists were making their mark. They were the first of a number of theologians and writers who recovered the traditionalism of Gardiner and Tunstall and preserved it during the tumultuous times of the Civil War and Commonwealth. Without their efforts—and those of the long-lived bishops who saved the episcopal succession—the Anglicanism of the Henrician and early Edwardian periods might have been lost forever.

The several theologians and writers became known as the "Caroline Divines," a reference to the two King Charleses whose reigns bracketed the Interregnum. Despite religious and political turmoil, the Caroline period was a golden age of Anglican scholarship. During that period "high-church" entered the religious vocabulary, probably coined by Archbishop Laud.

Lancelot Andrewes, Richard Neile, and William Laud are usually counted among the Caroline Divines, though Andrewes died just eighteen months after Charles I's accession, and both Neile and Laud died before the Civil War began. Andrewes (1555–1626), one of the most learned churchmen of his time, served as bishop of Chichester, Ely, and finally Winchester. His reverence for sacramental worship was coupled with a theology based on the works of the Greek Fathers. When James I commissioned his new translation of the Bible, he appointed Andrewes principal editor for the first twelve books of the Old Testament and general editor for the whole project. Ninety-six of Andrewes's sermons were published by command of Charles I in 1631, and his works fill eight volumes of the *Library of Anglo-Catholic Theology*, a tractarian initiative of the nineteenth century.

Neile (1562–1640), another student of patristic works, held various positions before being named archbishop of York in 1631. While he was serving as bishop of Durham in the 1620s, Charles I appointed him to the Privy Council and the Court of Star Chamber. During that period Neile hosted meetings of prominent clergy at his London home, Durham House. The "Durham House Group" acquired fame for resistance to growing puritan influence in the church. Among its members was the young William Laud.

Laud (1573–1645) was ordained in 1601, two years before Elizabeth's death, and steadily gained influence under James I and Charles I. He was appointed archbishop of Canterbury in 1633 and served for twelve years.

Laud had strong organizational abilities but was rigid in temperament and lacking in diplomacy. He angered Puritans by trying to restore more traditional worship in the Church of England. He even planned to appoint a bishop to congregationalist Massachusetts. His downfall was a plan to impose Anglican worship on the Presbyterians of Scotland. He was blamed for the proposed Scottish Prayer Book of 1637, which incited the Scots to invade England and helped provoke the English Civil War. Laud was condemned by a parliamentary bill of attainder and beheaded in 1645.

Prominent Divines who played important roles after the Restoration included John Cosin, Herbert Thorndike, Mark Frank, John Pearson, and Jeremy Taylor. Cosin (1594–1672) was master of Trinity College and eventually vice-chancellor of Cambridge University. After spending much of the Interregnum in Paris, he returned to England and was appointed bishop of Durham. He wrote a number of collects for the 1662 Prayer Book,[3] but most of his writings were published posthumously. His collected works fill five volumes of the *Library of Anglo-Catholic Theology*.

Thorndike (1598–1672) was lecturer in Hebrew and fellow of Trinity College, Cambridge. After the Restoration he was appointed prebendary of Westminster Abbey and is buried there. Thorndike promoted the early church and the decrees of the ecumenical councils as models for Anglican practices and beliefs.[4] He promoted prayers for the dead, urged a restoration of the sacrament of penance, and affirmed a mystical but objective real presence in the Eucharist. Greatly admired by Tractarians, his collected works fill six volumes of the *Library of Anglo-Catholic Theology*.

Frank (1612–65), fellow of Pembroke College, Cambridge, was strongly influenced by Andrewes. Dismissed in 1643, in the approach to the Civil War, he continued to preach during the Interregnum despite great personal hardship. His fellowship was restored after the Restoration, and he went on to serve as archdeacon of St Albans, prebendary of St Paul's, and eventually master of Pembroke College. Frank was a major proponent of Marian devotion. He was one of the great preachers of the Caroline period, and his sermons fill two volumes of the *Library of Anglo-Catholic Theology*.

Pearson (1612–86) served as a chaplain in the royalist army and preached at St Clement's, Eastcheap, London. After the Restoration he was appointed master of Trinity College, Cambridge, and in 1670 bishop

3. Stanwood, "The Prayer Book," 144–46.
4. Thorndike, *An Epilogue*.

of Chester. His best-known work, based on a series of sermons, was *Exposition of the Creed* (1659).

Taylor (1613–67), a protégé of Laud's and chaplain to Charles I, achieved fame as a poet and prose writer. He was imprisoned during the Civil War but later was appointed bishop of Down and Connor, Ireland, and vice-chancellor of the University of Dublin. His fifteen-volume collected works were published in 1822

In addition to Taylor, several men contributed to the religious culture of the time through their poetry. John Donne (1572–1631) converted from Roman Catholicism and was appointed dean of St Paul's Cathedral. His poetry enriched his preaching in a distinctively Anglican way that reached back to medieval times. Another poet of note was Henry Vaughan (1622–95), twin brother of alchemist Thomas Vaughan. After a religious conversion experience he came under the influence of the Welshman George Herbert, whereupon his work took on a mystical flavor; Wordsworth and Tennyson were influenced by his writings. Donne, Vaughan, and Herbert are counted among the "metaphysical poets" whose work won new appreciation in the twentieth century through the efforts of T. S. Eliot.[5] The poetry of this and other periods enriched not only preaching but hymnody.

The Nonjurors

Nonjuring English and Scottish clergy were dismissed after the deposition of James II (VII of Scotland) in 1689 when they declined to swear allegiance to William III and Mary II and the Hanoverian George I. They were the cream of high-church Anglicanism in their time, and their departure left the Church of England in the hands of latitudinarians and Evangelicals, and the Church of Scotland under the firm control of Presbyterians. Despite their dismissal, they were able to make far-reaching contributions to high-church beliefs and practices.

The highest ranking English Nonjuror was William Sancroft (1617–93). Appointed archbishop of Canterbury in 1677, he officiated at the coronation of James II in 1685 but was charged with sedition two years later for petitioning the king to withdraw the Declaration of Indulgence. Sancroft was dismissed from his archbishopric after refusing to take the oath of allegiance to William and Mary.

---

5. The American-born T. S. Eliot converted to Anglicanism and identified himself as Anglo-Catholic.

Thomas Ken (1637–1711), fellow of New College Oxford and bishop of Bath and Wells, was a lifelong high churchman. After losing his see in 1691 he retired to the home of his friend Lord Weymouth. Often considered the most eminent of the English Nonjurors, he made substantial contributions to modern English hymnology. One of his best-known collects is: "O God, make the door of this house wide enough to receive all who need human love and fellowship, narrow enough to shut out all envy, pride and strife. Make its threshold smooth enough to be no stumbling block to children nor to strained feet, but rugged and strong enough to turn back the tempters of power. God, make the door of this house the gateway to thine divine kingdom."[6] As he approached death Ken wrote a testimony to the nonjuring cause: "I am dying in the Holy, Catholic and Apostolic Faith professed by the whole church before the disunion of East and West; and, more particularly, in the Communion of the Church of England, as it stands distinguished from both Papal and Protestant innovation."[7]

William Law (1686–1761) was ordained in 1711 and elected a fellow of Emmanuel College, Cambridge. Three years later his fellowship was withdrawn when he refused to swear allegiance to George I. Law attained fame for a dispute with Benjamin Hoadly, bishop of Bangor. Hoadly promoted a Zwinglian interpretation of the Eucharist and preached against the validity of an institutional church. Law wrote three open letters to him, providing an important statement of high-church principles. In 1717 the Convocation of Canterbury moved to censure Hoadly, but George I suspended it before a vote could be taken. Apart from two brief sessions in the 1740s, it did not meet again for 130 years.

The only schismatic sect of any significance formed by English Nonjurors was the "Orthodox British Church," based in Manchester. Its leader was Thomas Deacon, consecrated in 1733 by the Scottish nonjuring bishop Archibald Campbell. Deacon was involved in the Jacobite cause; one of his sons was executed and another exiled for involvement in the failed rebellion of 1745. Deacon's son-in-law, William Cartwright,

---

6. Inscribed on the door of the Church of St Stephen Walbrook, London.

7. Middleton, *Eminent English Churchmen*, "Thomas Ken."

served as the sect's last bishop.[8] Thomas Podmore (1704–85), remembered for *A Layman's Apology* (1745), was an ordained deacon.[9]

Prominent among the early Scottish Nonjurors was Arthur Rose (1634–1704), chancellor of St Andrews University, archbishop of St Andrews, and primus of the Church of Scotland. After 1689 he retired to private life but was acknowledged as primus of the Scottish Episcopal Church until his death. Alexander Rose (c. 1645–1720), Arthur's nephew and bishop of Edinburgh, attained fame for attempting to persuade William III to recognize the Scottish episcopate. After his uncle's death the younger Rose became primus and participated in the consecration of seven new bishops. Despite his involvement in the nonjuring church, he maintained contacts with orthodox clergy in England, including Bishop Henry Compton of London.[10]

Archibald Campbell, a student of patristic writings, was consecrated bishop of Aberdeen in 1721 but resigned his see four years later and moved to London, where he developed a relationship with the English Nonjurors. He also made important ecumenical contacts, which will be discussed later. Thomas Rattray (1684–1743), bishop of Brechin and then Dunkeld, was elected primus in 1739.[11] He is remembered especially for his liturgical research, which influenced the 1764 Communion Service. His *Ancient Liturgy of the Church of Jerusalem* was published posthumously.

The nonjuring SEC was losing strength by the 1730s, but it maintained a substantial base in northeast Scotland. All six remaining bishops lived in the region, three in the diocese of Aberdeen.[12] Samuel Seabury's consecration was performed by Robert Kilgour, bishop of Aberdeen and primus; John Skinner, coadjutor and eventually Kilgour's successor; and Arthur Petrie, bishop of Ross and Moray. Both Skinner and his father, John Skinner (1721–1807), dean of Aberdeen, shared ideals with the Hutchinsonians to be discussed shortly.[13]

---

8. Overton, *The Nonjurors*, 354–70. The sect was sometimes referred to as the Primitive Catholic Church in Britain.

9. Various attempts have been made to revive the Orthodox British Church.

10. Overton, *The Nonjurors*, 435.

11. Bertie, *Scottish Episcopal*, 118.

12. Walker, William, *The Life*, 1.

13. Wilde, "Hutchinsonianism," 2.

Other High Churchmen

In 1686 English theologian George Bull (1634–1710) was appointed archdeacon of Llandaff, Wales, whose cathedral stands on the site of an ancient Celtic church. Nineteen years later he was appointed bishop of St David's. Bull sought to reconcile the conflict between Paul's Epistle to the Romans, which supported justification by faith, and the Epistle of James, which stressed good works. His conclusion that Romans should be interpreted in the light of James attracted puritan criticism. A generation later, John Johnson (1662–1725), vicar of Cranbrook, Kent, sympathized with the Nonjurors but remained loyal to the Church of England. He made a significant contribution to eucharistic understanding.

John Hutchinson (1674–1737), self-taught Hebrew scholar and natural philosopher, defended Anglican theology against rationalism.[14] The "Hutchinsonians" whom he inspired, had considerable influence in both England and Scotland. Among the English Hutchinsonians was Alexander Catcott, a Bristol clergyman, who promoted a mystical interpretation of Anglicanism. The two John Skinners of Aberdeen were allied with the group. Emergence of the Hutchinsonians marked the rebirth of a coherent high-church tradition in the Church of England after the Nonjurors' departure.

Joseph Butler (1692–1752) was raised a Presbyterian but joined the Church of England and studied at Oriel College, Oxford. He served as bishop of Bristol and then Durham. A theologian and philosopher, Butler gained renown for challenging the Enlightenment philosophy of Thomas Hobbes and John Locke. Butler's writings influenced the early twentieth-century high-church Anglican C. S. Lewis.

Alexander Jolly (1756–1838) was consecrated bishop of Moray in 1787, succeeding Arthur Petrie.[15] Jolly wrote extensively on high-church issues, including baptismal regeneration and the Eucharist; his work will be cited later. His best-known book is *The Christian Sacrifice in the Eucharist* (1831). James Walker, presbyter of St Peter's Chapel, Edinburgh, and an outstanding scholar, was appointed first Pantonian Professor of Theology[16] in the SEC's new Theological Institute. He was attacked for his views by two "qualified" clergy—even though his high-church views

14. Ibid., 1–24. Newton did not propose an atheistic, or even a deistic, view of the universe. Philosophers gave his mechanics that interpretation a few generations later.

15. Walker, William, *The Life*, 37, 43.

16. The chair was named for Kathrein Panton who endowed the institute in 1810.

were shared by most of his colleagues, and even though the SEC was by then officially recognized. Walker became bishop of Edinburgh in 1830 and primus seven years later.[17]

The "Hackney Phalanx" emerged early in the nineteenth century, named after the London district where members lived and worked. Leading members were John James Watson (1770–1839), rector of Hackney, his brother Joshua, and his brother-in-law Henry Norris, rector of South Hackney.[18] Norris was a leading figure in the SPCK, and his influence on ecclesiastical appointments earned him repute as "bishop maker."[19] In 1812 Norris and Joshua Watson purchased the *British Critic* and restored it as a voice of orthodox high-church Anglicanism.[20]

Two bishops of the nineteenth century deserve mention: Henry Phillpotts and Samuel Wilberforce. Phillpotts (1778–1869) entered Oxford University at thirteen years of age and graduated with a master's degree from Magdalen College at eighteen. He served as bishop of Exeter for thirty-nine years—the longest tenure of any English bishop since the Reformation. Phillpotts criticized both Evangelicals and the more extreme Tractarians. His obituary declared that he "held to the last to the via media of the Anglican Church as the strongest safeguard against Romish and Calvinistic errors, and probably rejoiced to die like Ken and Laud . . . expressing his firm faith in the [church] as essentially one and the same in doctrine and faith with the undivided Church of the first five centuries of the Christian era."[21] Phillpotts campaigned for reestablishment of the Convocation of Canterbury, and it finally met in 1854.

Among much else Phillpotts is remembered for his role in the Gorham case. George Gorham was an evangelical clergyman who, in the face of Article XXVII, denied the regenerative effects of baptism. Gorham "held, and persisted in holding, that spiritual regeneration is not given or conferred in that holy Sacrament—in particular that infants are not made therein members of Christ and the children of God."[22] In 1847 Phillpotts

17. Goldie, *A Short History*, 112.

18. The group was sometimes called the "Clapton Sect," referring to the neighborhood where a member lived. It called to mind the "Clapham Sect," associated with anti-slavery activists William Wilberforce and Henry Thornton.

19. Corsi, *Science and Religion*, 11.

20. Overton, *The English Church*, 200.

21. *The Times*, September 20, 1869.

22. *Gorham v. Bishop*, 3–4.

refused to install him in a parish in Devon. Gorham appealed to the ecclesiastical Court of Arches but lost. The Privy Council, however, ruled in his favor, noting that "from the first dawn of the Reformation . . . the Church was harassed by a great variety of opinions respecting Baptism and its efficacy" and that the articles of faith admitted "some latitude of interpretation."[23] Gorham was installed over Phillpotts's objection.

An attempt by the bishop's supporters to challenge the Privy Council's competence in the case failed in the House of Lords. Outraged by the decision, Henry Manning (1808–92), archdeacon of Chichester, converted to Roman Catholicism, eventually becoming cardinal archbishop of Westminster. Sadly, the Gorham case set a precedent for numerous appeals to the Privy Council during the nineteenth century. Politicization of internal church disputes ultimately hurt all church parties.

Samuel Wilberforce (1805–73), son of abolitionist William Wilberforce, was a high churchman but distanced himself from the Tractarians. He was appointed bishop of Oxford in 1844 and in 1854 founded Cuddesdon Theological College, Oxford. Wilberforce died three years after becoming bishop of Winchester.

Several other individuals had close contacts with the Tractarians but retained an orthodox high-church orientation. They included Hugh James Rose (1795–1838), Cambridge scholar, chaplain to the archbishop of Canterbury, and founding editor of *The British Magazine*; Robert Isaac Wilberforce (1802–57), Samuel's older brother; and William Patrick Palmer (1803–85), Dublin graduate and fellow of Worcester College, Oxford.

HIGH-CHURCH ANGLICANISM IN NORTH AMERICA

As the son of a "Yale apostate," Samuel Seabury (1729–96) was raised in an Anglican family that rebelled against New England Congregationalism. He served as an SPG missionary and initially supported the Tory cause in the American Revolution. His consecration in the nonjuring Scottish Episcopal Church, performed according to the 1549 *BCP*, reinforced an already high-church orientation. As noted, Seabury and the Scottish bishops signed a concordat urging the American church to adopt the 1764 Scottish Communion Service, which in essence it did.[24]

23. Ibid., 7.
24. *Concordat*, §V.

Upon his return to America, Seabury made New London, Connecticut, his base of operations and became rector of St James's Church as well as bishop of Connecticut. At the conclusion of the General Convention in October 1789 he was named presiding bishop of the PECUSA. Seabury began to wear a mitre on special occasions, and also by repute a scarlet hood.[25] Thomas Claggett, consecrated in 1792, followed his example. Their practice implied that bishops in the SEC also wore the mitre. By contrast, no English bishop did so from the time of Thomas Cranmer until the late nineteenth century.[26]

Though born in Ireland, Charles Inglis (1734–1816) acquired a high-church orientation from his work as an SPG missionary in New York City. A lifelong Tory, he served as chaplain to the First Battalion, New Jersey Volunteers during the American Revolutionary War and preached a rousing sermon in 1780 urging the citizens of New York to support the monarchy.[27] When British forces evacuated in 1783 Inglis fled, with numerous other colonists, to Nova Scotia. Four years later he was consecrated in the Church of England and appointed first bishop of Nova Scotia—and the first in British North America.

In 1793 Jacob Mountain (1749–1825) was appointed first Anglican bishop in the Roman Catholic stronghold of Quebec. He campaigned for clergy reserves, which, along with SPG funding, supported Anglican clergy. He also worked tirelessly for his diocese; during his tenure sixty churches were built and thirty-five missions created. Holy Trinity Cathedral, Quebec City, was consecrated in 1804, only nine years after the diocese was created. George Jehoshaphat Mountain, Jacob's son, served as rector of Fredericton, New Brunswick, and then as archdeacon of Lower Canada. In 1836 he was consecrated coadjutor bishop of Montreal, within the Quebec diocese.

The United States and BNA/Canada were both served by strong high-church bishops during the nineteenth century. The Colonial Bishoprics Council, founded in 1841 as an offshoot of the SPG in BNA, functioned as a lobbying organization to nominate suitable candidates.[28] Although it faced increasing evangelical opposition, its successes in-

25. Grafton, *The Lineage*, vol. 2, 221. See also DeMille, *The Catholic Movement*, 33.
26. Reportedly Cranmer wore a cope and mitre at John Hooper's consecration in 1651.
27. Inglis, "The Duty."
28. Hayes, *Anglicans*, 65.

cluded John Medley (1804–92), an Oxford Tractarian, appointed first bishop of New Brunswick in 1845. Eight years later Medley oversaw the dedication of Christ Church Cathedral, Fredericton, and organized a choir school. Not everyone in the diocese shared his high-church vision, however. Medley had an uneasy relationship with King's College, Fredericton, which had maintained a strong evangelical orientation since its creation in 1828.

Other nominees of the Colonial Bishoprics Council were Francis Fulford (1803–68), an Anglo-Catholic, appointed first diocesan bishop of Montreal in 1850, and George Hills, son of a Royal Navy admiral, appointed bishop of British Columbia in 1859.

In the United States John Henry Hobart, third bishop of New York and first dean of the General Theological Seminary, was the most powerful high churchman of the early nineteenth-century. Hobart shared his views on a variety of subjects by publishing tracts, setting a precedent for the Oxford tracts of a generation later. Also anticipating tractarian principles, he emphasized the historic episcopate, the sacraments, episcopal ordination, and prayers for the dead. Hobart insisted on conformity with Prayer Book rubrics, earning comparisons with Archbishop Laud.[29]

Other notable American high churchmen were George Washington Doane (1799–1859), bishop of New Jersey; his son William Croswell Doane (1832–1913), bishop of Albany, New York; and William Ingraham Kip (1811–93), first missionary bishop of California. Whereas most bishops in nineteenth-century England distanced themselves from the Catholic Revival, several high-church bishops in North America actively supported it. Levi Silliman Ives of North Carolina, John Henry Hopkins of Vermont, and Charles Chapman Grafton of Fond du Lac, Wisconsin, were strong supporters. Their work and others' will be discussed in later chapters.

HIGH-CHURCH PRINCIPLES AND PRACTICES

High-church Anglicans reinforced or moved beyond mainstream beliefs—and in a few cases mainstream practices—in areas including ecclesiastical authority, the apostolic succession, and the sacraments. Particularly important were their efforts to recover the early church's understanding of the Eucharist.

29. DeMille, *The Episcopal Church*, 69.

The Church

The early Caroline Divines took great pride in the traditions and authenticity of the Church of England. But at the time Anglicanism was fighting a life-or-death battle for survival; the episcopate had been abolished, the king was dead, and Puritans were in firm control of parliament.

Jeremy Taylor wrote an impassioned, fifteen-page letter to a "gentlewoman" who had defected to Rome. She had betrayed the church, he complained, at a time of persecution when it bore "the marks of the Cross of Jesus." Anglicans, Taylor went on, "suffered for a holy cause and a holy conscience, when the Church of England was more glorious than at any time before; even when she could show more Martyrs and Confessors than any Church this day in Christendom, even then when a King died in the profession of her Religion, and thousands of Priests, learned and pious Men suffered the spoiling of their goods rather than they would forsake one Article of so excellent a Religion."[30]

Taylor insisted that the Church of England was the legitimate successor of the catholic church of late antiquity:

> [The church] professes the belief of all that is written in the Old and New Testament, all that which is in the three Creeds, the Apostolical, the Nicene, and that of Athanasius, and whatsoever was decreed in the four General Councils.... This is the Catholic faith, so saith the Creed of Athanasius; and unless a company of Men have power to alter the faith of God, whosoever live and die in this faith, are entirely Catholic and Christian. So that the Church of England hath the same faith without dispute that the Church had for 400 or 500 Years, and therefore there could be nothing wanting here to saving faith, if we live according to our belief.[31]

Taylor promised to "pray to God to open your heart," but whether his correspondent returned to the Church of England is not recorded.

William Laud, responding to parliament's assault on the episcopate, insisted that bishops had certain inviolable rights: "Bishops may be regulated and limited by human laws in those things which are but incidents to their calling; but their calling, as far as it is *jure divino*, by Divine right, cannot be taken away."[32] On the other hand, church and

---

30. Taylor, Jeremy, *The Whole Works*, 645.

31. Ibid., 646.

32. Quoted in Hutton, *William Laud*, 238.

state were inseparably linked: "They, whoever they be, that would over-throw *sedes ecclesiae*, the 'seats of ecclesiastical government,' will not spare, if ever they get power, to have a pluck at 'the throne of David.'"[33] Laud's prophecy was validated a few years later when the monarchy and the episcopate were both abolished.

In 1843 Bishop Kip addressed the popular topic of how Anglicanism should position itself relative to other protestant churches and the Church of Rome. In language that Richard Hooker would have endorsed, Kip declared that "the Church bears her double witness against them both—and points out a middle path as the one of truth and safety."[34] Kip concluded by identifying "the true Catholic Churchman" as one who would "proclaim to the world the fact, that he is a disciple of Christ, and a member of His Holy Apostolic Church. He is ready to acknowledge his belief in all that his Master taught," either while on earth or through the church to which he had committed, "the lofty duty of being a Keeper and Witness of the Truth."[35] Kip's "true Churchman," presumably the high-church Episcopalian, paid due attention to scripture but also acknowl-edged his dependence on the corporate entity of the church.

The Authority of Tradition

Article VI affirmed that scripture contained "all things necessary to sal-vation: so that whatsoever is not read therein, nor may be proved thereby, is not to be required of any man." The intent was to refute Rome's claim of a teaching *magisterium* and the large body of doctrine formulated under its mandate—doctrine that, in the Reformers' view, perverted the true message of the Bible. High-church Anglicans accepted the primacy of scripture. But they urged the Church of England to claim its own magisterium, arguing, as the Roman and Orthodox churches did, that bishops inherited a teaching mandate from the apostles.

Luther and Calvin asserted that scripture was "self-authenticating," requiring no external authority to validate or interpret it. Some reformists in the Church of England embraced similar beliefs. But it soon became apparent that meaning was not self-evident: that even sincere, informed people could disagree over what pivotal scriptural passages meant. High

33. Ibid., 130.
34. Kip, *The Double Witness*, preface. Emphasis removed.
35. Ibid., 315.

churchmen throughout the period insisted that interpreting scripture was the church's right and responsibility. For example, Bishop Hobart tried to dissuade Episcopalians from joining the evangelical American Bible Society, which promoted a self-authenticating view of scripture.[36]

High churchmen acknowledged that the ecumenical councils were guided by the Holy Spirit and could legitimately define dogma, exercising what ecclesiastical lawyers called the *magisterium extraordinarium*.[37] Thorndike regarded the first six ecumenical councils as authentic. More commonly, Anglicans focused on the first four: Nicaea (325), Constantinople (381), Ephesus (431), and Chalcedon (451). Those four councils formulated the doctrines of the Trinity, Christ's co-equality with the Father, and the two natures of Christ "joined together in one Person, never to be divided." They also produced the Nicene Creed, which, along with the Apostles' and Athanasian Creeds, were identified in Article VIII as "thoroughly to be received and believed: for they may be proved by most certain warrants of Holy Scripture." The Nicene Creed referred to the "one holy, catholic and apostolic church," and the early church represented its purest expression.[38]

High-church Anglicans recognized that no ecumenical council had met since late antiquity, and another was unlikely since the catholic church was now fragmented. However, the church exercised a *magisterium ordinarium* through the routine, consensus teachings of its bishops. It was the magisterium of tradition.

Respect for tradition was one leg of Hooker's "three-legged stool." Thomas Podmore even declared: "*Tradition* is the only Method we now have, whereby we can come to the understanding of the Scriptures . . . . For a man may pore his eyes out upon an *hebrew* Bible and a *greek* Testament, and pray most heartily to understand them, and yet shall never be the wiser, if he get not a master to instruct him, or have not recourse to those authors, who have expounded those languages into what he doth understand."[39] "[N]either our blessed Lord, nor his Apostles,"

36. DeMille, *The Catholic Movement*, 179. Hobart was no Romanist, but on that issue he expressed a familiar Roman Catholic position.

37. Anglicans never acknowledged Roman claims that the pope could exercise the *magisterium extraordinarium* unilaterally.

38. Christianity was not totally unified at the time. But sixteenth–eighteenth century divines took that to be an article of faith.

39. Podmore, *A Layman's Apology*, 4. Emphasis in original.

he claimed, "did prescribe the scriptures as a sufficient rule of faith and practice."[40] Podmore should have reminded his readers that the New Testament canon was not finalized until forty-two years after the first Council of Nicaea.[41]

Tradition was the accumulated wisdom received from earlier periods, especially periods with a special claim to credibility.[42] The Durham House Group argued that the writings of the Church Fathers merited special attention because of proximity to apostolic times. High churchmen brushed aside any hesitation in appealing to the Church Fathers because of possible conflict with the Reformers' teachings. Notwithstanding, the patristic writings were often ambiguous and sometimes contradictory. Received tradition must be tested for reliability.

High-church Anglicans found the ideal test in the Vincentian Canon. Proposed by the Gallic scholar Vincentius of Lérins in 434 CE, it established three criteria of reliability: universality, antiquity, and consent. Specifically the canon stated: "We shall follow universality if we acknowledge that one Faith to be true which the whole Church throughout the world confesses; antiquity if we in no wise depart from those interpretations which it is clear that our ancestors and fathers proclaimed; consent, if in antiquity itself we keep following the definitions and opinions of all, or certainly nearly all, bishops and doctors alike."[43]

The Canon did not mention scriptural support. A doctrine that conflicted with scripture would obviously be rejected. But what of doctrines that passed the Vincentian test but on which the Bible was silent? For example, the Roman church offered the five nondominical sacraments, transubstantiation, the sacrificial intent of the Mass, the existence of purgatory, and the immaculate conception of Mary. High churchmen insisted that they might be permissible private beliefs but could not be required universally.

The argument that tradition could compensate for lack of specific scriptural support was applied to ritual. For example, kneeling to receive Holy Communion was not prescribed by the Bible; but it was an "edifying practice," backed by tradition and indirectly supported by First

40. Ibid., 7.

41. The final selection of New Testament books was provided in 367 CE by Athanasius, patriarch of Alexandria.

42. In Judaism the notion of received tradition is captured by the word *kabbalah*.

43. Vincentius, *The Commitorium*, vol. 4.

Corinthians 14:26. Another edifying practice was the wearing of clerical vestments. According to an addendum to the 1549 Prayer Book, a bishop presented for consecration must wear the surplice and cope.[44] Ridley decided to enforce the requirement, but John Hooper, nominated bishop of Gloucester in 1550, refused to comply. The Privy Council ruled that Hooper could not refuse a royal appointment, and after a stint in prison he consented to wear the vestments. Ridley and Hooper were both executed by Mary I.

The vestment controversy erupted again after Elizabeth came to the throne. Archbishop Parker gained royal encouragement to force parish clergy to wear the white surplice for the Communion Service. Hooker agreed; the surplice, he argued, was "comely" and not "unholy;" rather it made the priest resemble "the glory of the saints in heaven." To those who criticized the practice, he responded: "To solemn actions of royalty and justice their suitable ornaments are a beauty. Are they only in religion a stain?"[45]

Hooker also defended the propriety of including pre-Reformation prayers in the liturgy, including the *Gloria, Benedictus*, and *Magnificat*. Inclusion of saints' days and days of fasting in the liturgical calendar was also justified because "the law both of God and nature alloweth generally days of rest and festival solemnity to be observed by way of thankful and joyful remembrance."[46] The Puritans encouraged austerity of lifestyle but opposed the observance of fast days.

The Episcopal Succession

The authority of tradition rested on trust in the divine institution of the episcopate and the apostolic succession. The episcopal lineage, high churchmen argued, began with the apostles and continued through the first five centuries of "catholic" Christianity, and even through the medieval period, when western Christianity became corrupt. Regrettable as that latter period might be, the argument continued, the succession was not broken. It was not broken during the Reformation, when the bishops, as a body, seceded from Rome. It was threatened but not broken during the Interregnum.

44. *BCP* 1549, "Form of Consecrating a Bishop."
45. Hooker, *Of the Laws*, §XXIX, 129.
46. Ibid., §LXXI.7, 400.

William Law offered a strong defense of the apostolic succession and the power of the episcopate in a letter to Hoadly. "If there be no uninterrupted succession," he declared, "then there are no authorised ministers from Christ; if there are no such ministers, then no Christian sacraments; if no Christian sacraments, then no Christian covenant, whereof the sacraments are the stated and visible seals."[47] Bishops' authority flowed from the Holy Spirit through the consecration rite: "Receive the Holy Ghost." On the other hand, that authority was narrowly defined. "How absurd," Law asked, "is it therefore, to pretend to abolish, or depart from the settled Order of the clergy, to make new orders, and think any God's ministers, unless we had His [the Holy Spirit's] authority and could make new sacraments or a new religion?"[48]

Bishop Hobart addressed the General Convention of the PECUSA on the importance of the historic episcopate and episcopal ordination of clergy in 1814: "They are the principles, the declarations, the language of the venerable Church from which we derive our immediate origin; principles which at the period of the reformation she restored to primitive shape and form and laid at the foundation of her polity; principles, in her attachment to which, a revolution that for a while subverted them, served more to confirm." Those principles, he continued, "entitle our Church to the character of an Apostolic Church."[49]

In a sermon in 1858, J. H. Thompson, of the high-church Bishop's College, Lennoxville, Quebec, affirmed the apostolic succession and traditions of the faith as the basis of Anglican unity:

> [S]urely to us, members of one Common Church, linked together in a holy bond of brotherhood by the faith and sacraments of Christ—to us who accept as Apostolic the Episcopal form of Government . . . who recite the ancient Creeds, and are joined in spirit to the holy and the good of many generations by the use of that form of sound words, the Book of Common Prayer—to us, I saw, there can be little cause of disagreement.[50]

47. Nash, J. O. & Gore, *William Law's Defence*, 58.
48. Ibid., 102–3.
49. Hobart, "The Origin."
50. Thompson, "The Conditions," 12.

The Sacraments

Emphasis on the sacraments was a major issue dividing high- and low-church Anglicans. In the sixteenth century Calvinists questioned the value and propriety of sacramental rites and the need for a priesthood. In response Bishop Jewell explained: "Men cannot be gathered together to the profession of any religion . . . unless they be bound in the fellowship of visible signs or sacraments."[51]

Hooker agreed: "The Church is to us that very mother of our new birth, in whose bowels we are all bred, at whose breasts we receive nourishment," and "the Church [uses] to that end and purpose not only the Word, but the Sacraments, both having generative force and virtue."[52] Against charges that sacramental ritual lacked meaning, Hooker asked: "Which strange imagination is begotten of a special dislike they have to hear that ceremonies now in use should be thought significant . . . . Doth not our Lord Jesus Christ himself impute the omission of some courteous ceremonies even in domestical entertainment to a colder degree of loving affection?"[53]

Calvinists also attacked the doctrine of baptismal regeneration, arguing that it was not a prerequisite for salvation; in any case, only the elect would be saved. But even the 1552 Prayer Book declared that "none can enter into the kingdom of God except he be regenerate and born anew of water and the holy Ghost."[54] High churchmen fiercely defended the doctrine. Thorndike explained: "The necessity of the Sacraments of Baptism and of the Eucharist unto salvation consisteth in the Covenant of Grace . . . the one of them setteth and enacteth, the other reneweth and replenisheth."[55] Bishop Jolly added that baptism was not only a source of grace but an acceptance of responsibilities: "Baptism binds upon the receivers all the conditions of salvation, included in the solemn promise of vow then made to God, obliging to repentance or renunciation of sin, firm faith, and holy obedience."[56] Henry Phillpotts would have agreed.

High-church Anglicans urged that the marriage ceremony be enriched by receipt of Holy Communion. Hooker affirmed: "To end the

51. Quoted in Rowell et al., *Love's Redeeming Work*, 69.
52. Hooker, *Of the Laws*, §L.1, 219.
53. Ibid., §LXV.5, 320-21.
54. *BCP* 1552, "Ministration of Baptism."
55. Quoted in Rowell et al., *Love's Redeeming Work*, 197.
56. Jolly, *The Christian Sacrifice*, 193.

public solemnity of marriage with receiving the blessed Sacrament is a custom so religious and so holy, that if the church of England be blamable in this respect it is not for suffering it to be so much but rather for not providing that it may be more put in use."[57] High churchmen resisted puritan efforts to abolish wedding rings on the grounds that they perpetuated pagan superstition. Rings' ubiquitous use in the modern world testifies to their success.

The rite for the ordination of priests declared: "Whose sins thou dost forgive, they are forgiven; and whose sins thou dost retain, they are retained." Perhaps that declaration referred to the general absolution in the Daily Offices and the Communion Service, but certain high churchmen insisted that it also referred to private, auricular, confession. The sacrament of penance was unpopular among the Reformers because of abuses in the late Middle Ages. But Jewell declared: "I do not condemn [it]. It may do much good." "The use and practice hereof," he continued, "is not only to be allowed, but most needful and requisite, if so the superstition, and necessity, and conscience, which many have fondly used and put therein, be taken away."[58]

Andrewes preached on the benefits of private confession in 1600.[59] Three centuries later, Phillpotts recommended confession for "those sinners whose troubled conscience admits not of being quieted by self-examination however close and searching."[60] By the end of the nineteenth century many Anglicans were finding comfort in regular confession. Eventually the practice earned its place in the Prayer Book, but nobody has suggested making it mandatory.

The Eucharist

The English Reformers were cautious in formulating eucharistic doctrine, but receptionism emerged as mainstream Anglican belief, supported by Article XXVIII and embodied in the 1552–1662 *BCP*. Hooker was probably a receptionist. And so was Caroline Divine John Cosin. "[I]t is most evident," he wrote, "that the Bread and Wine . . . are neither changed as to their substance, nor vanished and reduced to nothing." But Cosin

---

57. Hooker, *Of the Laws*, §LXXIII.8, 433.

58. Quoted in Rowell et al., *Love's Redeeming Work*, 73.

59. Stevenson, K., "The Prayer Book," 139.

60. Phillpotts, *Letter*.

conceded that they "are solemnly consecrated by the words of Christ, that by them His blessed Body and Blood may be communicated to us."[61]

Thorndike and Andrewes—the latter thirty-nine years Cosin's senior—both understood the Eucharist in a more objective way. Thorndike kept the distribution of Communion in mind, even as he affirmed the localized real presence: "[T]he Body and Blood of Christ become present in the sacrament by the institution of our Lord . . . whereby His institution is executed by consecrating the elements to the purpose that the Body and Blood of Christ may be received."[62] Andrewes went further to affirm a transformation of the eucharistic elements.[63] Both he and Thorndike approved of adoration of the consecrated elements.

Andrewes also ventured beyond mainstream beliefs, represented by Article XXXI, in viewing the Eucharist as a sacrifice. He declared: "The Eucharist ever was and by us is considered both as a sacrament and as a sacrifice . . . . The sacrifice of Christ's death did succeed to the sacrifices of the Old Testament. The sacrifice of Christ's death is available for present, absent, living, dead yea, for them that are yet unborn."[64] Thorndike agreed, adding: "The sacrament of the eucharist must needs be the sacrifice of Christ on the cross, because the Body and Blood of Christ are present in it as sacrificed."[65] After studying patristic writings Podmore "took it for granted that Eucharist is a sacrifice."[66]

The most detailed affirmation of eucharistic sacrifice came from John Johnson. In *The Unbloody Sacrifice* (1714) he declared that Christ's sacrifice was not simply death on the cross "but commenced with the Paschal solemnity, and was finished at His ascension into heaven, there to appear in the presence of God for us."[67] At the Last Supper, when he instituted the sacrament of the Eucharist, Christ took the role of a sacrificing priest and offered his sacramental body and blood; moreover, "He has positively commanded us to do the same."[68] After exhaustive discussion, Johnson concluded: "I have fully established the doctrine of

61. Cosin, *The History*.

62. Thorndike, *The Theological Works*, 544.

63. Quoted in Ottley, *Lancelot Andrewes*, 202.

64. Ibid.

65. Thorndike, *The Theological Works*, 547.

66. Podmore, *A Layman's Apology*, 140.

67. Johnson, *The Theological Works*, 164.

68. Ibid., 170, 176.

the Sacrifice, not only from the monuments of the primitive Church, but from the words of Christ Jesus Himself, and of His Apostle St Paul."[69]

In a letter to the bishop of Norwich, who had encouraged his work, Johnson affirmed that he hoped "that by God's blessing on the labours of them who do now, or may hereafter contend for the perfect establishment of it, the prejudices of men may by degrees be conquered, and the Unbloody Sacrifice and Altar recover its pristine luster and esteem, not by the force and imposition of human authority, but by its own intrinsic excellence and reasonableness, and by the irresistible evidence of Scripture and antiquity."[70]

Andrewes, Thorndike, and Johnson left no doubt that they viewed the Eucharist as an offering of the consecrated elements, not just as a 1549-style self-oblation. By the end of the eighteenth century, the objective real presence, sacrificial intent, and the associated priestly role were well-established in high-church Anglicanism. For example, Bishop Seabury affirmed:

> When Christ commanded his apostles to celebrate the Holy Eucharist in remembrance of him, he . . . gave them power to do so; that is he communicated his own priesthood to them in such measure and degree as he saw necessary for his church— to qualify them to be his representatives—to offer the Christian sacrifice of bread and wine as memorial before God the Father of his offering of himself once for all . . . as a means of obtaining, through faith to him, all the blessings and benefits of his redemption."[71]

Bishop Jolly pursued the same theme, portraying the eucharistic sacrifice as the fulfillment of the temple sacrifices of biblical Judaism: "No longer confined to Judea, and the limited priesthood of Aaron, the divine and eternal High Priest after the order of Melchisedec [sic], having made the oblation of His all-prevailing sacrifice, under the symbols of bread and wine, left these symbolical pledges to be the sacrifice of his universal church."[72] Christ "is both Priest and Sacrifice, the Giver and

---

69. Ibid., 175.

70. Ibid., 24.

71. Quoted in Rowell et al., *Love's Redeeming Work*, 326.

72. Jolly, *The Christian Sacrifice*, 46. Genesis 14:18 records that Melchizedek made an offering of bread and wine.

the Gift; who condescends to take from among men . . . the gifts which He instituted for his memorial."[73]

An English clergyman offered the following devotional prayer in a work published in 1856:

> Hail, most holy and precious Body of Christ! which wast once offered on the Altar of the Cross for the saving of the world, and now in solemn mystery art daily offered upon the Altars of Thy Holy Church throughout all the world. I worship Thee, life-giving and enduring Sacrifice. By faith, I discern Thy Body under these outward veils of Bread and Wine. I believe that Thou art "verily and indeed" present, adorable Lord: therefore I will worship Thee: therefore I supplicate Thee; therefore I praise and magnify Thee.[74]

Orthodox high-church Anglicans were not assertive ritualists. But they attached importance to the environment in which the Eucharist was celebrated and to participants' attitudes. Even during times of puritan minimalism, a few brave souls preserved elements of sacred ritual. Elizabeth I placed a cross and candles on the communion table in her private chapel, despite clerical opposition and occasional sabotage.[75] Andrewes incorporated ceremony into his private services and burned incense.[76] Archbishop Laud ordered that wooden communion tables be replaced by stone altars, or at least that the table be placed behind an altar rail at which people could kneel.[77] He also sought to enforce the wearing of the surplice during worship services—a custom that had fallen into disuse since Parker's time. John Craddock, a fellow member of the Durham House Group, was a useful ally in enforcing the practices because of his political clout in the North of England.

High churchmen campaigned, with little success, for more frequent offering and receipt of Holy Communion. From medieval times onward ordinary people had felt a strong sense of unworthiness with respect to Communion. The gentry and nobility had fewer scruples, but hardly anyone received Communion more than once a month. During the late Stuart and early Hanoverian eras, some parishes offered it no more than

73. Ibid., 150–51.
74. Prynne, *The Eucharistic Manual*, 70.
75. Spinks, "From Elizabeth," 46.
76. Ibid., 50.
77. Ibid.

once per year. Among those who supported frequent Communion in the eighteenth century was John Wesley: "[I]t is the duty of every Christian to receive the Lord's Supper as often as he can . . . because the benefits of doing it are so great."[78] Weekly, or even daily, Communion Services became a hallmark of the Catholic Revival in the nineteenth century.

The Eucharistic Liturgy

The 1549 *Book of Common Prayer* is often regarded as a transitional form between the Sarum Rite and the 1552 and later versions of the English *BCP*. Others have regarded it as the first "high-church" Anglican liturgy and the starting point for developing new liturgies that preserved the sacramental tradition.

The authors of the proposed Scottish *BCP* of 1637—"Laud's Book"—concluded that the Communion service in the English Prayer Book was deficient. After the Savoy Conference of 1661 it was clear that the latter would retain its character for the foreseeable future. But the Nonjuror schisms provided opportunity for experimentation, free from evangelical resistance in the Church of England.

A group of Nonjurors, led by Jeremy Collier and Thomas Brett in England and Bishop Rattray in Scotland, took advantage of that opportunity in the early eighteenth century. Known as the Usagers, they sought to restore four practices, or "usages," that they believed had apostolic precedent: the mixed chalice, recognition of sacrificial intent, the *epiclesis*, and prayers for the dead. The "mixed chalice" is the practice of mixing water with the sacramental wine. The epiclesis will be discussed shortly. Tension developed between the Usagers and other Nonjurors who were content with the English Prayer Book.[79]

Influenced by Johnson's work, two English and two Scottish Usagers prepared the "1718 Liturgy."[80] Its full title: *A Communion Office, Taken Partly from Primitive Liturgies and Partly from the First English Reformed Common Prayer Book* revealed links with ongoing liturgical research as well as with the 1549 *BCP*. The 1718 Liturgy attracted considerable attention, particularly in Scotland.

78. Wesley, "Duty."
79. Hefling, "Scotland," 170.
80. *A Communion Office* 1718.

The 1637 Scottish Prayer Book[81] and the 1718 Liturgy influenced the 1764 Scottish Communion Service.[82] In turn, language from the Scottish rites was incorporated into the 1789 *BCP* of the newly formed Episcopal Church in the United States.[83] The sequence of four liturgies represents an unfolding high-church eucharistic tradition. Table 5.1 compares key passages whose inclusion, placement, and wording provide invaluable insight into underlying beliefs. Specifically the table shows the *anamnesis*, the *epiclesis*, and the prayer of oblation.

Anamnesis appears in the words of institution: "do this in remembrance [*anamnesis*] of me" (1 Cor 11:24). More commonly the term refers to a prayer depicting the Eucharist as a commemoration of Christ's passion and death, and sometimes also to his resurrection and ascension. The 1718 Liturgy even relates it to his "second coming with glory and great power to judge the quick and the dead"; *anamnesis* evidently can mean more than "remembrance."

The *epiclesis* is an invocation addressed to God the Father. "Weak forms" of the epiclesis ask the Father to send the Holy Spirit to bless and sanctify the eucharistic elements; "strong forms," characteristic of Eastern Orthodox liturgies, also ask that the Spirit give effect to the real presence. The epiclesis in the 1549 *BCP*—albeit weak, but unique in the western church at that time—was eliminated in subsequent versions of the English Prayer Book.[84]

The oblational prayer portrays the Eucharistic rite as a sacrifice and specifies what is being offered. In the Sarum Rite the consecrated elements were offered to God. The 1549 *BCP* contained a self-oblation, but it was eliminated in the 1552 and later versions.

All four liturgies in Table 5.1 contained an epiclesis. The strong form in the 1764 Scottish Communion Service—no doubt reflecting Orthodox influence—asked the Father "to bless and sanctify, with thy word and holy Spirit, these thy gifts and creatures of bread and wine, that they may become the body and blood of thy most dearly beloved

81. *BCP for the Use of the Church of Scotland* 1637, "Order for the Administration."

82. *Communion-Office* 1764. Emphasis in original.

83. *BCP* PECUSA 1789, "Order for the Administration."

84. The Sarum rite did not contain an explicit epiclesis. The *Quam oblationem* ("Which oblation") prayer had similar intent but did not mention the Holy Spirit; see Table 3.1. An epiclesis has been restored in the most recent Church of England liturgies—and also now appears in the Roman Catholic Mass.

TABLE 5.1. SIGNIFICANT PASSAGES IN FOUR EUCHARISTIC LITURGIES

1637 "Laud's Book"	1718 Nonjurors' Communion Service
Epiclesis Hear us, O merciful Father, we most humbly beseech thee, and of thy almighty goodness vouchsafe so to bless and sanctify with thy word and holy Spirit these thy gifts and creatures of bread and wine, that they may be unto us the body and blood of thy most dearly beloved Son; so that we receiving them . . . may be partakers of the same his most precious body and blood . . . . [Words of Institution] **Anamnesis and Oblation** Wherefore, O Lord and heavenly Father . . . we thy humble servants do celebrate and make here before thy divine Majesty, with these thy holy gifts, the memorial which thy Son hath willed us to make, having in remembrance his blessed passion, mighty resurrection, and glorious ascension . . . . And we entirely desire thy Fatherly goodness, mercifully to accept this our sacrifice of praise and thanksgiving . . . . And here we offer and present unto thee, O Lord, our selves, our souls and bodies, to be a reasonable, holy, and lively sacrifice unto thee	[Words of Institution] **Anamnesis and Oblation** Wherefore, having in remembrance his Passion, Death, and Resurrection from the dead; his Ascension into heaven, and second coming with glory and great power to judge the quick and the dead, and to render to every man according to his works; we offer to thee, our King and our God, according to his holy Institution, this Bread and this Cup; giving thanks to thee through him, that thou hast vouchsafed us the honor to stand before thee, and to Sacrifice unto thee. **Epiclesis** And do thou Accept them to the honor of thy Christ; and send down thine Holy Spirit, the witness of the passion of our Lord Jesus, upon this Sacrifice, that he may make this Bread the Body of thy Christ, and this Cup the Blood of thy Christ.

Son." Laud's Book was unique among the four liturgies in placing the epiclesis before the words of institution. That placement could imply, as the Roman church insists, that the elements are changed into the body and blood of Christ as soon as the priest utters the words of institution. However Eastern Orthodox theologians insist that the real presence does not take full effect until the priest recites the epiclesis, which in Eastern liturgies always follows the institution narrative.

TABLE 5.1. SIGNIFICANT PASSAGES IN FOUR EUCHARISTIC LITURGIES

1764 Scottish Communion Service	1789 *BCP* Episcopal Church (USA)
[Words of Institution] **Oblation and Anamnesis** Wherefore, O Lord, and heavenly Father, according to the institution of thy dearly beloved Son our Saviour Jesus Christ, we thy humble servants do celebrate and make here before thy divine majesty, with these thy holy gifts, which we now offer unto thee, the memorial thy Son hath commanded us to make; having in remembrance his blessed passion, and precious death, his mighty resurrection, and glorious ascension . . . . **Epiclesis** [W]e most humbly beseech thee, O merciful Father, to hear us, and of thy almighty goodness vouchsafe to bless and sanctify, with thy word and holy Spirit, these thy gifts and creatures of bread and wine, that they may become the body and blood of thy most dearly beloved Son.	[Words of Institution] **Oblation and Anamnesis** Wherefore, O Lord and heavenly Father according to the institution of thy dearly beloved Son our Saviour Jesus Christ, we, thy humble servants, do celebrate and make here before thy Divine Majesty, with these thy holy gifts, which we now offer unto thee, the memorial thy Son hath commanded us to make; having in remembrance his blessed passion and precious death, his mighty resurrection and glorious ascension . . . . **Epiclesis and Anamnesis** And we most humbly beseech thee, O merciful Father, to hear us; and, of thy almighty goodness, vouchsafe to bless and sanctify, with thy Word and Holy Spirit, these thy gifts and creatures of bread and wine; that we, receiving them according to thy Son our Saviour Jesus Christ's holy institution, in remembrance of his death and passion, may be partakers of his most blessed Body and Blood.

All four liturgies also included an oblational prayer. Laud's Book included the self-oblation from the 1549 *BCP*: "[W]e offer and present unto thee, O Lord, our selves, our souls and bodies, to be a reasonable, holy, and lively sacrifice." But it also spoke of offering "these thy holy gifts." The Nonjurors' 1718 Liturgy stated explicitly that the consecrated elements were being offered: "[W]e offer to thee, our King and our God, according to his holy Institution, this Bread and this Cup." The 1764 Scottish liturgy and 1789 American *BCP* simply offered "these gifts."

As noted in chapter 3, the words of administration of Holy Communion provide another indicator of attitudes to the real presence. The language in both the 1718 Liturgy and the 1764 Scottish Liturgy was taken from the 1549 *BCP*: "The body of our Lord Jesus Christ which was given for thee, preserve thy body and soul unto everlasting life . . . . The blood of our Lord Jesus Christ which was shed for thee, preserve thy body and soul unto everlasting life." The 1718 and 1764 Liturgies also incorporated the rubric from the 1662 *BCP* that instructed the priest to deliver Communion to the people *"all meekly kneeling."* The 1789 American Prayer Book, which represented more of a compromise between high- and low-church interests, used the words of administration from the 1662 *BCP*, but a rubric referred to the people *"all devoutly kneeling."*

The 1549 *BCP* provided for reservation of the Sacrament. Following its example, the 1718 Liturgy included the rubric: "*If there be any persons who through sickness or any other urgent cause are under a Necessity of communicating at their houses, then the Priest shall reserve at the open Communion so much of the Sacrament of the Body and Blood, as shall serve those who are to receive at home.*"[85] Provision for reservation continued in the Scottish tradition, but no corresponding rubric was included in the 1552 and subsequent English Prayer Books.

The rite for the consecration of a church or chapel offered by the 1789 American *BCP* referred, in distinctly high-church terms, to "the blessed Sacrament of the Body and Blood of Christ."[86] A rite for the induction of ministers into parishes or churches was added in 1804, based on a form developed earlier in Connecticut. The bishop charged the priest: "[W]e hereby do institute you into said Parish (or Church), possessed of full power to perform every Act of sacerdotal Function among the People."[87] "Sacerdotal Function" was not defined, but it could be interpreted to mean the priestly function of sacrifice. The induction rite also referred to the communion table as "the altar" and used the term "Holy Eucharist" throughout.

85. *A Communion Office* 1718.
86. *BCP* PECUSA 1789, "Form of Consecration."
87. Ibid. (amended 1804), "Office of Institution." Parentheses in original.

OTHER ISSUES IN HIGH-CHURCH ANGLICANISM

Marian Doctrine and Devotion

The continental Reformers felt that devotion to Mary in medieval times had become excessive, even idolatrous. Yet they subscribed to the Ephesus doctrine on the argument that "Mother of God" was supported by scripture and the traditions of the early church. Luther declared: "Not only was Mary the mother of him who is born [in Bethlehem], but of him who, before the world, was eternally born of the Father, from a Mother in time and at the same time man and God."[88] Zwingli went so far as to say: "I esteem immensely the Mother of God, the ever chaste, immaculate Virgin Mary."[89] Later generations of Protestants were not nearly so generous.

The English Reformers shared the sentiments of their continental counterparts but, mindful of the strong tradition of "Mary's Dowry," proceeded with caution. They accepted her perpetual virginity, and the collect and preface for Christmas Day in the 1662 *BCP* referred to Mary as "a pure Virgin." Cranmer retained the *Magnificat* ("My soul doth magnify the Lord") in Evening Prayer. The liturgical calendar of 1561 included five feasts, celebrating Mary's conception, nativity, annunciation, visitation, and purification. Bishop Latimer referred to her as "our blessed lady,"[90] though the context of his remarks raises questions about his sincerity. Latimer strongly criticized Marian intercession and applauded the destruction of her shrines and images. Marian devotion steadily declined in popularity as reformist, and particularly puritan, attitudes took hold.

The Caroline Divines sought to revive Marian devotion in the seventeenth century. Andrewes, Taylor, Frank, and Pearson all urged greater focus on Mary in Anglican worship. In his Christmas sermon for 1609 Andrewes modified Psalm 2:7 to create a Marian affirmation: "Thou art my Son, this day I brought Thee into the world."[91] In his private devotions, published posthumously, Andrewes commemorated "the allholy, immaculate, more than blessed mother of God and evervirgin Mary."[92]

88. Luther, *Works*, vol. 7, 572.
89. Quoted in Stakemeier, *De Mariologia*, 456.
90. Latimer, *Sermons*, 60.
91. Quoted in Dorman, "Andrewes."
92. Andrewes, *Preces Privatae*, 85. Concatenations in original.

Frank was the most assertive in promoting Marian devotion. In a sermon preached on the feast of the annunciation, "Lady Day," he proclaimed: "Give we her in God's name the honour due to her. God hath styled her 'blessed' by the Angel, by Elizabeth; commanded all generations to call her so." The first Christians, he observed, "speak of her as the most blessed among women, one 'highly favoured' . . . . But all the while give *Dominus tecum* ["The Lord be with you"] all the glory, the whole glory of all to him; give her the honour and blessedness of the chief of the saints."[93] One day, he added encouragingly, we shall "be partakers of the blessedness she enjoys, when the Lord shall be with us too, and we need no angel at all to tell us so."

John Pearson referred to Mary as "most pure immaculate Virgin,"[94] recalling Zwingli's affirmation and suggesting belief in the immaculate conception. Pearson may have remembered that Homily XX, in the second volume, declared that Christ took upon himself "our frail nature, in the blessed Virgin's womb, and that of her *undefiled* substance" (emphasis added).[95]

A sermon by Bishop Bull began with the usual cautionary statement: "The blessedness of the holy Virgin is not so altogether proper to her." But he warmed to his subject, proclaiming that Mary "was more blessed by conceiving Christ in her heart by faith, than by conceiving him in her womb. And in this her chieftest blessedness the meanest Christian, that is a sincere one, may be a sharer with her." He concluded on the optimistic note: "And if we be true Christians, though all generations do not call us blessed, as the holy Virgin, yet together with her we shall be indeed blessed beyond all generations."[96]

The Religious Life

A conspicuous outcome of the Reformation was the abolition of religious orders. For Luther it was prompted by his negative experience as an Augustinian friar. Henry VIII was interested in confiscating assets but exploited public perceptions of monastic laxity and materiality—carefully nurtured by Thomas Cromwell—to project a worthier motive. The bish-

93. Frank, "Sermon."
94. Pearson, *Exposition*, 324.
95. Homily XX, second vol., 528–29.
96. Quoted in Rowell et al., *Loves Redeeming Work*, 232.

ops were not disposed to criticize the dissolution because of long-standing rivalry with the religious orders, which lay outside their jurisdiction.[97] Ideals of renunciation and asceticism persisted in the western Christian consciousness, however. Mennonites and Amish created communities on a substantial scale on the continent of Europe and later in America. The Shakers would do the same in eighteenth-century England.

Small Anglican communities were established from time to time. In 1626 Nicholas Ferrar founded a community consisting of his extended family at Little Gidding, Cambridgeshire. The same year he was ordained a deacon by Archbishop Laud.[98] Members were committed to recitation of the Daily Offices. Among the community's many visitors was Charles I, who sought refuge there after the Battle of Naseby in 1645. The community was disbanded by parliamentary edict the following year, but it inspired T. S. Eliot to write the poem *Little Gidding* (1942).[99]

In 1740 William Law established a small community, dedicated to "the Serious Call," on his estate in Northamptonshire. Law served as spiritual director, and his charges included two women. One was the rich widow of his friend Archibald Hutcheson, who had asked Law to provide for her pious retirement. The other was the sister of a former pupil. The little group lived a life of devotion, study, and charity until Law's death in 1761. Much of its income of nearly £3,000 per year was spent on charitable work.[100]

In one of the ironies of English history, the cloistered colleges of Oxford and Cambridge—the academic bastions of the Anglican establishment—operated on semi-monastic lines, following traditions established before the Reformation, when they *were* monastic institutions. Divinity studies, leading to ordination to the priesthood, formed a major part of the curriculum. Only men were admitted, chapel attendance was mandatory, subscription to the Thirty-Nine Articles was a matriculation requirement, and fellows of the colleges were required to remain unmarried.[101]

97. Monasteries and religious orders in the West traditionally lay outside episcopal jurisdiction.

98. Rowell et al., *Loves Redeeming Work*, 163–66.

99. The poem was included in his *Four Quartets*.

100. Overton, *William Law*, 223–24.

101. Cranmer's fellowship at Jesus College, Cambridge, was withdrawn upon his first marriage, but it was reinstated after his wife died in childbirth.

Oxford and Cambridge lost much of their monastic character due to secularization in the mid-nineteenth century. By that time numerous Anglican religious orders were being created in the wake of the Tractarian Movement. They will be discussed in chapter 6.

Church and State

Generalizations must be treated with caution, and the precise correlation between religious and political opinion has not been measured. Nevertheless, high-church Anglicans embraced a strong sense of a divinely ordained social order in which episcopal lineage and hereditary monarchy and aristocracy played parallel roles. The constitutional concept of the Divine Right of Kings may have ended to all intents and purposes in the Stuart era, but notions of divine sanction of the English constitution were pervasive until well into the nineteenth century.

Most high churchmen in England supported the monarchy and had Tory political leanings—though, to quote a modern writer, "by no means always in a narrowly political party sense."[102] They were predominantly royalist in their sympathies ahead of and during the English Civil War. Later they celebrated the feasts of "Charles the Martyr" on January 30 and the restoration of the monarchy on May 29. By contrast, they tended to ignore the anniversaries of the Gunpowder Plot, the "Glorious Revolution" of 1689, and the Hanoverian succession, which found their way into the liturgical calendars of low-church Anglicans.

The coronation oath represented a solemn covenant in which the monarch accepted responsibility for protecting and nurturing the Church of England. The form established in 1689 required the presiding archbishop to ask: "Will you to the utmost of your power maintain the laws of God, the true profession of the gospel and the Protestant reformed religion established by law, and will you preserve unto the bishops and clergy of this Realm, and to the churches committed to their charge, all such rights and privileges as by law do or shall appertain unto them, or any of them?" To which the monarch responded: "All this I promise to do . . . . The things which I have here before promised, I will perform and keep: So help me God."[103] High-church Anglicans applauded George III when he declined to endorse Roman Catholic emancipation on the

---

102. Nockles, *The Oxford Movement*, 26.

103. See for example Gillis, *The History*.

grounds that it violated his coronation oath—and felt betrayed when William IV signed the Catholic Relief Act of 1829.

A growing problem, over the course of centuries, was the shift in power from the crown to parliament and from the House of Lords to the Commons. It was one thing to argue that the monarch was in some way divinely guided; it was quite another to believe that the monarch's "advisers" in parliament were similarly guided. Parliament was not bound by a coronation oath, and politicians answered to the electorate. As rival political parties jockeyed for power, and governments rose and fell, parliament's ability and willingness to act in the church's best interests were called into question. When non-Anglicans and even non-Christians began to take seats in parliament the problem became acute. By 1830 it was obvious that parliament could no longer be portrayed as a "lay synod" complementing episcopal governance of the Church of England.

The Nonjurors sacrificed their appointments because of the oaths they had taken to James II (VII of Scotland). Many Scottish Nonjurors supported the Jacobite claim to the throne, even actively participating in the rebellions of 1715 and '45. Penal laws targeting the SEC were enacted when the rebellions failed. Yet, when the Jacobite cause became hopeless in the 1780s, the Nonjurors gladly transferred their allegiance to George III.

High churchmen in the American colonies disproportionately sided with the Tories in the Revolutionary War and suffered when the patriots won. Those who found a new homeland in BNA had opportunities to retain their imperial loyalties. Those who stayed in the United States faced persecution and, in many cases, poverty; they also found themselves in an environment where traditional political affiliations were no longer relevant. High-church Episcopalians, however, were soon swept up in the strong national sentiment in the early years of the republic. George Washington commissioned Pierre Charles l'Enfant to create a visionary plan for the nation's new capital. In addition to the National Mall and government buildings, the plan included "a great church for national purposes."

William Reed Huntington, rector of Grace Church, New York City, published *The National Church* in 1898. Huntington urged that the Episcopal Church be viewed as the national church of the United States because it best reflected the nation's democratic and inclusive ideals. The Episcopal Church never gained the recognition Huntington envisioned; on the other hand it avoided the pitfalls of legal establishment.

Cathedrals

By definition a cathedral is a bishop's primary church and base of opera-tion. Size or splendor is not necessarily implied; the grandeur of England's cathedrals reflected the spiritual ideals of medieval Christianity rather than canonical requirement. Nevertheless, English tradition dictated that every bishop should have a cathedral—and a suitably impressive one. Every diocese at the time of the Reformation had its cathedral, and normally the inventory of abbey churches and other large build-ings was enough to satisfy demand when new dioceses were created. Construction was rare, except to replace cathedrals destroyed by natural disasters, fire, or war.[104]

Other Anglican provinces had no heritage of cathedrals and did not always acknowledge the need for them. The decision to construct a new cathedral depended not only on budget priorities but on attitudes to English tradition and on the churchmanship balance in the particu-lar province or diocese. High churchmen generally favored cathedrals. Evangelicals, by contrast, regarded the construction and maintenance costs as wasteful; they even opposed conversion of existing churches into "pro-cathedrals." Cathedrals, in their view, encouraged unwanted pageantry, and the staffs of deans, canons, and music directors were po-tential hotbeds of high-church intrigue.

Reverence for English customs may not have been strong in Scotland. But the SEC had a strong high-church tradition, and ca-thedrals were built as soon as resources became available. St Ninian's Cathedral, Perth, Scotland, consecrated in 1850, was the first Anglican cathedral built in Great Britain since the Reformation. The founda-tion stone for St Mary's Cathedral, Edinburgh, was laid in 1874 by the Duke of Buccleuch and Queensberry, whose family had long supported the episcopal cause, and the nave was completed in 1879. St Andrew's Chapel, Aberdeen, which had been constructed in 1817 became St Andrew's Cathedral a century later.

The Anglican church in British North America began with a high-church orientation, strong English traditions, and even some funding from the mother country. As new dioceses were created, they all ac-quired cathedrals. Charles Inglis promptly converted St Paul's church, Halifax—Nova Scotia's oldest church—into the Cathedral of St Paul. King

---

104. Guildford Cathedral was constructed for a new diocese in the twentieth cen-tury. Coventry Cathedral was rebuilt after its destruction in World War II.

George III paid for the construction of Jacob Mountain's Holy Trinity Cathedral, Quebec City—the first Anglican cathedral built outside the British Isles. When the diocese of Toronto was created in 1839, its first bishop, John Strachan (1778–1867) a native of Aberdeen, converted the parish church of St James into a cathedral. It was destroyed by fire in 1849, but construction of a new cathedral began almost immediately and services were held just four years later.

In 1845 the foundation stone of Christ Church Cathedral, Fredericton was laid by the lieutenant governor of New Brunswick in full ceremonial attire. When the cathedral was dedicated in 1863 the high altar was decked with candles, and the guest preacher, Bishop Edward Feild (1801–76) of Newfoundland, took the opportunity to denounce the Privy Council's decision in the Gorham case.[105] The altar decoration—which anticipated the Ritualist Movement—the sermon, and the cathedral itself combined to make a strong high-church statement.

By the time the churchmanship balance shifted to the left, BNA/ Canada already had several cathedrals. Moreover, favorable attitudes to English tradition and the softening of evangelical opposition allowed construction to continue into the twentieth century.

In the United States, attitudes toward English tradition were mixed, the high-church party gained strength more slowly, and money was tight. A few high churchmen favored the cathedral concept, including the two Bishop Doanes. But no cathedrals were built, or even converted from existing churches, during the first half of the nineteenth century. A bishop's parish church served as his base of operations, without any special designation.

The first Episcopal cathedral constructed in the United States was the Cathedral of Our Merciful Savior, Faribault, Minnesota. James Lloyd Breck (1818–76), first dean of Nashotah House, and Henry Benjamin Whipple, first bishop of Minnesota, discussed the need for a cathedral in the Midwest and architect James Renwick was entrusted with the design. Whipple laid the foundation stone in 1862, and the building was dedicated in 1869. Wealthy businessman Erastus Corning donated land for William Doane's Cathedral of All Saints, Albany, and construction began in 1884.

Other cathedrals also sprang up from Maine to Utah in the latter half of the nineteenth century. When cathedrals were constructed they took on—as Evangelicals feared—the ceremonial trappings of great

105. Hayes, *Anglicans*, 125.

European churches, including pageantry and extensive music programs. Not surprisingly they played an important role in the Catholic Revival as well as reflecting its influence.

Plans for a cathedral in Honolulu began in 1862, when Hawaii was still an independent kingdom. The islands were served by Thomas Stanley, missionary bishop of the Church of England. King Kamehameha IV and Queen Emma, who were Anglicans, donated land. The king died on the feast of St Andrew, 1863, before ground was broken. But construction proceeded, and St Andrew's Cathedral was dedicated in his honor in 1886. When Hawaii was annexed by the United States the cathedral was deeded to the Episcopal Church. The Cathedral of the Holy Trinity, Paris, was consecrated in 1886 to serve American émigrés and temporary residents in France.

Huntington's discussion, in *The National Church*, of the role of the Episcopal Church revived Pierre l'Enfant's vision of "a great church" in the nation's capital. At a meeting in 1891, hosted by financier and philanthropist Charles Carroll Glover, the decision was made to build Washington National Cathedral. Fundraising began, and the foundation stone was laid in 1907; construction was completed in 1990. Washington Cathedral became a national symbol and the crowning glory of cathedral construction in the United States.

The cornerstone of the Cathedral of St John the Divine, New York City, was laid in 1892, but construction was delayed, and in the 1910s the architectural design was changed. Construction was delayed again by the Great Depression and World War II; it was not restarted until 1979 and the twin towers remain unfinished.

Ecumenical Outreach

Bishop Campbell established contacts with the Greek Orthodox Archbishop Arsenius of Thebas in the early eighteenth century. Based on those contacts he proposed that Nonjurors seek union with the East under the auspices of the patriarchate of Jerusalem.[106] The initiative came to nothing after the eastern patriarchs showed no inclination to compromise. Despite the rebuff, the Nonjurors maintained their interest in Orthodox liturgy and theology.

---

106. Langford, *"The Non-Jurors."*

The nineteenth century witnessed renewed interest in Christian unity. Understandably, attitudes depended on churchmanship. Low-church Anglicans wanted closer connections with Protestant denominations, whereas high churchmen envisioned union with the Roman and Orthodox churches.

In 1870 Huntington proposed "a basis on which approach may be by God's blessing, made toward Home Reunion"; "Home" referred to the one holy, catholic, and apostolic church.[107] Influenced by Frederick Denison Maurice,[108] Huntington identified four principles that defined Anglicanism and should serve as minimum conditions for merger negotiations. The principles, distilled from the Thirty-Nine Articles, were: the centrality of scripture, the Nicene Creed, the sacraments of baptism and the Eucharist, and the historic episcopate. Clearly they focused on Articles VI, VIII, XXV, and XXXVI, implying that the others were either taken for granted or negotiable.

Huntington's proposal was adopted by the House of Bishops in Chicago in 1886. The bishops affirmed that "all who have been duly baptized with water, in the name of the Father, and of the Son, and of the Holy Ghost, are members of the Holy Catholic Church." They explained that "this Church does not seek to absorb other Communions, but rather, co-operating with them on the basis of a common Faith and Order, to discountenance schism, to heal the wounds of the Body of Christ, and to promote the charity which is the chief of Christian graces and the visible manifestation of Christ to the world." Two years later, the Lambeth Conference endorsed the proposal and formulated what became known as the Chicago–Lambeth Quadrilateral, or just the Lambeth Quadrilateral:

- The Holy Scriptures of the Old and New Testaments, as "containing all things necessary to salvation," and as being the rule and ultimate standard of faith.
- The Apostles' Creed, as the Baptismal Symbol; and the Nicene Creed, as the sufficient statement of the Christian faith.
- The two Sacraments ordained by Christ Himself—Baptism and the Supper of the Lord—ministered with unfailing use of Christ's Words of Institution, and of the elements ordained by Him.

107. Huntington, *The Church Idea*.

108. Maurice, *The Kingdom of Christ*. Maurice was an early proponent of Christian Socialism.

- The Historic Episcopate, locally adapted in the methods of its administration to the varying needs of the nations and peoples called of God into the Unity of His Church.

EROSION OF TRADITIONAL CHURCH PARTIES

Starting in the eighteenth century, and accelerating in the nineteenth, the neat division into high- and low-church Anglicans began to break down. The two-party system never captured Anglican opinion in its entirety; labels are attached to stereotypes rather than real people. Moreover, the composition of the low church changed over time as Evangelicals displaced Puritans as its dominant subgroup. Nevertheless, the categorization was meaningful and easily understood. The emergence of new parties clouded the picture but also softened the previously stark polarization.

"Latitudinarian" was first applied to the bishops and clergy who accepted positions in the Church of England vacated by the Nonjurors, with the implication that they put ambition, or at least pragmatism, ahead of conscience. Over time the term came to denote a more general attitude of indifference toward the liturgy, doctrine, and the historic episcopate.[109] Enlightenment philosophy, German rationalism, and liberal theology played into that attitude. In their attempt to defend Christianity against assault by skeptics, latitudinarians felt that the miracles of Jesus, the real presence in the Eucharist, and other mysteries were expendable. The Hutchinsonians sought to counter their influence.

The "broad church" emerged in the mid-nineteenth century. Drawn from moderates across the spectrum, it respected the traditions of the Prayer Book and the Thirty-Nine Articles but embraced aspects of latitudinarianism, rationalism, and liberalism. *Essays and Reviews* (1860), with contributions from prominent clergy, including a future archbishop of Canterbury, Frederick Temple, became a broad-church manifesto.[110] The broad church soon became the largest party in the Anglican church, whereupon the high- and low-church parties found themselves treated as fringe groups.

Each of the three parties—high, broad, and low—came under attack. For example, high churchmen criticized the broad church for denying sa-

109. Among the early latitudinarians were the Cambridge Platonists who saw in Plato's writings important lessons for Christianity.

110. Parker, *Essays and Reviews*.

cred mystery and the low church for indifference toward the sacraments. From time to time, two of the three parties would join forces to attack the third. High and low churchmen attacked the broad church: the former committed to preserving traditions of ecclesiology, liturgy, and doctrine; the latter committed to opposing liberalism. High and broad churchmen defended the episcopal tradition against low-church indifference. Broad and low churchmen accused the high church of "popery." Such alliances were fragile and short-lived; traditional hostilities soon reasserted themselves, or changing priorities necessitated new alignments.

The broad church may have lacked conviction and fervor; but its tolerant, non-threatening, and optimistic demeanor helped maintain the cohesion of Anglicanism and the ability of right and left to function within a common pluralistic structure. The "big tent" was as much the broad church's creation as it was Elizabeth I's.

Romanticism emerged in the nineteenth century as a reaction against the dehumanizing aspects of the Industrial Revolution—and not incidentally against Enlightenment rationalism. It helped the Catholic Revival gain traction. In turn the Catholic Revival added a new dimension to Anglican churchmanship. Some parishes, clergy, and laity identified themselves as "Anglo-Catholic," to emphasize continuity with the early catholic church, while maintaining a healthy distinction from Roman Catholicism. Actually the term was not new. "Anglo-Catholic" originally described the Church of England in general and then became a label for orthodox high churchmen.[111] But it was appropriated by the Tractarians in the 1840s. Eventually the term would expand to capture all adherents to, or aspects of, the Catholic Revival.

Anglo-Catholics considered themselves high-church. But more conservative high churchmen distanced themselves from major parts of the Anglo-Catholic agenda, which in their view undermined the legacy of the Reformation. Considerable tension arose between the two subgroups. Accordingly, it became necessary to distinguish "orthodox high-church" from "Anglo-Catholic high-church."

In the twentieth century "high-," "broad-," and "low-church" largely gave way to "catholic," "liberal," and "evangelical." By then still more parties were emerging, cutting across traditional lines. The catholic and evangelical parties, for example, were—and still are—deeply split over the ordination of women and persons in same-sex relationships. The

111. Bishop Phillpotts's obituary used the term in that sense as late as 1869.

growth of Anglicanism in Africa, South Asia, and South America created further confusion. Southern-hemisphere Anglicans, whose cultures are very different from those of Europe and North America, tend to be socially conservative but open to liturgical experiments that worry traditionalists elsewhere.

The Scottish Episcopal Church has been the most consistently high-church province in the Anglican Communion. The religious polarity that gave it birth has relaxed in recent decades, however, and the SEC's orientation is softening. Considerable interest has been shown in reunion with the Church of Scotland. As a gesture toward Presbyterians in 1982 the large crucifix and altar candles in St Andrew's Cathedral, Aberdeen, were removed.

REFLECTIONS

High-church Anglicans preserved a thread of sacramental Christianity against powerful opposition. They emphasized belief in the divine institution of the church and episcopate, the authority of tradition, the efficacy of the sacraments, the centrality of the Eucharist, the scripted liturgy, and Marian devotion. Thus they laid the groundwork for the Catholic Revival in the nineteenth century.

Traditionalists successfully resisted pressure to align England with continental Protestantism in the immediate post-Reformation period. They lost influence under Edward VI, became irrelevant under Mary I, and only slowly regained strength under Elizabeth I. A strong high-church tradition finally reemerged at the end of Elizabeth's reign to preserve the thread of sacramentalism during the turbulent period of the English Civil War and the Commonwealth. A modern collect honoring Caroline Divine Lancelot Andrewes, whose feast is celebrated September 26, is as follows: "Almighty God, who gavest thy servant Lancelot Andrewes the gift of thy holy Spirit and made him a man of prayer and a faithful pastor of thy people: Perfect in us what is lacking of thy gifts, of faith, to increase it, of hope, to establish it, of love, to kindle it, that we may live in the life of thy grace and glory."[112]

It was clear, however, both before and after the Interregnum, that Puritanism was so strong that to move the Church of England to the right was not feasible. The most the Caroline Divines could do after

---

112. Source: Standing Commission on Liturgy and Music, ECUSA.

the Restoration was to return the church to where it was during the Elizabethan era.

The revolution of 1689 created a dilemma for Anglican clergy: whether to support a king whose Roman Catholicism they abhorred or betray their oaths of ordination by supporting monarchs of questionable legitimacy: William and Mary, Anne, and eventually the Hanoverians. At great personal sacrifice the Nonjurors chose the former path and were forced out of the church. The twofold outcome was that Calvinists took control of the Church of Scotland, and the Church of England went into decline for 150 years.

The silver lining in a very dark cloud was the Nonjurors' freedom to explore high-church Anglicanism without the need to compromise. Those in England left a legacy of writings that proved of inestimable value in the Catholic Revival. The Nonjurors in Scotland not only preserved an Anglican presence, where it would otherwise have been extinguished, they created the Scottish Episcopal Church, whose high-church orientation eventually spread far beyond its home base.

"Laud's Book," the Nonjurors' 1718 Liturgy, and the 1764 Scottish Communion Service formed a continuum of unfolding belief in the objective real presence and sacrificial intent of the Eucharist. It extended to the nascent Episcopal Church in the United States through the consecration of Samuel Seabury. In the twentieth century the Scottish/American sacramental tradition reinvigorated liturgies in Canada, England, and other provinces of the Anglican Communion.

Seabury was the first of a line of strong high-church American bishops whose work supported, and in a few cases foreshadowed, the Catholic Revival. Under their influence the Episcopal Church in the United States moved to the right throughout the nineteenth century. British North America did not have a Seabury. But Charles Inglis was a high churchman who took refuge in Nova Scotia at a time when the colony was absorbing immigrants from both the United States and Scotland. BNA/Canada developed its own long line of high-church bishops, distinguished among much else by preserving the English tradition of cathedral building.

6

Catholic Revival I:
Church, Doctrine, and the Spiritual Life

THIS CHAPTER DISCUSSES TWO of the overlapping phases of the Catholic Revival: the Tractarian Movement and the revival of Anglican religious orders. It examines the Tractarian Movement's theological and ecclesiological focus and its encouragement of personal and collective sanctity. The movement reinforced orthodox high-church beliefs and, in a few cases, moved beyond them to recover more of the richness of early Christianity. The encouragement of sanctity led directly to the revival of religious orders. The Tractarian Movement attracted support, but also strong opposition, for its perceived convergence with Roman Catholicism.

CRISIS IN THE CHURCH OF ENGLAND

The mood in England at the turn of the nineteenth century was depressed. The American Revolution had left deep wounds in the English psyche, only partly relieved by colonial successes in Africa, Asia, and Australia. The French Revolution had upset long-standing stability on the continent of Europe and disturbed religious as well as political and military sensibilities at home.[1] The Napoleonic Wars were still to come.

After a century or more of spiritual decline, the Church of England seemed to have lost its vitality, lost its sense of direction. An American observer commented that the church had fallen from a position of power to the condition of "a victim, dressed for the slaughter." It was a a ghastly

---

1. Nockles, *The Oxford Movement*, 46–49.

picture, he declared, "when skepticism was rampant, and an insufferably insolent individualism paraded itself on the platform; when the men most alive were the Evangelicals, amongst whom there was hardly one who combined scholarship, intellect, and address in a considerable degree, nor one who represented the principles and system in the Book of Common Prayer."[2]

Challenges to the Church of England were compounded by union with Ireland (1800), Catholic emancipation (1829), the Reform Act of 1832, and the Church Temporalities (Ireland) Act of 1833. The "Irish Church Act," as the last was known, reformed the Anglican church in Ireland. Steered through Parliament by Whig Prime Minister Lord Charles Grey, it reduced the number of Irish archbishoprics from four to two, consolidated twenty dioceses into ten, abolished religious taxes, and gave tenants on church lands opportunities to purchase their holdings. The measure was intended to improve resource utilization, and certainly the Irish church was top-heavy, considering the small Anglican population it served. But ecclesiastical authorities were not consulted, and the government's unilateral action outraged many people. Reorganization of the Church of England itself might be next on the Whig agenda.

Parliamentary legislation affecting the church was not new. The Act of Supremacy of 1534 declared the monarch to be head of the Church of England; it was revoked in 1554 and reinstated in 1559. Parliament dismantled the episcopate in 1650 and restored it 1662. Parliament authorized successive versions of the Prayer Book. But church and state had always been viewed as partners in a divinely ordained social order. That partnership was now threatened not only by parliamentary action but also by changes in parliament itself. Parliament was no longer restricted to members of the Church of England; Nonconformists and Roman Catholics sat in the Commons, even in the House of Lords. The prospect that non-Anglicans, or even non-Christians, could make decisions for the Church of England was intolerable.[3]

The church's problems were the more serious because senior churchmen lacked an official forum where they could express concerns; the Convocations of Canterbury and York had been suspended since the reign of George I.

2. Dix, M., *The Oxford Movement*, 6, 8.

3. Eligibility for election to parliament was extended to Jews in 1858 and to atheists in 1886.

Informal suggestions for action came from all quarters. Evangelicals and liberals concluded that Anglicanism should broaden its appeal and relax its links with the state. Richard Whately, archbishop of Dublin, proposed disestablishment of the Church of England while retaining public financing—an irony not lost on his critics. Thomas Arnold, headmaster of Rugby School, published a pamphlet, *Principles of Church Reform*, offering a vision of the church as an inclusive institution that could embrace all Christians except Roman Catholics, Quakers, and Unitarians. Arnold called for increased lay participation in the church and criticized as "groundless superstition" the "mischievous confusion of the Christian ministry with a priesthood."[4] Latitudinarians proposed discarding the Creeds and eliminating any mention of the Trinity, baptismal regeneration, and absolution from the liturgy.[5]

High-church Anglicans drew totally different conclusions. They believed that the bishops should assert themselves and resist parliament's meddling in ecclesiastical affairs. Bishops who voted for Irish Church Act should be shamed as traitors.[6] Evangelical influence in the church must be stopped. The Church of England's traditional self-understanding should be restored and traditional Christian doctrine reinvigorated.

THE TRACTARIAN MOVEMENT

The Oxford Initiative

In the 1830s a group of high-church clergy at Oxford University decided to write tracts to share their views on the issues at hand and stimulate informed discussion. Tract writing was not a novel way for academics to express concerns. Many others had done likewise. Bishop Hobart of New York had shared his own experiences during a visit to Oxford in 1823.

The group came together in a "meeting of minds," with no formal organization. But soon it was apparent that a movement was underway. It was referred to by a variety of names, including "Tractarian Movement," coined in 1839 and used here, and "Oxford Movement," which entered

---

4. Arnold, *Principles*, 62.

5. Church, *The Oxford Movement*, 90.

6. Eleven bishops voted in favor of the Irish Church Act, including Edward Vernon Harcourt, archbishop of York; Charles James Blomfield, bishop of London; and Richard Whately.

the vocabulary in the 1880s.[7] Participants were referred to as "Tractites," "Apostolicals," "Oxfordites," "Newmanites," and "Puseyites," the last two referring to the group's leaders. We shall use "Tractarians." The movement's goals, in the words of Richard William Church (1815–90), tutor of Oriel College, Oxford, and later dean of St Paul's Cathedral, London, were "to rouse the Church from its lethargy, and to strengthen and purify religion, by making it deeper and more real."[8]

The principal characters were John Keble, Richard Hurrell Froude, John Henry Newman, and Edward Bouverie Pusey. Keble (1792–1866) was a fellow of Oriel College, high-church Tory, respected scholar, and accomplished poet.[9] In 1823 he had left Oxford to become curate at his father's parish in Gloucestershire, planning to live the quiet life of a country parson. But that was not to be. He was appointed professor of poetry in 1831, and two years later he preached the sermon that launched the Tractarian Movement.

Froude (1803–36), son of an archdeacon, had studied under Keble and absorbed many of his mentor's ideals. He was cautious and scholarly in his public statements but more radical in private correspondence. That radicalism damaged the tractarian cause when his papers were published after his untimely death. Froude was one of the first Tractarians to propose disestablishment of the Church of England: "[L]et us give up a national church," he declared, "and have a real one."[10]

Newman (1801–90), son of a London banker, was another fellow of Oriel College. He had once been influenced by Richard Whately, and eventually he would convert to Roman Catholicism. But in the 1830s he identified strongly with high-church Anglicanism. Froude introduced him to Keble, and Newman soon became the movement's leader. As Dean Church put it, "Keble had given the inspiration, Froude had given the impulse; then Newman took up the work."[11] Newman was inspired by notions of the "one, holy, catholic, and apostolic church." His search for "Catholicity"—and he liked to capitalize the word—colored much of his work.

7. Nockles, *The Oxford Movement*, 36, 38.

8. Church, *The Oxford Movement*, 111.

9. Keble's *The Christian Year* (1827) became a best-seller.

10. Quoted in Church, *The Oxford Movement*, 32

11. Ibid., 28.

Pusey (1800–82), yet another fellow of Oriel, was Regius Professor of Hebrew and canon of Christ Church Cathedral, Oxford. He had studied in Germany and showed an early interest in pietism, but by the 1830s he had become a strong high churchman. Pusey had contacts with the Tractarians from the beginning but did not become fully involved until 1835. After Newman's defection he found himself in the leadership role, whereupon "Newmanites" became "Puseyites."

Others who played significant roles in the Tractarian Movement were poet and religious writer Isaac Williams; Arthur Philip Perceval, former student of Keble's, rector of a Surrey church, and chaplain to the king; Newman's brother-in-law Thomas Mozley; James Bowling Mozley, Thomas's brother and fellow of Magdalen College; John W. Bowden, a friend of Newman's; and Benjamin Harrison of Christ College. Orthodox high churchmen who played supporting roles included Hugh James Rose, Robert Isaac Wilberforce, and William Patrick Palmer of Worcester College.[12]

Beginning of the Movement

On July 14, 1833—300 years, almost to the day, after the pope excommunicated Henry VIII—John Keble delivered the Assize Sermon at St Mary's Church, Oxford.[13] His theme was "National Apostasy," and he chose for his text First Samuel 12:23: "As for me, God forbid that I should sin against the Lord in ceasing to pray for you: but I will teach you the good and the right way." The sermon summed up high-church concerns. "What," Keble asked, "are the symptoms, by which one may judge most fairly, whether or no a nation, as such, is becoming alienated from God and Christ. And what are the particular duties of sincere Christians, whose lot is cast by Divine Providence in a time of such dire calamity?"[14] Those duties included both prayer and activism. Keble ended on an optimistic note: a "true Christian" can trust that he will be on "the winning side, and that the victory will be complete, universal, eternal."[15]

---

12. William P. Palmer (1803–85) of Worcester College, later Sir William, is not to be confused with fellow Tractarian William Palmer (1811–79) of Magdalen College.

13. Preachers during the Assizes—meetings of the English circuit courts—often chose subjects of current political relevance.

14. Keble, Assize Sermon.

15. Ibid. Emphasis removed.

Two weeks later, Hugh Rose hosted a strategy meeting at his deanery in Suffolk. Palmer, Perceval, and Froude attended, the last serving as spokesperson for Keble and Newman who were otherwise engaged.[16] No firm decisions were made, but Froude announced that he and his academic colleagues would write a number of tracts addressing the issues at hand.

The first three tracts, written by Newman but published anonymously, appeared in September 1833 and were distributed to parish clergy and interested laypeople.[17] The ninetieth and last, written by Newman, appeared in 1841. The tracts addressed a broad range of topics related to church organization, doctrine, and religious practices. Only a few bore their authors' names, but we know that Keble, Froude, Pusey, Bowden, Harrison, Perceval, and Williams contributed, as well as Newman. The first few tracts were short, on the order of three or four pages. The later ones were longer, and some ran to more than one hundred pages. Pusey's Tracts 67–69 on baptism ran to a combined total of 300 pages and, in a second edition, to 400 pages. Periodically the tracts were collected into volumes and published as *Tracts for the Times*.

The tracts were not intended to form an official statement of the group's views—still less an official confession of faith, like the Homilies. They were intended to stimulate discussion. No formal steps were taken to ensure consistency, and the views expressed were entirely their authors'. The Tractarians formed a fairly cohesive, though not homogeneous, group. Newman and Froude, for example, were more radical than Keble.

In a preface, or "advertisement," to the first bound volume, Newman identified the tracts' purpose as "contributing something towards the practical revival of doctrines, which, although held by the great divines of our Church, at present have become obsolete with the majority of her members, and are withdrawn from public view even by the more learned and orthodox few who still adhere to them."[18] The Tractarians drew upon the writings of the Caroline Divines and Nonjurors, and some tracts were reprints of those writings. But they did not acknowledge the contributions of the Hutchinsonians, the Hackney Phalanx, or Americans like Hobart.

---

16. Ollard, *A Short History*, 28–32.

17. They were sold for one penny each.

18. Newman, "Advertisement."

The tracts provoked great interest at Oxford and, before long, other parts of Britain and abroad. To quote Dean Church, they "almost monopolized for the time both the intelligence and the highest religious earnestness of the University, and either in curiosity or inquiry, in approval or in condemnation, all that was deepest and most vigorous, all that was most refined, most serious, most high-minded, and most promising in Oxford was drawn to the issues it raised."[19] The tracts "touched many consciences, they won many hearts, they opened new thoughts and hopes to many minds."[20]

Rarely has a small group achieved so much in a short time. In addition to publishing the tracts, the Tractarians wrote articles and books, gave speeches, preached sermons, and exchanged numerous letters. They published a fifty-volume collection of the patristic writings[21] and began work on the ninety-five volume *Library of Anglo-Catholic Theology*.[22] The Tractarians acquired the *British Critic* from the Hackney Phalanx and made it a voice for the movement; Newman served as its first editor, succeeded in 1841 by Thomas Mozley.

THE TRACTS AND THEIR MESSAGE

The Church

Several of the early tracts addressed issues of Anglican catholicity, continuity with the early church, and the historic episcopate. Tract 5, authored by "a laymen" (Bowden), focused on the Church of Christ, "bequeathed to the world, to be cherished and enjoyed as a precious legacy, until His coming again." It proceeded to explain that a "branch of this holy Catholic (or universal) Church has been, through God's blessing, established for ages in our island; a branch which . . . we denominate the Church of England."[23] Presumably that branch also extended to the British Empire and other countries, like the United States.

Tract 5's thesis received strong support from William P. Palmer's influential *Treatise on the Church of Christ*, published in 1838. Palmer made the bold claim that the Anglican, Roman, and Orthodox churches

---

19. Church, *The Oxford Movement*, 159.

20. Ibid., 131.

21. Pusey et al., *Library of the Fathers*.

22. Copeland et al., *Library*.

23. Parenthesis in original.

comprised three authentic branches of the one, holy, catholic, and apostolic church.[24] Each branch preserved the apostolic succession and, to
different degrees, the purity of apostolic Christianity. The branch theory
was rejected by the Roman and Eastern Orthodox churches, each of
which claimed to be the sole legitimate successor of the apostolic church.
The Church of Rome also rejected the Anglican claim to an unbroken
episcopal succession. The branch theory did not attract much excitement
within the Church of England either. Evangelicals emphasized ties with
continental Protestantism, which the theory excluded, while many broad
churchmen considered continuity with the early church unimportant.

Tract 7: "The Episcopal Church Apostolical," made the familiar
claim that "our present Bishops are the heirs and representatives of
the Apostles." But Tract 15 went farther to declare: "There was no new
Church founded among us [at the Reformation], but the rights and the
true doctrine of the Ancient Church were asserted and established." Its
account of the English Reformation was highly abridged: "In the year
1534, the Bishops and Clergy . . . assembled in their respective convocations of Canterbury and York, and signed a declaration that the Pope or
Bishop of Rome had no more jurisdiction in this country."

Pusey made a similar point in a letter to his bishop. The Anglican
church was not "a new Church of the Reformation" but a "purified"
form of the unified catholic church.[25] Pusey contrasted the Church of
England, which had preserved its episcopate from pre-Reformation
times, with the new churches founded by Luther and Calvin. Henry VIII
had preserved medieval beliefs and practices, and both Elizabeth I and
the Caroline Divines had initiated restoration movements. In a letter
dated 1834 but published posthumously, Froude confessed: "You will
be shocked at my avowal, that I am every day becoming a less and less
loyal son of the Reformation."[26] In the quest for catholicity, the English
Reformation was being erased from the Anglican memory. Critics re-
torted that the Tractarians were trying to rewrite history.

Tract 34, which will be discussed in more detail shortly, reaffirmed
trust in the authority of the patristic writings, even in matters on which
scripture was silent. Newman expressed a similar belief in a lecture
given in 1837: "[W]hatever doctrine the primitive ages unanimously at-

24. Palmer, *A Treatise*, especially ch. 10.

25. Quoted in Chandler, *An Introduction*, 48.

26. Ibid., 46.

test, whether by consent of Fathers, or by Councils, or by the events of history, or by controversies, or by whatever way may fairly be considered to be the universal belief of those ages, is to be received as coming from the Apostles."[27] Newman endorsed the Vincentian Canon: "Catholicity, Antiquity, and Consent of Fathers, is the proper evidence of the fidelity or Apostolicity of a professed Tradition."[28]

In Tract 89 Pusey defended the Church Fathers against charges that they stooped to allegorical interpretation of scripture or were "mystics." Those charges may seem odd to us today. The Alexandrian school was well-known for its use of allegory, contrasting with the school of Antioch, which held to a literal reading of scripture. And we might side with Eastern Orthodox theologians who insist that rational formulations can never capture the whole of divine truth. But the negative light cast on mysticism by the Reformation and the Enlightenment was still pervasive in the nineteenth century.

In his defense of the Fathers Pusey expressed confidence that they were sufficiently capable of critical thinking to avoid allegory.[29] He acknowledged that, in many people's minds, mysticism "implies a sort of confusion between physical and moral, visible and spiritual agency, most abhorrent to the minds of those, who pique themselves on having thoroughly clear ideas, and on their power of distinctly analyzing effects into their proper causes, whether in matter or in mind. [It] conveys the notion of, something essentially and altogether remote from common sense and practical utility."[30] Pusey added that the "man of the world" rejects mysticism and accordingly "is saved all trouble of research."

Pusey insisted, however, that the pitfalls of mysticism could be avoided by moral development, "repentance, devotion, and self-denial" so that we may "draw near, with Moses, to the darkness where God is. And this so much the more, the more that darkness is mingled with evangelical light; for so much the more he may hope to see of God; and we know Who it is, that has inseparably connected seeing God with purity of heart."[31]

27. Newman, *Lectures*, 62.
28. Ibid., 63.
29. Tract 89, §V.
30. Ibid., §I.
31. Ibid., §V.

Religious Practices

Several tracts addressed issues of spiritual discipline and personal sanctity. The thrust of Pusey's Tract 18 was obvious from its title: "Thoughts on the Benefits of the System of Fasting, Enjoined by Our Church." Tract 21 continued in the same vein: "[C]ertain bodily privations and chastisements are a very essential duty to all who wish to serve God, and prepare themselves for his presence." It listed precedents in the Old and New Testaments and also in the primitive church. However, Tract 21 did not address Luther's objection to "good works" or the Thirty-Nine Articles' grudging acknowledgement of their merits.

Tract 26, based on a sermon preached by William Beveridge, an eighteenth-century Welsh bishop and well-known preacher, promoted the desirability of frequent Communion. The Prayer Book required that all Anglicans "shall communicate at least three times in the year, of which Easter to be one." But the tract declared, "the Church . . . hath taken all the care she can, that the Holy Sacrament should be everywhere administered, if it was possible, every day, at least every Sunday and Holy-Day in the year."

Newman's Tract 34, "Rites and Ceremonies of the Church," discussed a number of customs of primitive Christianity, including the sign of the cross, kneeling or standing for certain prayers, head-covering for women during worship, sacramental use of oil and salt, and invocations before and after the consecration of the Mass. Tract 34 was significant for two reasons. Ritual had been scorned by the Puritans as romish superstition and had received only lukewarm support from orthodox high churchmen. The new interest foreshadowed the Ritualist Movement of a decade or two later.

Furthermore, several of the rites discussed were not explicitly mentioned in scripture, raising the issue of authority noted earlier. "If any parts of [a religious practice] are contrary to Scripture," the tract explained, "that is of course a decisive reason at once for believing them to be additions and corruptions of the original ceremonial." Article VI required no less. "[B]ut till this is shown," Tract 34 continued, "we are bound to venerate what is certainly primitive, and probably is apostolic." The sixteenth-century controversy over "edifying practices" comes to mind.

Tract 34 quoted Church Father Tertullian: "[A] tradition, even though not in Scripture, still binds our conduct, if a continuous usage be preserved as the witness of it." It also cited Basil of Caesarea's argument that "the Apostles and Fathers . . . were accustomed to lodge their secret doctrine in mystic forms, as being secretly and silently conveyed. This is the reason why there is a tradition of observances independent of Scripture, lest doctrines, being exposed to the world, should be so familiar as to be despised."[32]

Pusey never rivaled Keble or Newman as a preacher, but his tracts on baptism assured his intellectual leadership in the Tractarian Movement. With the title: "Scriptural Views of Holy Baptism," Tract 67's main purpose was to reinforce the doctrine of baptismal regeneration against evangelical contention that baptism simply prepared the person for the conversion experience later in life. James Mozley's *The Primitive Doctrine of Baptismal Regeneration* (1856) expanded on Pusey's arguments, and the two works should be read together.

"Regeneration," according to Pusey, was "the act by which God takes us out of our relation to Adam and makes us actual members of His Son."[33] He explained the doctrine thus:

> Baptismal regeneration, as connected with the Incarnation of our Blessed Lord, gives a depth to our Christian existence, an actualness to our union with Christ, a reality to our sonship to God, an interest in the presence of our Lord's glorified Body at God's right hand, a joyousness amid the subduing of the flesh, an overwhelmingness to the dignity conferred on human nature, a solemnity to the communion of saints who are the fullness of Him Who filleth all in all, a substantiality to the indwelling of Christ, that to those who retain this truth the school which abandoned it must needs appear to have sold its birthright.[34]

Pusey blamed evangelicals' flawed understanding of baptism on Calvinist influence, arguing that it ignored multiple passages in the New Testament whose meaning was abundantly clear. Mozley identified several of those references in his book "signifying or implying a new or second birth," for example: "dead to sin," "dead with Christ," "buried with Christ," "risen with Christ," "quickened," "alive from the dead," and

---

32. Thomas Podmore made a similar claim that certain rites were deliberately omitted from scripture because of safety concerns. See *A Layman's Apology*, 7–8.

33. Tract 67, 23.

34. Ibid., 12–13. See also Liddon, *Life*, vol. 1, 349.

"alive unto God."[35] Mozley insisted that baptism imparts real, permanent grace—"*final* grace"—as distinct from a capacity for grace.[36]

On the other hand, both the high- and low-church views of baptism raised many questions concerning justification by faith, post-baptismal sin, repentance, and forgiveness. Faced with criticism of Tract 67 Pusey exclaimed: "I should have written on Christian repentance, on confession and absolution."[37] An even more important issue—one pertaining not just to baptism but to all the sacraments—was the efficacy of sacramental rites: did Christ institute sacraments and guarantee their efficacy or did he not? If baptism was nothing more than a symbol, what about the Eucharist?

Nowhere in the tracts do we find any encouragement for Marian devotion. Keble's Tract 54 was a sermon for the feast of the Annunciation, but the only reference to Mary was: "This day, though named for the Blessed Virgin, is one of the greatest festivals of our Savior";[38] the rest of the sermon spoke of Christ. In Tract 71, "On the Controversy with the Romanists," Newman identified "the worship of Mary," along with suggestions that Mary retained a kind of maternal authority over Christ, as important objections to Roman doctrine.[39] As late as 1865, Pusey argued that the reunion of the Anglican and Roman churches was impeded by "that vast system as to the Blessed Virgin, which to all of us has been the special 'crux' of the Roman system."[40]

On the other hand, Keble wrote several poems with Marian themes. In one he declared, with enthusiasm recalling Mark Frank's writings of two centuries earlier: "Ave Maria! thou whose name / All but adoring love may claim."[41] Furthermore, Keble did not reject the notion of intercessionary prayer. Froude had a personal affection for Mary, and he may have influenced Newman, whose attitude began to change after the 1840s.[42] Newman wrote extensively on the subject of Mary after his conversion to Roman Catholicism.

---

35. Mozley, J., *The Primitive Doctrine*, xi.
36. Ibid., 2–3, 44. Emphasis in original.
37. Liddon, *Life*, vol. 1, 252.
38. Tract 54.
39. Tract 71.
40. Pusey, *The Church of England*."
41. Quoted in Rowell, *The Vision*, 31.
42. Boyce, *Mary*, 25–26.

The Controversial Tracts

Controversy began almost as soon as the first tracts were published, but it became strident in the late 1830s. Critics claimed, unfairly, that the tracts expressed views that deviated substantially from accepted Anglican doctrine. The problem was that the Church of England had been dominated by Evangelicals and latitudinarians for 150 years, and what many people regarded as accepted doctrine was significantly to the left of center. For the most part the tracts reiterated orthodox high-church positions.

Suspicions also arose that the Tractarian Movement was some kind of conspiracy, and the fact that most of the tracts were published anonymously gave the fears credibility. Suspicions were heightened when Tract 80 appeared with the title: "On Reserve in Communicating Religious Knowledge." Written by Isaac Williams, it began with the provocative line: "The object of the present inquiry is to ascertain, whether there is not in God's dealings with mankind, a very remarkable holding back of sacred and important truths, as if the knowledge of them were injurious to persons unworthy of them. And if this be the case, it will lead to some important practical reflections."

After exhaustive discussion Williams ended with a twofold conclusion. First, sacred things must be approached with awe and trepidation; to say too much, too soon, destroyed that sacredness. If we exercise due care, however, "the means of grace faithfully cherished will lead us, as it were, step by step, into all these treasures, inexhaustible in their nature, limitless in their duration, and exceeding all conception of man, the blessing of the pure in heart, that they shall see God."[43] Second, some truths were too dangerous to be revealed to the masses. In the early church the most important teachings were shared only with members of the Christian communities who had professed belief in Christ and accepted baptism. Tract 34 had pointed out that, during the times of Roman persecution, missionaries were careful to avoid betraying innocent Christians, or themselves, to potentially hostile third parties.[44]

Although Williams cited many precedents in the early church for "reserve" in communicating religious knowledge, Tract 80 was not well-received. Critics likened the Tractarians to the Jesuits who, according to

43. Tract 80.

44. Tracts 34 and 80 did not mention that the Gnostics inherited the notion of secret teachings from the ancient mystery schools.

an enduring stereotype, were foreign agents plotting against Anglicanism and the monarchy.

Early nineteenth-century England was still caught up in anti-Roman sentiments that dated back to the time of Mary I, Guy Fawkes, and James II. Those sentiments had been reinforced by Catholic Emancipation, increased visibility of Roman Catholic worship and religious orders, and the prospect of a Roman hierarchy in Britain. However, Froude argued for an end to the customary polemic and urged a more balanced view of Roman Catholicism. In his private papers he suggested that, on certain issues, Roman Catholicism was closer than Anglicanism to the truth, and that some of the church's problems resulted from the Reformation.

Newman argued that the Anglican position would be strengthened by conceding its own weaknesses, while focusing on areas of Roman Catholicism where abuses and corruption had destroyed the purity of early medieval Christianity. In Tract 71 Newman declared: "We have . . . too often fought the Romanists on the wrong grounds." Anglican doctrine might be incomplete, but Roman teachings contained "positive errors," such as belief in purgatory, the granting of pardons and indulgences, the veneration of images, or the necessity of yearly confession. The same year, 1836, Newman delivered a series of lectures on "Romanism and Popular Protestantism." Reflecting on the lectures later, he asserted: "My desire hath been to have Truth as my chieftest friend, and no enemy but error. If I have had any bias, it hath been desire for peace, which our common Saviour left as a legacy to His Church, that I might live to see the re-union of Christendom, for which I shall always bow the knees of my heart."[45]

The Tractarians, in Dean Church's words, "declined to commit themselves to the vulgar and indiscriminate abuse of [Roman Catholicism] which was the discreditable legacy of the old days of controversy. They did what all the world was loudly professing to do, they looked facts in the face."[46] Unfortunately, to minimize differences, assess the relative merits of Roman and Anglican teachings, and express a desire to heal the wounds of schism were all viewed as betraying the very foundations of the Church of England. The perception developed that the Tractarians were subversives, plotting to surrender the church to Rome.

45. Newman, *Lectures*, Advertisement.
46. Church, *The Oxford Movement*, 225.

If the Tractarians were trying to move Anglicanism closer to Roman Catholicism, their efforts certainly were not reciprocated. Nicholas Patrick Wiseman, future archbishop and cardinal, who had recently arrived from the English College in Rome, became an outspoken critic of the Tractarian Movement. In an article published in the *Dublin Review* in 1839 he likened Anglicans to the Donatists of the fourth century, who refused to accept the sacraments from priests who had returned to the church after renouncing their faith under persecution.[47] Roman Catholic leaders launched an aggressive campaign for the "conversion of England," which lasted until the latter part of the twentieth century.

The Tractarians often came across as deliberately confrontational. They were brilliant men, but they lacked diplomacy and political skills. Keble's and Newman's decision to publish Froude's personal papers was a case in point. Newman believed so strongly in his mission that he overlooked the need to build a political base. By the late 1830s he had lost the support of the Hackney Phalanx, moderates like Rose and Palmer, and high-church bishops like Henry Phillpotts.

The bishops, whom the Tractarians had set out to rescue from religious indifference and parliamentary interference in 1833, did not return the favor. Prime Minister Grey was long gone, the Whig party was weakened, and the threat of a major reorganization of the Church of England had receded. Suspicion of the Tractarians was now as great as it had been of the Whigs. Episcopal attitudes toward the movement in 1840 ranged from lukewarm support to fierce opposition. Bishop John Bird Sumner of Chester described the tracts as the work of Satan.[48]

Meanwhile, opposition was steadily growing within the university. By 1840 a coalition of powerful enemies had emerged, committed to driving Tractarianism from Oxford. The "heads of houses," who collectively governed the university, might have urged caution. Instead, to quote Dean Church, they "found themselves going along with the outside current of uninstructed and ignoble prejudice, in a settled and pronounced dislike, which took for granted that all was wrong in the movement."[49]

47. Donatism was attacked by Augustine of Hippo and condemned by the Council of Arles in 314 CE. Later, "donatism" was applied to the claim that unworthy priests could not administer valid sacraments.

48. Church, *The Oxford Movement*, 219.

49. Ibid., 216.

Tract 90

When Newman's Tract 90 was published in January 1841, opposition turned into outrage. The tract entitled: "Remarks on Certain Passages in the Thirty-Nine Articles," examined issues that traditionally had distanced the Church of England from Rome, including ecclesiastical authority, justification by faith, good works, purgatory, indulgences, the veneration of images, the sacraments, transubstantiation, and the Mass. Newman's goal was to show that the Articles and associated homilies rightly took issue with the errors and exaggerations of later Roman Catholicism—particularly the Council of Trent—but were consistent with the teachings of the Fathers and the early church.

The strategy Newman adopted in the tract can be illustrated by his discussion of the Eucharist. Three Articles of Faith addressed that topic. For example, Article XXVIII stated:

> Transubstantiation (or the change of the substance of Bread and Wine) in the Supper of the Lord, cannot be proved by Holy Writ; but is repugnant to the plain words of Scripture, overthroweth the nature of a Sacrament, and hath given occasion to many superstitions. The Body of Christ is given, taken, and eaten, in the Supper, only after an heavenly and spiritual manner. And the mean whereby the Body of Christ is received and eaten in the Supper, is Faith.

Newman contended that it refuted "superstitions" and abuses relating to the medieval doctrine of transubstantiation, not to the understanding of the real presence that prevailed in apostolic and patristic times. Article XXVIII did not insist that the eucharistic elements remained entirely unchanged:

> We see then, that, by transubstantiation, our Article does not confine itself to any abstract theory, nor aim at any definition of the word substance, nor in rejecting it, rejects a word, nor in denying a "mutatio panis et vini," ["change of the bread and wine"] is denying every kind of change, but opposes itself to a certain plain and unambiguous statement . . . that the material elements are changed into an earthly, fleshly, and organized body.[50]

Newman noted the explanation in the Prayer Book that "the natural body and blood of our Savior Christ are in heaven, and not here, it

---

50. Tract 90, §8.

being against the truth of Christ's natural body to be at one time in more places than one." But, he pointed out, "in the Communion Service itself, Catechism, Articles, and Homilies, it is plainly declared, that the Body of Christ is in a mysterious way, if not locally, yet really present." "Christ's Body and Blood are locally at God's right hand," but, he argued, they could also be present here "because they are spirit." We encounter the "sacramental presence" of the Eucharist through the agency of the Holy Ghost. Accordingly Eucharistic adoration is appropriate: "We kneel before [God's] heavenly throne, and the distance is as nothing; it is as if that throne were the Altar close to us."[51]

Article XXIX scoffed at the belief, attributed to Augustine of Hippo, that even unworthy communicants "carnally and visibly press with their teeth . . . the Sacrament of the Body and Blood of Christ." The suggestion that, unless communicants swallowed the host whole, they would bite into the arms and legs of the baby Jesus entered the pious imagination in the late Middle Ages and survived in Roman Catholicism to the twentieth century. Newman found it "shocking."

Article XXXI rejected "the sacrifices of Masses, in which it was commonly said that the Priest did offer Christ for the quick and the dead, to have remission of pain or guilt." But, Newman argued, it did not necessarily exclude belief that the Mass could be viewed as a sacrifice in some *other* way.

Newman's treatment of the other issues in Tract 90 followed a similar pattern. For example, Article XXV declared that "Confirmation, Penance, Orders, Matrimony, and Extreme Unction, are not to be counted for Sacraments of the Gospel" and, though "allowed in the Scripture," should be distinguished from baptism and the Eucharist, which were ordained by God. However, Newman insisted: "The Article does not deny the five rites in question to be sacraments, but to be sacraments *in the sense* in which Baptism and the Lord's Supper are sacraments" (emphasis in original). Article XXII's condemnation of "the Romish Doctrine concerning purgatory," did not necessarily exclude belief in *some* form of purification after death. And so on, and so forth. In every case, the issues were closely argued; and in every case Newman concluded that the language of the Articles did not automatically conflict with the teachings of primitive Christianity.

51. Ibid., including "extracts from a pamphlet published several years since."

Newman insisted that the Articles of Faith had intentionally been couched in language providing flexibility of interpretation. They accommodated both traditionalist and reformist opinions in the sixteenth century as well as the many shifts in emphasis since that time. Indeed, the Evangelicals and liberals of Newman's own time demanded even greater interpretational latitude than he proposed.[52]

In the highly charged atmosphere of Oxford in 1841, however, any suggestion that pivotal statements in the Thirty-Nine Articles might be compatible with Roman Catholic teachings aroused indignation. Four senior tutors, including Archibald Campbell Tait, future archbishop of Canterbury, denounced Tract 90 as "suggesting and opening a way by which men might violate their solemn engagements to the University." Subscription to the Articles was still a matriculation requirement. The heads of houses sided with the tutors, stating in their ruling: "That modes of interpretation, such as are suggested in the said Tract, evading rather than explaining the sense of the Thirty-Nine Articles . . . defeat the object and are inconsistent with the due observance of [university] statutes."[53] Newman was convicted of undermining a university regulation; but in the eyes of the world he was a heretic.

Newman offered his apologies and regrets, and expressed a willingness to reexamine the assertions made in Tract 90. He also wrote a conciliatory letter to the previously sympathetic Richard Bagot, bishop of Oxford, stressing his commitment to the church and deference to episcopal authority. Several prominent individuals stepped forward to defend him. But the heads of houses were unyielding. The tract was condemned by bishops throughout England, and Bagot ordered that no more tracts be published. Keble, who was writing Tract 91 on mysticism in the early church, was allowed to publish it as Part II of Tract 89.

OUTCOME OF THE TRACTARIAN MOVEMENT

The Leaders

Unable to appease the university authorities and bishops, Newman retired to the village of Littlemore, near Oxford, and lived there in se-

---

52. For example, Evangelicals rejected the Athanasian Creed mentioned in Article VIII.

53. Church, *The Oxford Movement*, 253.

clusion with a small band of followers.[54] He was seriously contemplating conversion to Roman Catholicism and resigned his benefice at St. Mary's, Oxford, in 1843. But his inner struggle continued for two more years. One factor in his hesitation was dislike for the Irish activist Daniel O'Connell.[55]

Newman was influenced in his soul searching by William George Ward, professor of mathematics and fellow of Balliol College. Ward not only supported Tracts 71 and 90 but felt they did not go far enough. In *Ideal of a Christian Church* (1844) he declared that the only hope for the Church of England lay in communion with Rome. The suggestion outraged university authorities, and Ward was stripped of his degrees. He converted to Roman Catholicism in September 1845. Newman followed him one month later, after requesting that his name be stricken from the records of Oriel College and Oxford University. In 1846 Newman was ordained in the Church of Rome. He would not meet Keble and Pusey again for nearly twenty years.

Robert Wilberforce became archdeacon of the West Riding of Yorkshire and wrote his influential *Doctrine of the Incarnation in Relation to Mankind and the Church* (1848) and *Doctrine of the Holy Eucharist* (1853). Soon after the latter was published, he followed his friend Henry Manning to Roman Catholicism. Wilberforce died in 1857 while preparing for ordination. Ward, Newman, and Wilberforce were just three of more than a dozen prominent individuals who defected to Rome within a quarter-century, confirming many people's suspicions about the Tractarian Movement. In 1850 the prime minister, Lord John Russell, said that he regretted to see "Tractarians leave the church, but if it can only remain Protestant at the cost of their secession I shall be ready for one to pay the price."[56]

Yet Keble, Pusey, Williams, Mozley, and many others remained loyal to the Church of England. When Keble left Oxford upon the expiration of his professorship in 1841, he retired to All Saints' Church, Hursley, Hampshire. He published another book of poetry, *Lyra Innocentium*, and five of his compositions were included in the *English Hymnal*.

---

54. Newman built a small church at Littlemore, about three miles from Oxford, He also bought ten acres of land on which he planned to construct a monastery. A few old farm buildings currently stood there.

55. Newman, *Apologia*, 230. See also Nockles, *The Oxford Movement*, 78.

56. Scherer, *Lord John Russell*, 191.

In May 1843, Pusey preached a sermon at Christ Church, Oxford: "The Holy Eucharist, a Comfort to the Penitent." It did little more than summarize orthodox high-church teachings, but he was charged with heresy and suspended from preaching for two years.[57] Vice-Chancellor Philip Wynter ignored a memorial signed by high-court judge John Coleridge, William Gladstone, and others expressing dismay over the sentence. The outcome was that Pusey attained martyr status and sold 18,000 copies of the published sermon.

Pusey turned his attention to ascetic spiritual practices and restoring Anglican religious orders. But he was still regarded as leader of the Tractarian Movement. Indeed he would be credited with—or blamed for—much of the Catholic Revival. For decades he was the most talked-about man in the Church of England. Pusey's lifelong friend William Ewart Gladstone (1809–98) went on to serve four terms as prime minister.

Various publications promoted the tractarian cause. The *British Critic* ceased operation in 1843 but was replaced by the *Christian Remembrancer*, reconfigured as a tractarian quarterly by James Mozley.[58] Richard Church and others founded *The Guardian* newspaper.[59]

Looking back on the Tractarian Movement, Newman observed that from small beginnings it "suddenly became a power in the National Church, and an object of alarm to her rulers and friends."[60] Anti-tractarian sentiment continued both at Oxford and elsewhere in Britain. But the university establishment's victory over the Tractarians was short-lived. Subscription to the Thirty-Nine Articles was eliminated as a matriculation requirement in 1854, and Oxford became the university of choice for many Roman Catholics, Nonconformists, and Jews. In 1878 it admitted women.

The tractarian leaders eventually won due recognition. After Keble died in March 1866, a new Oxford college was planned in his honor. The foundation stone was laid in 1868 by Charles Longley, archbishop of

---

57. Church, *The Oxford Movement*, 284–91. Neither the accuser's identity nor the specific charges were disclosed, but Pusey learned that the accuser was Godfrey Faussett, a professor of divinity. In addition to bringing the charges, Faussett served on the investigating tribunal.

58. The *Remembrancer*, which began in 1819, was originally sponsored by the Hackney Phalanx.

59. Church's *Guardian* had no connection to the modern newspaper of that name.

60. Newman, *Apologia*, 156.

Canterbury,[61] and Keble College opened two years later. Keble was quiet and cautious by nature but willing to take decisive action when needed. His life also exemplified the finest Anglican tradition of scholarship, poetry, hymnody, and preaching.

Pusey died in September 1882 and was buried in Christ Church Cathedral, where he had served as canon for fifty-four years. In his memory, friends acquired a building in Oxford to house his library and named it the Pusey House. Newman revisited Oxford in 1878, after thirty-two years, to accept an honorary fellowship of Oriel College. The following year Pope Leo XIII named him a cardinal. He died in 1890 and was buried in Birmingham, next to the remains of his long-time companion Ambrose St John. In 2010 Benedict XVI beatified him, the first step to possible sainthood.

The Broader Impact

The Tractarian Movement spread beyond Oxford and beyond England. Many students were drawn to the cause by personal contacts with Keble, Newman, or Pusey. When they graduated and accepted parish or other appointments they took tractarian ideals with them. A generation of Anglican clergy grew up with a new vision of their faith. Frederick Oakeley, fellow of Balliol College, was appointed to St Margaret's Chapel, London, in 1839. "It was the first church in London," a commentator wrote, "where a real attempt was made to preach the almost forgotten truth of the whole of the Church's faith."[62] Oakeley is remembered for translating the carol *Adeste Fideles* into English. But he later converted to Roman Catholicism.

Two Tractarians rose to the episcopate. Alexander Penrose Forbes (1817–75) developed a strong friendship with Pusey at Oxford and studied the teachings of the Nonjurors. With Gladstone's help he was appointed bishop of Brechin, Scotland, in 1847. Ten years later Forbes instructed his parish clergy in the objective real presence in the Eucharist, sacrificial intent, and the propriety of eucharistic adoration.[63] In his brother's words, he did his utmost "to bring the whole body of

---

61. Longley died six months later and was succeeded by Archibald Tait.

62. Ollard, *A Short History*, 62. In 1859 the chapel was replaced by All Saints Church, Margaret Street, still a famous center of Anglo-Catholic worship.

63. Goldie, *A Short History*, 109–10.

Catholic truth before his people."[64] That went beyond what even high-church Scottish Episcopalians could accept. He was charged with heresy and brought to trial in 1860. The ecclesiastical court censured him, but Forbes retained his bishopric until his death.

Forbes is often acclaimed as the first Tractarian bishop.[65] But that honor rightly goes to another Oxford graduate, John Medley, appointed bishop of New Brunswick in 1845. Earning the appellation "Tractarian Patriarch," Medley did much to promote high-church Anglicanism in his diocese. But often he was forced to compromise to avoid conflict with the low-church King's College, Fredericton.[66]

Tractarianism received mixed reactions in British North America. When reprints of the tracts and related articles were published in the high-church periodical *The Church*, in the late 1830s and early 1840s, complaints by Evangelicals were so strong that the editor was forced to resign.[67] By then BNA's early high-church orientation was being eroded by immigration. Irish immigrants saw in tractarian ideas a resemblance to Roman Catholicism, which "stood for persecution, superstition, priestly autocracy, idolatrous sacramental practices, and deviant views on the Blessed Virgin Mary."[68] Nevertheless, high-church bishops like Francis Fulford and George Hills continued to support Tractarianism and the larger Catholic Revival.

The Episcopal Church shared none of the political concerns that provoked the Tractarian Movement. Yet the tracts' theological content provoked considerable controversy. The 1844 General Convention was the scene of polarizing debate. Nine state delegations to the House of Bishops, including New Hampshire and Virginia, supported an evangelical motion condemning tractarian theology. But twelve, including New York, North Carolina, and Tennessee, defeated the motion.[69] Delegates then sidestepped the issue by noting that the tracts were written by individuals and the General Convention was not the appropriate body to rule on individual orthodoxy or heresy.

64. Forbes, *A Memoir*, 18–19. George Forbes, the bishop's brother, died one month after Alexander.

65. Strong, R., *Alexander Forbes*, 47.

66. Craig, *Apostle*, 143.

67. Hayes, *Anglicans*, 119.

68. Ibid., 117.

69. Prichard, *A History*, 142–43.

At the same meeting Evangelicals also called for an investigation of the General Theological Seminary in New York City, where interest in Tractarianism had been particularly strong. A group of low church-men submitted forty-three "inquisitorial questions" to the dean and faculty. One question was: "Are the works of the Rev. Dr. Pusey, Messrs. Newman, Keble, Palmer, Ward, and Massingberd, or any of them, used as text books, or publicly or privately recommended in the Seminary?" Another was: "Are the doctrinal and other errors of the Roman Church . . . duly exposed in the instruction of the Seminary?"[70] The investigation was disruptive but produced no evidence of heresy.

The 1844 ruling left judgments concerning Tractarianism to indi-vidual bishops. Some tractarian supporters were suspended, but most secured appointments in other dioceses. Powerful high-church bishops, like Hobart and George W. Doane, prevented any large-scale persecu-tion. Moreover, the United States had no dominant institution, like Oxford, to serve as a focus of opposition.

Educator and philanthropist William Augustus Muhlenberg (1796–1877) was inspired by the tracts. In the 1820s he had served as rector of St George's, Flushing, Long Island, and headmaster of the Flushing Institute, claimed to be the first Episcopal school in the United States. Muhlenberg became rector of the Church of the Holy Communion, New York City in 1846, and five years later founded *The Evangelical Catholic*, a widely read journal. What became known as "Evangelical Catholicism" was his attempt to put Tractarianism to practical use.

Muhlenberg envisioned an arrangement in which the Episcopal Church would provide the apostolic succession to a larger Christian entity. In 1853 he petitioned the House of Bishops to create "a system broader and more comprehensive than that which you now administer, surrounding and including the Protestant Episcopal Church as it now is, leaving that Church untouched, identical with that Church in all its great principles, yet providing for as much freedom in opinion, disci-pline and worship as is compatible with the essential faith and order of the Gospel."[71] Muhlenberg's initiative, which attempted to combine high- and low-church principles, came to nothing.

---

70. Grafton, *The Lineage*, vol. 2, 211. Also DeMille, *The Catholic Movement*, 61–3. The inclusion of Massingberd's name was surprising since he was an orthodox high churchman.

71. Muhlenberg et al., Memorial.

By the latter part of the nineteenth century Tractarianism was indistinguishable, in the minds of most Americans, from the Catholic Revival as a whole. James DeKoven (1831–79), warden of Racine College, Wisconsin, emerged as a strong supporter of ritualism and a powerful exponent of high-church eucharistic doctrine. In a letter to clergy at the 1875 Illinois Convention, he affirmed the real presence: "We refuse to explain away the mystery by saying that the holy elements are *mere figures* or *images* or *symbols* of Christ's absent body and blood . . . . Thus, whenever and wherever I have asserted that Christ is present 'in the elements,' 'under the form or species of bread and wine,' I mean thereby that He is there present sacramentally and spiritually, and thus really and truly."[72] DeKoven also emphasized the sacrificial intent of the Eucharist. "There is," he wrote, "an earthly altar, and a human priest-hood, and bread and wine; but Christ is really present as priest, and offering, and the food of the faithful who feed upon the sacrifice."[73]

Another exponent of high-church eucharistic doctrine was Morgan Dix of Trinity Church, New York City. Writing in 1884 he commented that the Catholic Revival "brought to light the truth of the Real Presence of Christ in the Sacrament of the Altar. The adversary denied, advancing either the Zwinglian notion of a memorial feast or the Calvinistic notion of a virtual presence, with symbols to help the faith; anything . . . except that our Lord spake literal truth when He said: 'This is My Body, this is My Blood.'"[74]

Ferdinand Cartwright Ewer (1826–83), rector of a parish in San Francisco and later of Christ Church, New York City, stressed the catholicity of the Anglican tradition. The principle of the English Reformation, he declared in *What is the Anglican Church?* (1883), was to recapture the purity of early Christianity in the face of the errors of both Rome and the continental Reformers. The restoration of catholicity "is the bounden duty of every true son of the Anglican Reformation."[75] Elsewhere, Ewer affirmed that the church was "the perpetual Incarnation of God on Earth, wrought by the marvelous miracles of Font and Altar." He also called for a revival of "the five lesser as well as the two greater" sacraments.[76]

72. DeKoven, *Letter to the Clergy*, §I. Emphasis in original.

73. Ibid.

74. Dix, M., *The Oxford Movement*, 12.

75. Ewer, *What Is the Anglican*, preface to 2nd ed.

76. Ewer, *Catholicity*, 102–3, 278.

Shortly after Ewer's work appeared, Frederick Swartz Jewell, chancellor of All Saints' Cathedral, Wisconsin, discussed the efficacy of the sacraments. Baptism, he affirmed, secures "forgiveness of all past sin, both original and actual; regeneration, or the implanting of the germ of a new nature in the soul; and the incorporation of the baptized into the organic Body of Christ."[77] The Eucharist provides "absolution from post-baptismal sin; the cleansing of both body and spirit . . . and the nourishing of the divine life within by the communicating Body and Blood of Christ."[78] The Eucharist, Jewell added, offers "direct access to the blessed Communion of Saints; and the efficient union of the believer's prayers with the intercession of our Lord before the Throne."[79]

Jewell sought to reconcile notions of catholicity with the existence of national churches: "[W]e claim that there may rightfully exist . . . diverse national branches of the One Catholic Church; with substantially the same divinely instituted Faith, Order, and Worship; but with each its own national uses, and its own distinct local autonomy under its own patriarchal or conciliar rule, always subject, however, to the decisions of the one undivided Church, and to the Royal Law of Charity, intercommunion and co-operation."[80] His remarks remain applicable to the Anglican Communion in the early twenty-first century.

Further Discussions

The *Tracts for the Times* touched on issues that had long been controversial and continued to elicit discussion. One such issue was where souls go after death and whether it is appropriate to pray for them. The 1552 Prayer Book eliminated prayers for the dead on the grounds that the soul's fate was already sealed. Article XXII rejected the Roman doctrine of purgatory as being "repugnant to the Word of God." However, John Wesley affirmed the existence of an "intermediate state between death and the resurrection."[81] He and others raised the possibility of a state in which a soul, not condemned to hell, could acquire the sanctity needed to merit heaven.

77. Quoted in Armentrout & Slocum, *Documents*, 84.
78. Ibid., 84–85.
79. Ibid., 85.
80. Ibid., 83.
81. Wesley, "Letter to Miss B," 322.

In addition to discussing purgatory in Tract 90, Newman preached a sermon on the intermediate state in 1836. The sermon was based on the passage in Revelation commenting that martyrs "should rest yet for a little season, until their fellow servants also and their brethren, that should be killed as they were, should be fulfilled" (Rev 6:11). Another relevant passage was: "Blessed are the dead which die in the Lord . . . that they may rest from their labours; and their works do follow them" (14:13). Newman portrayed the intermediate state as a place where imperfect souls "may have time for growing . . . and perfecting the inward development of the good seed sown in their hearts . . . a time of maturing that fruit of grace."[82]

Interest in the intermediate state increased in the latter part of the nineteenth century. Lloyd Russell, vicar of the Church of the Annunciation, Chislehurst, England, preached on the intermediate state in 1885. The departed, he declared, "are in possession of consciousness, memory, and sensibility to pain and pleasure" and must experience "progressive purification of the soul." Otherwise, he insisted, "we must conclude either that that absolute holiness is not a necessity for admission to Heaven, which is contrary to Scripture, or else that each person when he dies is at once fitted either for the Presence of God or the abode of the lost."[83]

James Strong (1822–94), the Methodist biblical scholar better known for his *Concordance*, produced the most detailed work on the subject. In *The Doctrine of a Future Life* (1891) he cited numerous scriptural passages in support of continued consciousness after death. The intermediate state, he said, could be understood as a condition of "enjoyment as in a pleasant dream of interior consciousness."[84] The stories of the widow's son, Jairus's daughter, and Lazarus showed that persons could temporarily return from the intermediate state, though they might remember nothing of their experience. As to the length of time spent there, Strong speculated that it could be "immense," but the soul would experience it "in the twinkling of an eye."[85] Anglican, and in Strong's case Methodist, teachings on the intermediate state offered a welcome alternative to protestant doctrine of a stark heaven–hell dichotomy and to Roman Catholic doctrine of a punitive purgatory.

82. Newman, "The Intermediate State," 720–21.
83. Russell, "The Intermediate State," 8.
84. Strong, J., *The Doctrine*, 57.
85. Ibid., 65.

Other issues provoking intense debate in the nineteenth century concerned the relationship between traditional beliefs and the findings of academic scholarship. A major source of conflict was higher scriptural criticism, which began early in the century in Germany. Higher criticism sought to identify the sources, authorship, date, place, and circumstances of a Biblical text's composition and to examine the historicity of the events described.

Higher critics asserted that the gospels were written decades after Jesus's death, not by eyewitnesses to his ministry. They suggested that Jesus may not have been born in Bethlehem. They also noted that Matthew's story of the flight to Egypt seemed to contradict Luke's account of the presentation in the temple and that Mark and John did not agree on the timing of the Last Supper, relative to the Jewish Passover. Higher critics did not question the relevance of scripture. Rather they urged that it be seen in a new light—as a collection of sacred stories of Christianity's origins rather than as biographically or scientifically accurate history. Belief in divine revelation, they argued, would be strengthened, not diminished, by the new perspective.

Broad churchmen tended to embrace higher criticism, but, except perhaps for Froude, Tractarians were scriptural literalists.[86] Pusey's defense of the Church Fathers in Tract 89 against charges of allegorical interpretation exemplified prevailing attitudes. Tractarian hostility toward higher criticism and other controversial areas of academic scholarship lasted until the last decades of the nineteenth century.

A major milestone in eventual change was the publication of *Lux Mundi* (1889),[87] a set of essays edited by Charles Gore (1853–1932), principal of Pusey House and future bishop of Oxford.[88] *Lux Mundi's* thesis was that advances in knowledge, democratic movements, biological evolution, and other aspects of progress were not antithetical to Christianity but provided evidence of Christ's continuing incarnation and redemptive work in the world. Canon Henry Liddon, Puseys' biographer, attacked *Lux Mundi* from the pulpit of St Paul's Cathedral. But the book was strongly supported by many others, including Bishop Hollingsworth Kingdon of New Brunswick.[89]

86. DeMille, *The Catholic Movement*, 171.
87. Gore, *Lux Mundi*.
88. Gore served successively as bishop of Worcester, Birmingham, and Oxford.
89. Hayes, *Anglicans*, 149.

By the early twentieth century most Anglo-Catholics were as comfortable with scriptural criticism, evolution, and other areas of academic scholarship as were their broad-church brethren. No longer on the defensive, Anglo-Catholics could use modernity as a springboard for proclaiming their faith. Lecturing in 1927 Gore reaffirmed the message of *Lux Mundi*: "We must lend our ears, then, not only to the wisdom of the gospels but to the wisdom of the ages and of the present age. We must learn to preach 'the everlasting Gospel' so that the men of our time may catch in it the reflection of their own best thoughts and aspirations. We must interpret the old creed into modern speech."[90]

ANGLICAN RELIGIOUS ORDERS

Attempts to establish Anglican religious communities in the seventeenth century had little lasting impact. The Tractarian Movement gave the concept new force, and the 1840s witnessed growing interest in religious orders on both sides of the Atlantic. By the end of the nineteenth century scores of Anglican religious orders and communities had been created. The revival of religious orders recovered one more feature of pre-Reformation English Christianity.

The circumstances of their creation, the themes and vows adopted, and the names they took provide interesting insight into evolving Anglican consciousness. Similarity of names makes taxonomy difficult, and many orders and communities were small or short-lived. But a few survived and grew, adding to the richness of Anglican spirituality and offering opportunities—aside from the priesthood—for individuals who aspired to express their faith at a higher level than the lay ministry might permit.

Women's Orders

Pusey strongly supported the revival of religious orders and was involved in the formation of several. He received vows of poverty, chastity, and obedience from Marion Rebecca Hughes in 1841—the year when Tract 90 appeared. Hughes was the first professed nun in the Church of England since the reign of Mary I. Eight years later she became superior of the Convent of the Holy Trinity at Oxford.[91]

90. Gore, "Christ and Society."
91. Chandler, *An Introduction*, 96.

Priscilla Lydia Sellon (1821–1900) responded to an appeal in 1848 by Bishop Phillpotts for women to teach poor children in Plymouth, England. In her father's words, she heard "a genuine call from God." The following year Sellon founded the Sisters of Mercy of the Most Holy Trinity. The sisters wore plain black dresses and wooden crosses. They organized orphanages and a "College for Sailor Boys." Evangelicals campaigned to suppress the sisterhood, making the familiar accusations of romanism and even persuading three former nuns to testify against the order. Phillpotts supported Sellon, however, and William Wordsworth wrote a sonnet in her honor.[92]

Another Englishwoman, Anne Ayres (1816–96), emigrated to the United States when she was twenty years old to find work as a teacher. She came into contact with William Muhlenberg and, impressed by his preaching, resolved to devote her life to God. Muhlenberg received her pledge to the religious life at a private ceremony in 1845. Muhlenberg himself had taken a vow of celibacy a quarter-century earlier.[93] In 1850 they jointly established the Sisterhood of the Church of the Holy Communion, the first religious order in the Episcopal Church.[94] In place of lifetime vows, Ayres's sisters pledged themselves to remain unmarried and to serve renewable three-year terms.[95] The sisters provided nursing care at St Luke's Hospital, which Muhlenberg founded in 1858. They also worked at the Church Industrial Community of St Johnland, a home on Long Island Sound for special-needs children and the aged. Muhlenberg is buried in the St Johnland cemetery.

In 1852 Canon Thomas Thellusson Carter and Harriet Monsell, widow of a clergyman, founded the Community of St John the Baptist at Clewer, near Windsor, England. Its charge was to care for "penitent women," and Monsell became mother superior. Carter "believed in the power of ladies, whose lives were dedicated to Christ, to deal with this terrible social evil." Their first clients were six women "of the lowest and coarsest kind."[96] The community soon established women's shelters, hostels, and orphanages. Within fifty years it had branches in England, North America, India, and elsewhere.

92. Jackman, *Deviating Voices*, 97–102.

93. DeMille, *The Catholic Movement*, 133.

94. Douglas, "Anne Ayres."

95. Hein & Shattuck, *The Episcopalians*, 163.

96. "Canon Carter," 419.

John Mason Neale (1818–66), whose work in the architectural revival and in hymn-writing will be discussed in the next chapter, founded a nursing sisterhood, the Society of St Margaret, in 1854; an American branch was formed nineteen years later. One of its principles was "our worship, prayer and service are offered as acts of joyful celebration." Neale commented on the importance of joy in the religious life: "There is nothing I should dread more than that unreal, melancholy way of going on which one sometimes sees among those who are in earnest in serving God: as if it were impossible to be holy without ceasing to be natural." "On the contrary," he continued, "remember that cheerfulness, that the capacity of being amused and amusing, nay more, that high spirits are a gift from God."[97]

In 1870 Bishop Forbes of Brechin, Scotland, founded the Sisterhood of St Mary and St Modwenna. The nuns founded a nursing home and an orphanage and worked in five poor parishes in Dundee.[98] Anglicans, who had once eliminated saints' days from the liturgical calendar, showed a surprising affinity for saints in the dedication of religious orders.

A Canadian woman, Hannah Coome Grier (1827–1921), took vows at the Sisterhood of St Mary in Peekskill, New York. Upon her return to Canada in 1884, she founded the Sisterhood of St John the Divine, the first permanent Anglican religious order for women in the dominion. The sisterhood, whose house was dedicated by the bishop of Toronto, adopted a modified form of the Rule of St Benedict.[99] In 1886 the General Synod formally authorized the creation of both deaconesses and sisterhoods. The measure was a compromise between the low church, which supported deaconesses, and the high church that sought recognition of sisterhoods.[100]

Opposition to the revival of Anglican religious orders was directed primarily at women's orders, and much of it was channeled through innuendo. Attitudes to religious orders in BNA/Canada and elsewhere were colored by Maria Monk's *The Hidden Secrets of a Nun's Life in a Convent Exposed* (1836), even though repeated investigations failed to find any evidence of wrongdoing at the Roman Catholic convent in Montreal, and even though Monk exhibited symptoms of mental illness.

97. Source: Sisters of St Margaret, United States.

98. Bertie, *Scottish Episcopal Clergy*, 666.

99. Hayes, *Anglicans*, 173.

100. See the discussion in Hayes, *Anglicans*, 174.

Walter Walsh's *Secret History of the Oxford Movement* (1899) offered salacious descriptions of life in tractarian-affiliated religious communities in England. Penances allegedly included use of "the Discipline
. . . secretly used by the fanatics at Elton [community]." The Discipline,
Walsh explained, "is a kind of cat-o'-nine tails, knotted, and made with
either cord or steel."[101] The practice "is of so secret a character that it
seems almost impossible to discover the priestly culprits who order
English ladies to be thus whipped on their bare backs."[102]

Men's Orders

The creation of religious orders for men might have been considered
less urgent, since men had access to the priesthood. But Froude had
considered the merit of establishing "colleges" of unmarried priests to
serve large populations.[103] And Newman's Littlemore community provided an early example of Anglican monastic seclusion and asceticism.
Nashotah House, Wisconsin, was founded in 1842 as a mission, monastic community, and seminary.

Also in 1842, Levi Silliman Ives (1797–1867), Hobart's son-in-law
and second bishop of North Carolina, founded a residential community
at Valle Crucis, in the western mountains of his diocese. It took the name
Society of the Holy Cross. Members wore black habits and observed the
traditional Daily Offices while performing missionary work and training
for the priesthood.[104] In 1847 William Skiles, a local farmer, took vows
of poverty, chastity, and obedience, becoming the first Anglican man to
do so since the Reformation. The diocese withdrew its support and the
community collapsed when Ives revealed that he had defected to Rome.
Ives was the first bishop in the Episcopal Church to be deposed by the
General Convention. Skiles remained in Valle Crucis as an ordained
deacon and eventually founded the chapel of St John the Baptist to serve
the mountain people. He is buried in the churchyard, and December

---

101. Walsh, *Secret History*, 35. The book was published by the Church Association,
notorious opponent of the Ritualist Movement.

102. Ibid., 40–41.

103. Oxford colleges still required men to resign their fellowships if they married.

104. Wright, L., "Anglo-Catholicism." See also Haywood, *Lives of the Bishops*, 110–
26. Valle Crucis and the Society of the Holy Cross were named for a configuration of
creeks in the valley that form a cross.

8, the date of his death, honors his memory in the Episcopal Church calendar.

Another Society of the Holy Cross was formed in London in 1855. Among its founders was Anglo-Catholic priest Charles Fuge Lowder. The order's stated mission was "To defend and strengthen the spiritual life of the clergy, to defend the faith of the Church, and to carry on and aid Mission work both at home and abroad." Restricted to ordained clergy, it placed strong emphasis on discipline and in that regard resembled the Jesuits. Several foreign bishops were members, but suspicion of the order's activities was one factor leading to passage of the Public Worship Regulation Act of 1874.

Also in the 1850s, Bishop Edward Feild of Newfoundland turned the struggling Queen's College, St John's, into a semi-monastic theological college, at which working-class men from Britain trained as missionaries or for the priesthood. It embraced strict high-church principles: for instance, any student who denied baptismal regeneration was suspended. The British evangelical magazine *The Record* branded Feild as "an ultra-Tractarian of the Exeter school."[105]

The Society of St John the Evangelist was founded in 1865, with Pusey's support and encouragement, by clergyman Richard Meux Benson. Members affirmed: "I promise and vow to Almighty God, the Father, the Son and the Holy Ghost, before the whole company of heaven and before you, my fathers, that I will live in celibacy, poverty and obedience as one of the mission priests of St John the Evangelist unto my life's end. So help me God."[106] The group met in a house on Cowley Road, Oxford, thereby acquiring the popular name "Cowley Fathers." Among the three charter members was Charles Chapman Grafton (1832–1912), future bishop of Fond du Lac, Wisconsin.

After returning to the United States in 1872 Grafton became rector of the Church of the Advent, Boston. Conflict between loyalty to his bishop and obedience to his superior in England led him to petition for release from his vows. He wanted to avoid the perception, common in the Middle Ages, that religious orders undermined episcopal and national authority. The Society of St John the Evangelist continued without him, and any problem of national authority was resolved in 1914

105. As we shall see in the next chapter, riots broke out in the diocese of Exeter in response to ritualist practices.

106. Ramsey, "Charles C. Grafton."

when the American province was granted autonomy.[107] The problem of episcopal authority never became serious, because the order remained small. Roland Ford Palmer, who taught at Nashotah and also served as rector of the Church of the Advent, San Francisco, founded a Canadian province in 1927 and became its first superior.[108]

Dedication to the cross inspired several religious orders. Unrelated to either Ives's or Lowder's orders, the Order of the Holy Cross was formed in the United States in 1884. Its founder, James Otis Huntington (1854–1935), made his profession to Bishop Henry Potter of New York. Potter's involvement signaled episcopal support for religious orders in America, but it did not go unchallenged; Presiding Bishop Albert Lee of Delaware expressed "astonishment and distress," complaining that taking vows was "romish."[109] Fortunately other bishops supported the new religious order, and Huntington worked at a mission in New York's East Side. The order, committed to a strong social ministry, established a community at West Park, New York, and eventually opened three other houses in the United States and a priory in Toronto. One of its members, Robert Erskine Campbell, was consecrated a missionary bishop in 1925, becoming the first active member of a religious order to hold an Anglican bishopric since the Reformation.[110] Campbell served for ten years in Liberia.

Charles Gore and five other men founded the Community of the Resurrection in 1892. Gore served as its first superior until his appointment to the bishopric of Worcester in 1902. Modeled on the Roman Catholic Dominican Order, the Community of the Resurrection originally had houses in Britain and South Africa. Currently, its only functioning house is the College of the Resurrection at Mirfield, Yorkshire. The college, an Anglo-Catholic seminary established in 1903, now educates both men and women for the priesthood.

The Society of the Sacred Mission was founded in England in 1893. Known as the "Kelham Fathers," the order adopted the motto *Ad gloriam Dei in eius voluntate* ("To the glory of God in his will"). It recruited men of ordinary ability rather than an intellectual or saintly elite. Originally conceived as a missionary society, the order at various times ran a theo-

107. DeMille, *The Catholic Movement*, 135–42.

108. Palmer is also known as a hymn writer. One of his compositions was "Sing of Mary, Pure and Lowly" (1938).

109. DeMille, *The Catholic Movement*, 141–44

110. Ibid., 145.

logical seminary in South Africa, offered retreats, and provided welfare services to the poor.

The Anglican Order of St Benedict was established in 1906. The most famous member of its Nashdom Abbey, Buckinghamshire, was the liturgical scholar Gregory Dix whose *The Shape of the Liturgy* (1945) still influences Prayer Book revisions. In the 1930s a group of Americans studied at Nashdom before returning to the United States to found the St Gregory's Abbey at Three Rivers, Michigan. The Benedictine tradition emphasizes a life of prayer and labor, *ora et labora*. Nashdom Abbey is no longer active, but other Anglican Benedictine monasteries are located in Britain, the United States, and elsewhere.

Other Associations

In addition to formal religious orders, a variety of associations, confraternities and guilds sprang up to bring together laypeople and clergy committed to devotion or service. The Confraternity of the Blessed Sacrament was founded in 1862 by Canon Carter, who also founded the Community of St John the Baptist.[111] Similar associations were the Guild of All Souls,[112] the Confraternity of Our Lady, and the Union of the Holy Rosary. The two latter were significant, because no Anglican religious order was dedicated to Mary.

An interesting ladies' guild formed in the nineteenth century was the Society of St Alphege whose members embroidered eucharistic vestments, altar cloths, and other materials for distribution to ritualist parishes.[113] The Order of St Luke the Physician, originally an Anglican order dedicated to the healing ministry, now accepts members from across the religious spectrum.

REFLECTIONS

Oxford was a study in paradox. Bastion of Church of England orthodoxy, it embodied little of that orthodoxy in its own affairs. The Prayer Book required worship to be conducted in English, but the Latin Communion

---

111. Alexander Mackonochie was a priest-associate of the confraternity.

112. The Guild of All Souls, formerly the Guild Burial Society, was founded in 1873. Arthur Tooth, a member of the Society of the Holy Cross, served as its first president.

113. Reed, *Glorious Battle*, 89, 190.

Service was permitted at Oxford as early as 1560.[114] Cranmer and others of his time scorned the "superstition" of elaborate ceremony, but Oxford colleges preserved ceremonies that competed with the best of medieval pageantry. The monasteries were dissolved and clergy allowed to marry, but the fellows of Oxford colleges were celibate Anglican clerics living in a cloistered world.

Despite its contradictions, Oxford provided the environment in which a few men of exceptional ability examined the identity, beliefs, and sacramental practices of the Anglican tradition and sought to put them on a firmer basis. What transpired there in the 1830s and early '40s had profound impact on Anglican thought. The Tractarian Movement reinforced orthodox high-church teachings but also offered important new insights. It influenced generations of theologians, bishops, and parish clergy who added their own insights.

The Tractarians embraced traditional high-church belief in the church as a visible, corporate entity, divinely ordained to bring Christ's message to the world and administer the sacraments that he instituted. They asserted that the Church of England was a rightful successor of the undivided, catholic church of late antiquity. The church had stripped away the perversions of the later Middle Ages and more closely approximated the purity of primitive Christianity, but it had also lost some of its pre-Reformation richness. The Tractarians sought to restore vital theological, sacramental, and ecclesiological principles that were rightly hers.

The Catholic Revival inevitably narrowed the differences between Anglicanism and Roman Catholicism. The convergence in doctrine distinguished Tractarians from orthodox high-church Anglicans. Critics accused Tractarians of trying to undermine the Reformation and open the door to Roman encroachment. Some individuals defected to Rome. Newman, in the words of Bishop Grafton, "invented a *via media* of his own."[115] It was an unstable one, and eventually he and others saw conversion to Rome as the only viable path. Most Tractarians remained loyal to the more traditional via media. Moreover, defection has not been a one-way street; numerous Roman Catholic clergy and laity have seen in Anglo-Catholicism a superior form of sacramental Christianity.

Considering the short period of their efforts—less than ten years—the Oxford Tractarians' achievements were astounding. Their judgment

114. Wright, J., "Early Translations," 56–57.
115. Grafton, *A Journey*, 27.

that the church faced imminent danger lent a sense of urgency to their endeavors. Yet the speed with which they moved and their indifference to warnings frightened the university establishment, orthodox high-church clergy, and the English episcopate. Had the Tractarians proceeded more slowly they might have carried conservatives with them, even in the face of growing evangelical and liberal influence in the church and the very real fear of institutional Roman Catholicism. High-church Anglicanism became divided into "orthodox" and "Anglo-Catholic." Opposition from orthodox high-church bishops was worrisome to the Tractarians since they placed so much emphasis on the episcopate's divine authority.

Whether or not the Tractarians attracted unnecessary hostility, they made enormous personal sacrifices for a cause in which they passionately believed. Without their enthusiasm, determination, and self-sacrifice, Anglo-Catholicism might never have emerged. Even greater sacrifice lay ahead for the ritualists.

The Tractarian Movement moved away from Oxford and away from England. Its tenets of ecclesiology, doctrine, and religious practice were examined, debated, and built upon in the latter half of the nineteenth century. The movement established the intellectual and spiritual framework on which other elements of the Catholic Revival found their place.

Tractarian teachings reached North America when the Episcopal Church and the Anglican Church in Canada were still in their formative stages. Patterns of churchmanship, never identical to Britain's, were also evolving. Tractarianism was embraced by high-church bishops in both countries with fewer reservations than their English counterparts had. The General Theological Seminary in the United States emerged as a center of interest, though it never abandoned the orthodox high-church Anglicanism of Hobart. New seminaries in the Midwest emerged as the strongest supporters of Tractarianism—and Anglo-Catholicism.

The revival of Anglican religious orders was linked to the Tractarian Movement both by the involvement of people, like Pusey, and also by tractarian emphasis on personal and collective holiness. Anglican orders further strengthened spiritual continuity with the medieval English church in which monasticism played such a prominent role.

More than one hundred Anglican orders now exist, worldwide. They continue to be small, posing no threat to the dioceses, provinces, or nations in which they operate—and enabling them to preserve integrity. Nevertheless, members of religious orders have made a disproportionate contribution to Anglican thought and religious practices and have held their own with counterparts from the Roman and Orthodox churches. Like monastic institutions everywhere, Anglican orders suffer from declining membership. Whether they can survive in the twenty-first century remains to be seen, though there is no indication that the path of renunciation has been abandoned.[116]

A few male and female monastic institutions now accept members from different religious traditions. Anglicans, Lutherans, Orthodox, Roman Catholics, and others share communal lives under the Rule of St Benedict. Ecumenical religious orders make a strong statement of catholicity and may prove more successful in reuniting Christianity than negotiated mergers and acquisitions.

116. Nash, J. F., *Christianity*, vol. 2, 337–41.

7

Catholic Revival II:
Sacred Spaces and Ceremony

THIS CHAPTER CONTINUES THE story of the Catholic Revival with a focus on the architectural revival and the Ritualist Movement. The individuals and groups discussed in this chapter believed that aesthetics, drama, and symbolism were essential elements of worship. They also believed that adoration was our appropriate response to an infinite, beneficent Creator.

Efforts to enhance the external aspects of public worship created conflict in both Britain and North America. The conflict stemmed largely from Anglicanism's ongoing struggle to define its boundaries, particularly those with Roman Catholicism and Eastern Orthodoxy. Nevertheless, by the end of the nineteenth century, Anglican worship was graced by colorful ceremony, conducted in beautiful church buildings.

The chapter ends with some comments on the interesting side-effect of ritualism—though one of major importance—the emergence of a strong social conscience and expansion of ministries to the marginalized elements of society.

EXTERNAL FORMS AND INNER REALITIES

Whether the external aspects of worship should be of any concern is a legitimate question. Persuasive arguments can be made that inner spirituality is all that matters—and that a focus on externals is distractive, even idolatrous.

John Henry Hopkins, bishop of Vermont, addressed those issues in *The Law of Ritualism* (1866). He distinguished the inner life of faith from the form through which it was expressed; "The *life* of religion is indeed a spiritual principle, but that is no reason why the Lord should be indifferent to its *form*." Moreover, "the love of form and order [was] implanted by the Deity Himself, in every human bosom."[1] Every Christian made use of form and order in worship, even the puritans in their bare meeting houses. The important question, therefore, was: "which is the *best* system of form and order?"[2]

The best system, Hopkins argued, was the one divinely prescribed for Jewish temple worship. Exodus 28:2–5 described the priestly vestments designed, "for glory and for beauty," for Moses's brother Aaron, the first high priest. Those vestments included "a breastplate, and an ephod [tunic], and a robe, and a broidered coat, a mitre, and a girdle." To make those vestments, the priests "shall take gold, and blue, and purple, and scarlet, and fine linen." Temple furnishings included: "the pure candlestick," "the altar of incense," "the altar of burnt offering," "the cloths of service," and "anointing oil, and sweet incense" (Exod 31:8–11). The rubrics for temple worship formed "a statute for ever unto [Aaron] and his seed after him" (28:43). The Jewish priests, or *kohanim*, were Aaron's descendents.

In the Jewish temple, according to Hopkins (not without some creative imagination),"we see the largest provision for the praise of God accompanied by all the instruments of music, in the Psalms given by inspiration and chanted morning and evening, every day, by trained and skillful choristers, in which the royal David sometimes bore his part."[3] Hopkins's thesis—his training was in ecclesiastical law—was that the divine statute had never been revoked. Altars, candles, incense, vestments, music, and so forth were adopted by the early Christian church, so far as their circumstances allowed, and should still be used. Hopkins might have mentioned Revelation, which referred to lamps (Rev 4:5), incense (8:3–4), elders in white robes (7:13–14), and angelic musicians and choristers (5:8; 14:2; 15:2).

Nothing is more external to religion than houses of worship, but those buildings tell us much about people's faith and the state of the church. Chapters 6–7 of 1 Kings record God's instructions for construction of Solomon's temple, and chapter 8 describes its dedication. The

1. Hopkins, *The Law of Ritualism*, 1–2. Emphasis in original.
2. Ibid., 3. Emphasis in original.
3. Ibid., 7.

best architect, Hiram, was hired, and by all accounts the building he constructed was impressive. The temple was a "sacred space" where worshippers could sense the presence and glory of God. Writers of the rabbinic period referred to the indwelling, divine glory as the *Shekinah*.[4]

Christians were unable to acquire large houses of worship until the fourth century, but from then on vast resources were invested in the construction of churches, abbeys, and cathedrals. The Gothic cathedrals of medieval Europe made dramatic statements of the transcendence of God (and not incidentally the power of the church) as well as providing worthy settings for sacred pageantry. The "glory and beauty" of those buildings represented the very best successive generations of Christians could offer. Eight centuries later Gothic architecture is still revered as a timeless heritage of Christian faith and a model for emulation.

CHURCH ARCHITECTURE AND DECORATION

The Eighteenth Century

Pre-Reformation churches and cathedrals were sturdily built, and many still stood in the eighteenth century. But the Reformers had removed the altars. Mobs of iconoclasts had defaced statues and frescoes, smashed stained-glass, and torn organ pipes from churches during the English Civil War. Bells had been melted down to reclaim the metal. Oliver Cromwell's army had stabled horses in cathedrals.[5] After the Restoration came general neglect or misguided renovation. The "very stones cried out" for what had been lost. To quote Bishop Grafton:

> The whitewashed walls, the damp stone floors, the high, stiff pews . . . allotted to all the principal houses and farms in the parish, the hard benches . . . where the poor might sit, spoke eloquently of the two prevailing vices of the times, apathy and exclusiveness. The grand old fonts were frequently removed to the rectory garden to serve as flower pots . . . . In the place where the High Altar stood, vested in fair array, was to be found a mean table with a moth-eaten cloth upon it.[6]

4. Nash, J. F., "The Shekinah."

5. Among those so desecrated were Canterbury and Gloucester Cathedrals in England; St Mary's Cathedral, Kilkenny, and St Patrick's Cathedral, Dublin, Ireland; and St Magnus Cathedral, Kirkwall, Scotland.

6. Grafton, *The Lineage*, vol. 2, 193.

The seventeenth and eighteenth centuries by no means lacked good architecture. Christopher Wren's new St Paul's Cathedral, is considered a masterpiece, and the other fifty London churches he rebuilt after the Great Fire of London of 1666 won wide acclaim. St Martin's in the Fields, London, dedicated in 1726, was designed by James Gibbs, one of Wren's students. It was used as the model for St Paul's, Halifax, Nova Scotia, which later became the first pro-cathedral in North America. Holy Trinity, Quebec City, the first cathedral built for that purpose in North America, was based on, another Gibbs design. St Michael's, Charleston, South Carolina, dedicated in 1761, was constructed in the Wren style by Samuel Cardy, a master builder from Ireland. The interior of the Georgian Christ Church, Philadelphia, was redesigned in the 1830s by Thomas Walter, architect of the United States Capitol.

Some post-Reformation churches had been designed with chancels, and most of Wren's churches came with altars. By the eighteenth century, however, the altars had been removed or were used to display parishes' collections of silver plate.[7] Chancels were boarded up or used for other purposes.[8]

The typical eighteenth-century church may have been a fine building, but it resembled an auditorium or a courthouse. The Ten Commandments, Lord's Prayer, or Apostles' Creed might be displayed, but no decorative artwork relieved the stark interior. Furnishings were limited to the pulpit, pews, and a font. The pulpit was located in a prominent location, often at the center of a stage at the "east" end of the building.[9] Huge, three-tiered pulpits were common: the bottom tier for the parish clerk, the middle one for scriptural reading, and the top tier for the sermon.

Pews looked like polished or painted cattle stalls. Brass nameplates identified lease-holders, and door locks kept out squatters. The wealthiest families paid for private transepts or private balconies, like the skyboxes in today's sports stadiums. Worshippers of lower social class and casual visitors were relegated to benches at the back of the church. Slaves in the churches of the American South sat on rough-hewn benches in a gallery, where drafts would carry away the odor of caste along with body odor.

7. White, "Prayer Book Architecture," 110.

8. As late as the 1840s, the chancel in Bruton Parish Church in Williamsburg, Virginia, was converted into a Sunday School room, and the pews turned to face the west wall.

9. By then, not all churches were built with an East–West orientation.

Church buildings of the period provided shelter, where people could assemble to hear sermons and pray. But they lacked the aesthetics, symbolism, and sacredness of ancient houses of worship. They were not sacred spaces whose glory and beauty fostered a sense of the presence of God. The loss of sacredness was not unrelated to the decline in high-church influence.[10] Historian William Molesworth, exaggerating perhaps to make a point, declared that eighteenth-century churches were "debased and degraded," reflecting "bad taste and Puritanical prejudices."[11]

Gothic Revival

When change came, early in the nineteenth century, it was fueled not only by increasing high-church sentiment but also by romanticism. Nostalgia arose for all things ancient, noble, and beautiful. The Gothic style was soon identified as the architecture of choice. "Gothic," which a century earlier was still being used in a derogatory sense, came to symbolize everything good about medieval Christianity. From the 1840s onward, virtually every new Anglican church was designed in a neo-Gothic, or Gothic-revival, style. One concession to modern sensitivity: massive screens no longer separated chancel and nave.

Architect Archibald Simpson, already famous for his designs of buildings in "New Edinburgh," designed the neo-Gothic St Andrew's Chapel, Aberdeen, in 1817—later to become St Andrew's Cathedral. John Henry Hopkins built a Gothic-revival church in America a few years later.[12] In 1832 William Bulgin, an English builder and craftsman, began the construction of St Luke's, Hope, New Jersey. When Bishop George Washington Doane consecrated the church in 1839, he commented that it was "a singularly beautiful Gothic structure, of stone and furnished throughout in the very best of taste."[13] Two years later Doane made a trip to England and chose an old English church as the model for his own parish church of St Mary's, Burlington, New Jersey.

The Gothic revival was already in progress when the Cambridge Camden Society was founded. But the Society gave the revival focus and substantial support. Formed in 1839 by John Mason Neale, while he

10. Evangelical clergy's response to the Great Awakening in America was mentioned in chapter 4.

11. Molesworth, *History*, 375.

12. DeMille, *The Catholic Movement*, 28.

13. Walton, *A Short History*.

was still an undergraduate student, its goal was to promote "the study of Gothic Architecture, and of Ecclesiastical Antiques." Within two years the society counted, among its 700 members, university deans, members of parliament, and sixteen bishops. In addition to stimulating academic research on medieval architecture, it influenced church designs through-out the Anglican world.

The Camden Society did not address theological issues, but the implications of its reverence for medieval religious styles were hard to ignore. Local opposition forced the Society to move its offices from Cambridge to London in 1845, whereupon it changed its name to the "Ecclesiological Society."[14] Bishop Ives of North Carolina became a pa-tron of the New York Ecclesiological Society, formed in 1848.

Members became involved as architects or consultants in numer-ous church construction and renovation projects. Under their influ-ence, chancels and altars were restored, pulpits were reduced in size and placed to the side, and benches or movable chairs replaced rented pews. Not everyone welcomed the democratic ideal of open seating. A bishop of Nova Scotia protested that eliminating rented pews eroded proper social distinctions,[15] and an archbishop of York insisted on the right to seat people according to their station.[16] Notwithstanding, free-church movements gained strength in both Britain and North America. Within a few decades pew rental had become a rarity. Weekly plate collections were instituted to offset the loss of revenue.

Most famous of the architects associated with the Cambridge Camden Society was William Butterfield (1814–1900). Raised non-conformist, he was influenced by the Tractarian Movement and be-came a high-church Anglican. Butterfield was committed to the Gothic ideal, but his designs also reflected Victorian, French, and Italian in-fluence. Among his best-known designs were St Augustine's College, Canterbury; Keble College, Oxford; and St Paul's Cathedral, Melbourne, Australia. American architects associated with the Ecclesiological Society included Richard Upjohn and Henry Congdon.[17] Their work will be discussed in due course.

14. The Ecclesiological Society ceased operations in 1868, after Neale's death, but was reconstituted in 1879.

15. Hayes, *Anglicans*, 70.

16. Reed, *Glorious Battle*, 138.

17. Prichard, *A History*, 150.

Best-known architect of the Gothic revival school *not* associated with the Camden Society or the Ecclesiastical Society was George Gilbert Scott (1811–78), son of an Anglican clergyman. Whether any disaffection existed is unclear; he counted Butterfield among his "excellent friends" and fully supported the Society's goals.[18] Scott created the designs for the Albert Memorial and more than forty churches and cathedrals. ChristChurch Cathedral, New Zealand, and the St Nikolai Kirche, Hamburg, Germany, are counted among his best works.

Gothic Construction Boom

Gothic-revival styles were adopted for most of the new churches built in Britain to serve the expanding industrial areas. "[I]n every part of the kingdom," Molesworth observed, "churches began to rise, which vied with the churches of the Middle Ages, if not in size, at least in the splendour of their ornamentation, and were fitted up with a taste of magnificence which extorted the admiration even of those who feared that the revival of mediaeval ornaments would pave the way for a return to mediaeval doctrines."[19] That was the fear that drove the Camden Society from Cambridge.

All Saints', Margaret Street, London, provided an opportunity to illustrate and promote Camden Society principles. The Margaret Street Chapel, built in the 1760s as a deist chapel, was acquired by high-church Anglicans in 1839, and Tractarian Frederick Oakeley served as priest until his defection to Rome. In 1841 the vestry decided to build a new church. The physical constraints were severe: the church, choir school, and rectory all had to fit on a one-hundred-foot square lot. Among the specifications drawn up by the Camden Society was that "Its artist should be a single, pious and laborious artist alone, pondering deeply over his duty to do his best for the service of God's Holy Religion."

The "pious artist" chosen for the important assignment was William Butterfield. The foundation stone was laid by Edward Pusey in 1850, and the church was consecrated by Bishop Archibald Tait of London nine years later.[20] The interior was richly decorated, and, in a departure from the traditional Gothic stone, the exterior was contrasting colored brick. Artist and poet John Ruskin commented: "It is the first piece of archi-

18. Scott, G., *Personal*, 103–4.

19. Molesworth, *History*, 376.

20. Bishop Tait's involvement was ironical in view of his role in persecuting the Tractarians and ritualists.

tecture I have seen, built in modern days, which is free from all signs of timidity or incapacity . . . it challenges fearless comparison with the noblest work of any time. Having done this, we may do anything: there need be no limits to our hope or our confidence."[21]

The new St Andrew's Chapel, Aberdeen, was the first of many neo-Gothic designs in Scotland. Butterfield designed St Ninian's Cathedral, Perth (1850), and Gilbert Scott designed St Mary's Cathedral, Edinburgh (1879).

Opportunities were even greater in North America, where so many new church buildings were needed. Bishop John Medley of New Brunswick sought the assistance of the New York Ecclesiological Society in the construction of two new church buildings in Fredericton. The design of Christ Church Cathedral was inspired by St Mary's, Snettisham, England, and the result was "an outstanding Canadian example of the Camdenian allegiance to Pointed or Decorated Gothic and to ritualistic symbolism of the 1840s."[22] The new cathedral was consecrated in 1853. Scott's design for the Cathedral of St John the Baptist, Newfoundland, was an impressive cruciform structure in twelfth-century Gothic style. Construction began in 1847, the nave was completed in 1850, and the transepts and chancel were added three decades later.

Upjohn designed the new Trinity Church, Wall Street (1846), and St Paul's Cathedral, Buffalo (1851). Among Congdon's designs was St Andrew's Church, New York City (1872). Construction of Bishop William Croswell Doane's neo-Gothic Cathedral of All Saints, Albany, began in 1884. Renowned for its decoration and furnishings, the cathedral opened for services four years later but is still unfinished. By the end of the nineteenth century Gothic-revival churches and cathedrals graced most of North America. The crowning glory of cathedral construction in the United States was the neo-Gothic Washington National Cathedral, built in the twentieth century.

The only new cathedral built in England since the Reformation, the Cathedral of the Holy Spirit, Guildford, Surrey, was dedicated in 1961. Its architect, Edward Maufe, described the style as "undramatic Curvilinear Gothic."

21. Source: All Saints', Margaret Street, London.
22. Young, *Canada's First Parliament Buildings*, 12.

THE RITUALIST MOVEMENT

Ritual involves movements or gestures of symbolic significance, performed with some degree of solemnity and embodying tradition through repeated enactment. It is the oldest form of religious expression, long predating the formulation of creeds and possibly predating language. The notion of *order* is central; "ritual" comes, via the Latin *ritualis*, from the Sanskrit *rita*, a divine principle of cosmic order. The Apostle Paul declared: "Let all things be done decently and in order" (1 Cor 14:40). Ritual can be either public or private, sacred or secular. Public ritual overlaps in meaning with "ceremony" and the terms are essentially interchangeable. "Pageantry" connotes particularly elaborate ceremony.

"Ritual" in the present context will be understood to mean sacred ritual. Traditionally it is performed in a sacred space, like the Jewish temple, set aside for the purpose and undefiled by profane use. Ritual will be understood to include preparation of the sacred space; deliberate actions or gestures; wearing of vestments; use of symbolic objects or materials; and incorporation of visual, auditory, or other sensory stimuli. Ritual has obvious liturgical significance. But it is distinguished from a "rite": a tradition, custom, or liturgical script, accompanied or unaccompanied by significant ceremony.

"Ritualism" refers to the use or promotion of ritual practices in public worship—and particularly the promotion of practices beyond accepted norms; *some* ritual is unavoidable in any ongoing program of organized worship. This section discusses ritualism in general terms; the following two sections describe specific instances in Britain and North America and the reactions they provoked.

Ritual in the Anglican Church

Some rituals in the medieval church were simple; others very grand. High Mass in one of the great cathedrals, particularly on the occasion of a coronation or the consecration of a bishop, was rich in pageantry. The decorated chancel and altar, elaborately vested clergy and choristers, choreographed movements, consecrated bread and wine, candles, incense, bells, and music combined to raise the consciousness of a large body of participants. The occasion was anticipated with excitement, had great psychological and spiritual impact, and left warm memories.

The Reformers eliminated most ceremony from Anglican worship, regarding it as superstitious and "popish." Even the wearing of the white surplice was resisted and by the seventeenth century was falling into disuse. Nevertheless, Elizabeth I and prominent high-church Anglicans retained some ceremony in their private chapels. Vested choirs in college chapels and cathedrals offered sacred music. The choir of Holy Trinity Cathedral, Quebec City, wore surplices from the time of the cathedral's consecration in 1804.[23] No English bishop wore the mitre from Thomas Cranmer onward. Scottish bishops may have done so, however, and Samuel Seabury wore one upon his return to Connecticut in 1785. By the dawn of the nineteenth century Anglicanism was ripe for the restoration of ceremony.

Restoration arose spontaneously in different places and never was a coordinated effort. By the 1840s substantial numbers of people were involved, and the term "Ritualist Movement" became appropriate. People spoke of ritual "innovation." But the goal was not to break new ground but to revive practices that were part of the Anglican heritage. The Prayer Book, to which all Anglican clergy were committed by virtue of their ordination vows, was the accepted standard of propriety in styles of worship. Some of the restored rituals were at variance with the rubrics, whereas others were actually *prescribed* by the rubrics but had fallen into disuse. When controversy erupted, each side would appeal to the Prayer Book when it provided support or, when it did not, stretched an interpretation or argued that a rubric was no longer applicable.

Ritualism was encouraged by the revival of medieval architecture. The priest who found himself in the magnificence of a neo-Gothic church, to quote Molesworth, "sighed for vestments which accorded better with the temple in which, and the altar before which, he was appointed to minister." More importantly, ritualism was encouraged by new emphasis on the church's sacramental mission. Molesworth noted that vestment use helped satisfy a desire "to distinguish the eucharistic service from the other services of the sanctuary, and thereby to give greater honor and sanctity in the eyes of the multitude to that sacrament which was the very keystone of his system of doctrine."[24]

---

23. When the choristers became aware of the Ritualist Movement they discontinued the practice. Hayes, *Anglicans in Canada*, 123.

24. Molesworth, *History*, 377.

In 1832, the year before Keble's sermon launched the Tractarian Movement, William P. Palmer of Worcester College, Oxford, published a detailed study of liturgy through the ages. An appendix to the work described and illustrated a range of vestments and discussed them in the context of the "ornaments rubric" in the Prayer Book.[25] The rubric required clergy to use "such ornaments in the church, as were in use by authority of parliament in the second year of the reign of king Edward VI." Palmer and others interpreted "ornaments" to include clerical vestments as well as decoration of the altar and chancel.

Keble, Pusey, and the other tractarian leaders were lukewarm toward ceremony, but the emphasis they, and earlier high churchmen, placed on the real presence in the Eucharist made it an almost inevitable response. If the Son of God were really present on the altar, who would *not* feel obliged to decorate the chancel, wear special vestments, and express adoration through gestures, processions, and music? Not surprisingly, ritual restoration focused on the Communion Service—or what increasingly became known as "the Mass." Emphasis on the Eucharist and the restoration of elaborate ceremony in the Mass came to define Anglo-Catholicism in the eyes of the world.

Major Aspects of Ritualism

Ritual restoration began in a small way in the 1840s and gradually gathered momentum. Two decades later, the English Church Union reviewed developments and listed what it considered the most important elements of Anglo-Catholic ritual:
- Eastward facing celebration of the Eucharist
- Use of vestments such as the chasuble, stole, alb, and maniple
- Placement of candles on the altar for purposes other than illumination
- The mixed chalice
- Use of unleavened (wafer) bread in Communion
- The burning of incense in a thurible.[26]

The 1662 *BCP* prescribed that the priest stand at the north side of the communion table: that is to the left, as viewed from the congregation. Ritualists not only wanted a stone altar placed against the east wall

25. Palmer, "Ecclesiastical Vestures."
26. Roberts, *The History.*

of the chancel, where it stood in pre-Reformation churches; they wanted
the priest to face the altar, with his back to the people. The objective—
contrary to the Reformers' intent—was to affirm that the priest was offering a sacrifice on the people's behalf.

Ritualist clergy began to chant portions of the Communion service,
make the sign of the cross, bow toward the altar, and genuflect at critical
points in the service. They began to elevate the host and chalice at the
consecration. Bells were rung at the *Sanctus* and the consecration. The
Benedictus ("Blessed is he who comes in the name of the Lord") was
reinstated at the end of the *Sanctus*, and the *Agnus Dei* ("Lamb of God
who takes away the sins of the world") was returned to its place between
the consecration and the distribution of Communion.

Anglo-Catholic priests insisted on preaching in the surplice, rather
than the Geneva gown. The gown was not prescribed by the Prayer Book,
but the custom emphasized the importance and supposedly scholarly
level of preaching; it also hinted at admiration for Calvinism. Bishop
Hopkins criticized black robes on the grounds that black was the color
of "sin and mourning."[27]

By the 1840s some priests were wearing Roman-style chasubles for
the Communion Service.[28] The chasuble is a tunic, usually in liturgical
colors, slipped over the head like a poncho. Other vestments used were
the alb and maniple. The alb, a long, white garment reaching to the ankles,
is virtually indistinguishable from the Anglican surplice. A maniple is a
band of cloth worn over the left forearm, symbolizing a servant's towel.
A few priests began wearing birettas—the square, black hats of Roman
tradition. Ritualist bishops in America began to wear the cope and mitre.
A mitre is the traditional headdress symbolizing episcopal authority. Its
shape calls to mind the ogival arches of Gothic cathedrals. The cope is a
matching cape, usually in liturgical colors and often richly embroidered.

Acolytes were not needed in eighteenth-century worship services;
the celebrant's only assistant was the parish clerk. But acolytes began to
appear in numbers in ritualist parishes, all assigned specific responsibilities. Acolytes wore surplices or cassocks and cottas. A cassock is an
ankle-length garment of a dark color, usually black. The white *cotta* is
shorter than the surplice and may or may not have sleeves.

27. Hopkins, *The Law of Ritualism*, 47. Hopkins traced the Geneva gown to the
Black Friars of the Middle Ages.

28. White, "Prayer Book Architecture," 112.

Clergy, acolytes, and choristers processed into the church, led by a *thurifer* swinging an incense thurible and a *crucifer* carrying the cross or crucifix. The Church of England permitted the use of incense "in a standing vessel, for the two-fold purpose of sweet fumigation and of serving as an expressive symbol." But the Convocation of Canterbury expressed "its entire disapproval of the practice of censing persons and things." Ritualists definitely wanted to cense persons and things.

Ritualist clergy initially imported most of their vestments and equipment from continental Europe or shopped surreptitiously at Roman Catholic suppliers. But in 1864 Nelson Jarvis, an Anglican clerical outfitter in New York City, started carrying bishops' robes, clerical vests, cassocks, and stoles. At about the same time an English firm advertised chasubles, copes, and other items in "Anglican Patterns of the 12th and 13th centuries."[29] Advertisements soon appeared in the *Church Times* offering a wide range of products, including a clerical haberdashery line that attracted much comment: lace.[30]

Ritualists wanted to restore the crucifix, or at least the plain cross, to Anglican churches. They also wanted to bring back chancel lamps and altar candles. The chancel lamp traditionally indicated that the Sacrament was reserved in the tabernacle on the altar. Reservation for the purposes of visitation to the sick had been retained in the Scottish tradition but had fallen into disuse in England. Tabernacles had been outlawed at the Reformation, along with altars, to eliminate their symbolism and their role as a focus of adoration. Candles had been permitted only for purposes of illumination; ritualists wanted to burn candles on their altars during services, day or night.

Mixing water with the sacramental wine, customary in the Middle Ages, was variously interpreted to symbolize the blood and water that flowed from Christ's body on the cross, his dual divine and human natures, or Christ's divinity and our humanity. Unleavened bread had Old Testament precedents and was used in the Eucharist from early Christian times.

Some Anglo-Catholics organized outdoor processions, Benediction of the Blessed Sacrament, or the Stations of the Cross. Or they encouraged private confession, prayers for the dead, and Requiem Masses.

29. Prichard, *A History*, 149.
30. Reed, *Glorious Battle*, 91.

Veneration and invocation of the Blessed Virgin and the saints became popular toward the end of the nineteenth century.

New "Rubrics"

Some priests felt that the ritual practices they employed were worthy to become the norm: they wanted to create unofficial Anglo-Catholic rubrics. In 1856 George Rundle Prynne, rector of St Peter's, Plymouth, published *The Eucharistic Manual* offering instructions and devotions for the Communion Service; one of his prayers was quoted earlier.

John Purchas, a Brighton clergyman, published his *Directorium Anglicanum* in 1868. It provided detailed guidelines for sacramental and other rites, including "solemn religious processions—such for instance as at the Consecration of a Church, or the Benediction of a College, &c." Instructions for celebrating the Eucharist included the following:

> When the celebrant signs himself he places his left hand upon his breast; in blessing anything upon the Altar the left hand is laid upon the *mensa* [the top surface of the altar]; if such Benediction takes place during the Celebration of the Holy Eucharist, the hand is to be laid outside the corporal if before the consecration of the elements,—upon the corporal if afterwards.
>
> The celebrant should keep his head and body erect, but his eyes bent downwards even when turned towards the faithful, so as to avoid distraction. When he turns to the people, he turns from left to right, that is, standing in front of the altar facing eastwards, he turns round towards the south or right side, (epistle corner), when he turns again to his Normal Position at the altar with his face eastwards, he turns in the same way, i.e., from left to right.
>
> When the hands are "elevated," they are raised with the palms fronting each other, so that the tips of the fingers can be just seen above the shoulders.[31]

Nothing was left to chance. Purchas's list of recommended altar decorations included "the cross, two altar candlesticks, two standard candlesticks, candlesticks for *retables*, one desk for service-book for celebrant, one service-book for celebrant only, flower vases, antependia of the five "sacred" canonical or church colors, fair white linen cloth, the

---

31. Purchas, *Directorium Anglicanum*, 166. The "epistle side" and "gospel side" of the altar (right and left, respectively, as viewed from the pews) refers to Roman practice in which the missal is carried from one side of the altar to the other between readings.

corporal—enclosed in the burse—or corporal case, paten, chalice, and one silk chalice veil and pall."[32]

Carelessness can undermine the meaning and efficacy of ritual, but the usefulness of such detailed rubrics is questionable. Priests can be helped more by greater understanding of why certain gestures and movements are important. Ferdinand Ewer, founder of the Church of St Ignatius of Antioch, New York City, offered an example. He compared the practice of bowing or genuflecting when entering a church to the formality expected when entering a friend's library. "I should," he declared in 1878, "be deemed guilty of a great discourtesy should I not salute him in the customary manner on entering." The Anglo-Catholic should feel similarly negligent if he approached the Lord "without offering . . . that solemn, adoring salutation which is due from the creature to his God."[33]

Struggle for Acceptance

Ceremony clearly met a deep-seated need in the Anglican psyche, but it also faced stiff resistance. Evangelicals felt that ceremony had been abolished for good reason at the Reformation and that restoration smacked of romanism. The charge was not entirely fair. Eastern Orthodoxy employed just as much ritual as Rome did, and a number of ritualists, including John Mason Neale,[34] adopted or adapted Eastern liturgical forms. Some efforts were also made to devise liturgical ritual with a distinctively Anglican flavor. In any event, if ritual were "foreign," Anglo-Catholics could argue that Calvinist distaste for it was also foreign.

That said, ritual inevitably reminded people of Roman practices, and some practices were unashamedly imitative. Arguments that incorporating more ceremony into Anglican worship might deter further defections were refuted by the significant number of ritualists who converted to Roman Catholicism.

Whereas the Tractarian Movement exposed the major players to persecution, the Ritualist Movement provoked outright war on a broad front. For fifty years ritualist clergy faced disruption of worship

---

32. Ibid., 213. A *retable*, or *reredos*, is an ornate screen behind the altar, normally with ledges or niches for the cross, candles, statues, or flowers. The *antependia* is a cloth covering the front of the altar.

33. Ewer, *Catholicity*, 294–95.

34. Reed, *Glorious Battle*, 66.

services, denunciation by ecclesiastical and civil authorities, dismissal from benefices, fines, even imprisonment. Many of their parishioners were strongly supportive, others were hostile, and some were probably indifferent. All—as well as the general public—looked on with dismay as the war became progressively uglier. Over time, however, the sight of Anglican priests wearing chasubles, the sound of bells ringing, and the smell of incense became commonplace.

RITUALISM IN GREAT BRITAIN

In 1846 Neale, by then an ordained priest, became warden of Sackville College, an almshouse in East Grinstead, Sussex. He installed a large rood cross in the chapel and built a belfry. Several years later Neale and his sister Elizabeth founded the Society of St Margaret. Neale wore a chasuble in the convent chapel, used incense, placed flowers on the altar, introduced adoration of the Blessed Sacrament, and led the nuns in Latin hymns. The nuns observed the Daily Offices and participated in daily Communion. On Good Friday the altar was stripped, black draperies covered the windows, and nuns participated in the Stations of the Cross.[35]

What Neale did at Sackville and St Margaret's should not have attracted much attention. But he was denounced in the *Brighton Gazette* for the rood cross. The very privacy of the convent aroused suspicions; enemies claimed to have heard unusual sounds, seen suspicious lights, smelled unusual scents, and discovered incriminating residues in trash.[36] At the funeral of one of the nuns Neale placed a cross on the draped casket, whereupon her relatives snatched the body and had her buried elsewhere. Shortly thereafter a mob tried to burn down Neale's home.[37] At another funeral of a nun who had joined the order against parental wishes, he was attacked by a rock-throwing crowd incited by her father.

Henry Parry Liddon (1829–90) served as vice-principal of Cuddesdon Theological College, Oxford, in the 1850s. When he introduced limited ceremony into worship, Bishop Samuel Wilberforce, whose palace was across the street, was generally supportive. But the bishop demanded Liddon's resignation in 1859 when the practices attracted

35. Ibid., 54–55.
36. Ibid., 55.
37. Grafton, *The Lineage*, 194; Reed, *Glorious Battle*, 54.

adverse attention. Liddon went on to hold other prestigious positions at Oxford before being appointed prebendary of Salisbury Cathedral.

Ritual in Parish Churches

The introduction of ceremony in parish churches provoked more serious reactions. When Francis Courtenay, curate of St Sidwell's, Exeter, began preaching in a surplice in 1845, riots broke out in the city. Whether they were spontaneous or orchestrated remains an open question. The mayor called upon church leaders to intervene, and the bishops of Exeter, London, and Canterbury all got involved. After initial confusion they issued a joint statement that the vestment practice was incompatible with church custom and urged clergy to adhere to precedent.[38]

George Prynne, whose communion manual was mentioned earlier, was appointed in 1848 to one of the poorest parishes in the Exeter diocese. He preached in a surplice, chanted the service, and bowed at the name of Jesus.[39] In due course Prynne became a strong supporter of auricular confession. Opponents complained that confession was an assault on men's families; it enabled unmarried priests to pry into the sexual activities and fantasies of impressionable women.[40] Whether such accusations had any merit is debatable, but many Victorian men—including prominent clergy—also unburdened themselves in the confessional.

From 1842 onward Bryan King, rector of the London parish of St George's in the East, burned candles on the altar, wore eucharistic vestments, and intoned the psalms. For seventeen years his parishioners were either tolerant or indifferent. Then in 1859 opponents launched a well-orchestrated campaign of disrupting services. People turned their backs on the altar, drowned out the psalms, threw projectiles and set off firecrackers during sermons, turned dogs loose in the sanctuary, urinated in the pews, tore up and burned carpets, and smashed windows.[41] After several months, when bodyguards and even the police failed to stop the disruptions, the bishop of London ordered the church closed for six weeks. Eventually King was transferred to a parish in Wiltshire. Another incident of mob

38. Molesworth, *History*, 331–33.
39. Kelway, *George Rundle Prynne*, 34–39.
40. Reed, *Glorious Battle*, 195–201.
41. Ibid., 58.

violence occurred at St Alban's Church, Birmingham, where police had to use sabers to drive back a crowd bent on demolishing the building.[42]

In the 1850s John Purchas, rector of St John's Church, Brighton, and author of the *Directorium Anglicanum*, wore the alb, chasuble, cope, and biretta; burned candles and incense during the Communion Service; and placed crucifixes and a holy-water stoop in his church. The new Church of St Michael and All Angels, also in Brighton, was designed according to Purchas's recommendations. In the words of a modern commentator: "St Michael's was soon to become the most advanced ritualistic church in England, outstanding for its magnificent ceremonial, splendid vestments and operatic music."[43]

By mid-century ritualism had spread to Scotland. St John's Episcopal Chapel, Edinburgh, attracted attention for its practices. The bishop wrote a critical letter to the incumbent, complaining of "an ever-growing and ever-craving taste for a more symbolical and imaginative ritual" and urging him and his congregation "to be content with the simple but decent ritual which has been usual in well-ordered churches."[44] As noted in chapter 6, Bishop Alexander Forbes of Brechin was charged with heresy for his teachings on the Eucharist. In 1850 he reportedly anointed a sick person—the first time an Anglican churchman had administered the sacrament since the reign of Edward VI.[45] When ritualist clergy in England adopted the practice, unction had to be imported from Scotland because English bishops refused to bless it.[46]

Laypeople supported ritualism through money and political influence. William Gladstone, who had both, became involved in its struggles, as he had been in the Tractarian Movement's. Rumors circulated that he was converting to Roman Catholicism. The rumors proved untrue, but Gladstone did convert from Tory to Liberal in the 1850s, reflecting the changing relationship between high-church Anglicanism and British political parties.

42. Ibid., 93.

43. Brooks & Saint, *The Victorian Church*, 197.

44. Goldie, *A Short History*, 96–97.

45. Strong, R., *Alexander Forbes*, 235.

46. Reed, *Glorious Battle*, 146, 222.

Campaign "to Put Down Ritualism"

As the war over ritualism heated up, each side mobilized its forces. Ritualists formed the English Church Union (ECU) in 1859/1860, with Viscount Charles Halifax (1839–1934) as president. One of its goals was to "afford counsel and protection to all persons, lay or clerical, suffering under unjust aggression or hindrance in spiritual matters." Some 4,000 clergy and 38,000 laypersons joined.[47] The ECU's publication, the *Church Times*, became a potent propaganda weapon. Opponents founded the Church Association (CA) in 1865, with the goal of stamping out "Rationalism and Ritualism." The organization did little to counter rationalism, but with a war chest of £50,000, it became a formidable enemy of ritualism.

By the 1860s evangelicals had lost faith in the episcopal courts. Although the Gorham case had gone in their favor, the ruling had also shown that bishops had little authority over their clergy. So they decided to politicize the war. Most clergy vehemently opposed parliamentary interference in ecclesiastical matters, but militant Evangelicals were willing to use it to achieve their goals.

Attempts to persuade parliament to legislate against ritualism initially were unsuccessful. A Royal Commission appointed in 1867 ended inconclusively. Low-church fortunes improved dramatically, however, when Archibald Tait was appointed archbishop of Canterbury in 1868 and Tory/Conservative Benjamin Disraeli became prime minister in 1874.[48] Two months after Disraeli took office, Tait introduced a bill in the House of Lords "to put down ritualism." With the prime minister's support, the bill passed. Queen Victoria signed the Public Worship Regulation Act into law and personally congratulated Disraeli and Tait.[49] Approval of the measure by a Conservative government over Whig opposition was a major reversal of traditional party loyalties; the long-standing relationship between high-church Anglicans and the Tory party was over.

The Public Worship Regulation Act made disobedience of a bishop a criminal offense. A new court was established with former divorce

47. Grafton, *The Lineage*, 196.

48. Disraeli was born Jewish, but his father had him baptized in the Church of England following a dispute with their synagogue.

49. Chandler, *An Introduction*, 113–14. Victoria, who ascended the throne in 1837, had strong evangelical leanings. Her first tutor was George Davys, an evangelical preacher who became bishop of Peterborough. Later she was drawn to Scottish Presbyterianism.

lawyer Lord Penzance as presiding judge. Charges against offending clergy could be filed by a bishop or by a third party—and the Church Association eagerly assumed the latter role. Seventeen clergymen were prosecuted under the law. The first to go to prison was Arthur Tooth, a member of the Society of the Holy Cross and vicar of St James', Hatcham, in the diocese of Rochester; he was jailed for twenty-eight days in 1877. The longest prison term was imposed against Sidney Faithhorn Green of the diocese of Manchester. Green was convicted of contempt of court for ignoring an injunction issued by Penzance and was jailed from March 1881 until November 1882. The last clergyman imprisoned, James Bell Cox of the Liverpool diocese, served fourteen days in 1887.[50]

The most notorious case of persecution involved Alexander Heriot Mackonochie (1825–87), vicar of St Alban's, Holborn, London. Mackonochie wore eucharistic vestments, processed into the church led by a crucifer, burned candles on the altar, used unleavened bread and the mixed chalice, adopted the eastward-facing position, knelt during the consecration, elevated the host, burned incense, and inserted the *Agnus Dei* into the Communion Service. He also openly heard confessions.[51] St Alban's was the first Anglican church to hold a three-hour devotion on Good Friday and one of the first to organize a harvest festival. Mackonochie was also heavily involved in work for the poor and played a major role in the Society of the Holy Cross.

The Church Association first brought charges against Mackonochie in 1867. The Court of Arches ruled against him on two counts but dismissed three others. Mackonochie agreed to comply with the ruling, but the CA appealed and the Privy Council convicted him on all five charges and ordered him to pay costs. The CA continued to press charges, and Mackonochie was given a series of suspensions, including one for three years in 1878. He moved to St Peter's Church, London Docks, and after being suspended again in 1883 he resigned his living. He died four years later on the estate of the bishop of Argyll.[52] Mackonochie is revered as a martyr of the Anglo-Catholic cause, and St Alban's dedicated a chapel in his honor.

Not every case was successful. The CA filed a heresy charge in 1869 against William James Bennett, a Somerset vicar. Bennett had affirmed the

---

50. Ibid., 115–17.

51. Towle, *Alexander Heriot Mackonochie*, 148.

52. Ibid., 285–88.

"Real, objective Presence of our Lord, under the form of Bread and Wine, upon the Altars of our churches . . . and whom I myself adore, and teach the people to adore." The Privy Council acquitted Bennett on the grounds that his views lay within the permitted range of Anglican teachings.[53]

During the tenure of Dean Richard Church, chronicler of the Tractarian Movement, two canons of St Paul's Cathedral, London, tried to goad the Church Association into prosecuting them in what would have been a high-profile case. The CA declined the bait, preferring to target parish clergy.[54] After Church's death in 1890 the CA charged the dean and chapter with installing statues of the Virgin Mary and saints in the cathedral. The matter ended when Frederick Temple, bishop of London, exercised his episcopal veto.

The highest-ranking churchman prosecuted by the Church Association was Edward King (1829–1910), former principal of Cuddesdon College and currently bishop of Lincoln.[55] Although a few nineteenth-century English bishops tolerated ritualism, King was the only one who actively practiced it; for example, he was the first bishop in the Church of England to wear the cope and mitre since the sixteenth century. The CA charged King in 1889 with eastward-facing consecration, using a mixed chalice, and burning candles during daylight. Because of his rank the case was referred to a court of assessors, presided over by Edward Benson, archbishop of Canterbury. On the morning of the proceedings, Anglo-Catholics throughout England held prayer services, asking "that God might be pleased to overrule the trial to His greater glory and the good of His Church."[56] Their prayers were answered, and the court merely requested King to make minor changes. The CA appealed to the Privy Council but lost.

By the 1890s the *Church Times* had turned public opinion against the CA.[57] Ritualists were seen as martyrs persecuted by vindictive bullies, and no further charges were brought under the Public Worship Regulation Act. When Bishop King died in 1910 a Requiem Mass was celebrated with full honors in Lincoln Cathedral.[58]

53. Shepherd vs. Bennett; see also Grafton, *The Lineage*, 199.

54. Ibid., 116.

55. Chandler. *An Introduction*, 117–18.

56. Grafton, *The Lineage*, 199–200.

57. Reed, *Glorious Battle*, 103.

58. Bishop Edward Benson is not to be confused with his contemporary, Richard

In 1904 the Royal Commission on Ecclesiastical Discipline was appointed "to inquire into 'breaches or neglect of the Law relating to the conduct of Divine Service' in the Church of England and to devise remedies." Its report, issued in 1906, acknowledged that the machinery for discipline had broken down but declared that the laws governing religious practices in the Church of England were too narrow. The commission noted that eucharistic vestments were regularly worn at 1,526 churches in England and Wales, 167 in London alone; and "None of the present Bishops has taken any steps for the general prohibition of these vestments in his diocese." Clearly, vestment use had become routine: "What was [fifty years ago] a complete and startling novelty has become a practice . . . condemned by law, but for thirty years unrepressed in more than 1,500 English churches, and thousands of middle-aged persons now living have been accustomed to see those vestments worn as long as they can remember."[59]

The commission urged that the liturgy be expanded to "secure greater elasticity, which a reasonable recognition of the comprehensiveness of the Church of England . . . seems to demand."[60] The outcome, after years of work, was the proposed 1927/8 *Book of Common Prayer*. Unfortunately, the bill authorizing the new Prayer Book was defeated in the House of Commons. By then it was clear that machinery of a different kind had broken down.

RITUALISM IN NORTH AMERICA

The United States had no laws prohibiting ritualism and no judicial authority that could have ruled on them. Ritualism did not offend long-standing precedent, because the Episcopal Church was still in its infancy. Moreover, powerful bishops supported it. BNA/Canada might have experienced a situation more like England's, but it too was spared open warfare. Opposition to ritualism in North America was mild compared with that in the mother country.

William Muhlenberg's Evangelical Catholicism incorporated evangelical concepts like personal religious experience. But it also affirmed the seven sacraments and promoted ceremony, observance of daily of-

Meux Benson, founder of the Society of St John the Evangelist.

59. *Report of the Royal Commission*, "Present Breaches, §4.
60. Ibid., "Recommendations."

fices, and weekly Communion. Most of the graduates of Muhlenberg's Flushing Institute followed the ritualist path. One of them, John Ireland Tucker, introduced ritual practices at the Church of the Holy Cross, Troy, New York, which he founded in 1844.

In the late 1840s Bishop Levi Ives introduced ceremonial practices at his religious community in North Carolina. According to complaints by one of the state's United States senators, the Sacrament was reserved in the chapel, and prayers were offered to the saints and the Virgin Mary.[61] Eucharistic vestments and altar cloths were used, and private confession was encouraged. The practices came to an end when the diocese closed the community in 1852.

Bishop George Doane's close friend William Croswell became the first rector of the Church of the Advent, Boston.[62] Croswell, who had studied under Hobart, began offering daily services and weekly Communion in the 1840s. He preached in a surplice, knelt before the altar, and chanted the psalms. Shocking class-conscious Boston, he also introduced open seating. Bishop Manton Eastburn of Massachusetts reacted negatively and refused to make further visitations; candidates for confirmation had to go to neighboring churches. A few years later Eastburn charged Oliver Prescott, a priest at Advent, with hearing confessions. An investigation showed that he had not exceeded the authority given in the Prayer Book, but the bishop forced him to stop the practice. In 1856, after Eastburn's death, the General Convention enacted a rule that bishops must visit all parishes in their dioceses at least every three years.[63]

Soon after his ordination to the priesthood in 1855, James DeKoven (1831–79) was appointed professor of church history at Nashotah House, Wisconsin. By the 1850s Nashotah had ceased to be a mission or monastery, but its seminary had acquired a national reputation. DeKoven introduced daily celebration of the Eucharist as well as the use of vestments, candles, and incense. A few years later he left Nashotah to became warden of Racine College, Wisconsin, where he remained for the rest of his ministerial life.

The installation of crosses in American churches seems to have been relatively slow. Writing in 1867, Morgan Dix (1827–1908), rector of Trinity Church, Wall Street, commented on the practice:

61. Wright, L., "Anglo-Catholicism," 44–71.
62. Doane named his son, the future bishop of Albany, after Croswell.
63. DeMille, *The Catholic Movement*, 81–82, 92–93.

> There was a time, not long ago, when the cross was all but un-
> known among us as a symbol of our faith and an ornament of
> our holy places. It was left to the Romanists; by our permission
> they enjoyed a monopoly of it, as is still the case with other useful
> and excellent things. I can remember the day when a cross on an
> Episcopal church was hardly to be seen: the first one that I ever
> saw in such a position was on the Church of the Ascension of this
> city; I beheld it, and wondered, and rejoiced secretly, as not quite
> sure whether it was right or wrong.[64]

In British North America an archdeacon, George Coster, reportedly preached in a surplice before 1845, and Bishop John Strachan of
Toronto instructed clergy in two parishes to do the same.[65] Holy Trinity
Church, Toronto, began offering weekly Communion in 1858.[66] Three
years later Edmund Wood, rector of St John the Evangelist, Montreal,
celebrated daily Mass, offered private confession, and reserved the
Sacrament. When Herbert Binney was appointed bishop of Nova Scotia
in 1864, the congregation of St Paul's, Halifax, objected to his preaching in a surplice; Binney responded by moving his cathedral to the new
St Luke's Church. In 1868 Binney forced the resignation of a priest in
Halifax who persisted in preaching in a gown.[67]

Efforts began in 1868 to restrict ritual practices in both Canada
and the United States. At its meeting in that year the Provincial Synod
of Canada passed a resolution prohibiting "the elevation of the elements
during the celebration of Holy Communion, the use of incense during
Divine Service, and the mixing of water with the sacramental wine."[68]
The Provincial Synod also prohibited the use of candles on the altar and
wearing of the chasuble. Compliance seems to have been less than universal. The choristers of St Peter's, Charlottetown, Prince Edward Island,
which lay within the province, were vested from the time the church
opened in 1869. A rood cross was erected in 1872, altar candles were
introduced in 1877, eucharistic vestments in 1889, and daily celebration
of the Eucharist in 1890.

64. Dix, M., "A Sermon." Dix served Trinity Church for almost fifty-three years,
most of that time as rector.

65. Hayes, *Anglicans*, 122.

66. Ibid., 123.

67. Ibid., 122.

68. Quoted in Hayes, *Anglicans*, 261. The Province of Canada included dioceses
from Montreal to Newfoundland, including Nova Scotia.

The General Convention of the Episcopal Church debated ritual practices at meetings from 1868 through 1874. DeKoven, a delegate to the lower house, emerged as the chief spokesman for the ritualist cause in 1871 and 1874. He defended the use of candles, incense, and gestures like bowing and kneeling. DeKoven conceded that the church could make any rules it chose, but it could not dictate what occurred in people's hearts:

> [Y]ou may give us the most barren of all observances, and we will submit to you. If this Church commands us to have no cer- emonies, we will obey. But, gentlemen, the very moment anyone says we shall not adore our Lord present in the Eucharist, then from a thousand hearts will come the answer, as of those bidden to go into exile, "Let me die in my own country and be buried by the grave of my father and my mother!" for to adore Christ's person in His Sacrament, is the inalienable privilege of every Christian.[69]

Despite DeKoven's eloquence, the 1874 Convention ruled that bishops should investigate any "ceremonies or practices not ordained or authorized in the Book of Common Prayer."[70] As possible examples it cited elevation of the host and adoration of the eucharistic elements. DeKoven's prominence in the debate attracted enemies' attention and cost him promotion to the episcopate. He was nominated five times, but not elected; then in 1875 he was elected bishop of Illinois but did not receive the required consents from other dioceses. Interestingly his re- placement as bishop of Illinois was another prominent high churchman, William McClaren.

The 1874 ruling concerning "ceremonies or practices" affected Arthur Ritchie, rector of the Church of the Ascension, Chicago, and later of St Ignatius's, New York City. He came under fire from each bishop for reserv- ing the Sacrament and offering the service of Benediction. Under protest, he agreed to end the practices.[71] The problem was finally resolved when the prohibition against adoration of the Eucharist was lifted in 1904.

St Ignatius's had been founded in 1871 by Ferdinand Ewer. Writing several years later Ewer commented on how the typical Anglo-Catholic church had evolved: "It is made glorious not because an eloquent

69. Quoted in Armentrout & Slocum, *Documents*, 76.

70. DeMille, *The Catholic Movement*, 123–25.

71. Prichard, *A History*, 155, 191–92. Also DeMille, *The Catholic Movement*, 128– 29, 177.

preacher is to preach there, nor yet to please the eyes of fastidious taste; but that it may be a fitting casket to hold Christ in Real Presence at the Holy Altar, to hold the Antitype throughout the Christian ages, of which the Shekinah on the mercy seat in the Jewish Holy of Holies was but a type and shadow."[72]

The first bishop of the new diocese of Fond du Lac, established in northern Wisconsin in 1875, was John Henry Hobart Brown (1831–88), another of Muhlenberg's students.[73] Brown reached out to members of the Old Catholic Church, a denomination claiming the apostolic succession that had seceded from the Church of Rome after the First Vatican Council.[74] Upon his death in 1889 Brown was succeeded by Charles Chapman Grafton, former member of the Order of St John the Evangelist. Grafton routinely wore the cope and mitre. He also introduced all the typical ritual practices at St Paul's Cathedral, Milwaukee, and urged clergy throughout his diocese to do the same.

In November 1900 Grafton officiated at the consecration of Heber Weller as coadjutor bishop of Fond du Lac. He anointed Weller with chrism and presented him with an episcopal ring and pastoral staff, neither of which was customary at the time. The ceremony was attended by bishops from the Russian Orthodox Church and the Polish National Catholic Church, another Roman breakaway being courted. All wore vestments of their respective traditions. A photograph of the proceedings in *The Living Church* was dubbed the "Fond du Lac Circus." Within a relatively short time, however, the pomp of the investiture became the norm throughout the Anglican Communion.

THE CATHOLIC REVIVAL AND SACRED MUSIC

Music can be an important ingredient in sacred ritual. Anglicanism's rich musical heritage owes a great deal to royal patronage and to the resources of cathedrals, college chapels, and other large churches. That custom spread to Scotland, North America, and other parts of the Anglican world. St Andrew's Cathedral, Aberdeen, acquired a traditional choir of men and boys. As the new dioceses of BNA acquired cathedrals, they also organized choirs. The vested choirs at Holy Trinity Cathedral, Quebec City, and St Peter's, Prince Edward Island, have already been mentioned.

72. Ewer, *What is the Anglican*, §VI.

73. Brown's parents clearly were admirers of Bishop Hobart.

74. Prichard, *A History*, 153–54.

Although the United States was slow to build cathedrals, choirs were formed at some of the larger churches. Troy, New York, was blessed with three Episcopal church choirs before 1850: St Paul's, St John's, and Holy Cross. The choir at William Croswell's Holy Cross performed Gregorian Chant. Bishop William Croswell Doane created a choir of men and boys and also a choir school at All Saints' Cathedral, Albany. The choir school later closed, but All Saints' remained famous for its music program as well as for its Anglo-Catholic worship. The residential choir school at St Thomas's, Fifth Avenue, New York, is the only surviving school in the United States. Its students and professional male choristers have attained an international reputation. Every large Anglican church and cathedral in North America now invests considerable resources in its music program.

During the nineteenth century, choirs were organized even at smaller churches, allowing them to offer the Sung Communion, or High Mass, on Sundays and major festivals. Choirs also became more visible, moving from a loft at the rear of the church to positions closer to the chancel—sometimes behind the high altar or in the traditional "choir," or *quire*, between chancel and nave. Choristers processed into the church, along with clergy and acolytes, singing hymns or litanies. Choirs chanted the psalms and responses, led congregational singing, and sang polyphonic anthems. Anthems by the English baroque composers, like William Byrd and Henry Purcell, and their continental counterparts, Giovanni Pierluigi da Palestrina and Tomás Luis de Vittoria, all became popular. Scruples about singing Latin anthems or works by Roman Catholic composers were soon overcome.

The Cambridge Camden/Ecclesiological Society's primarily concern was church architecture, but it also supported sacred music. In a work published in 1843, John Merbecke's settings of the 1549 Prayer Book were modified for use with the 1662 liturgy.[75] The chants were performed in St Margaret's Chapel, London, as well as St George's Chapel, Windsor, where Merbecke had served as organist. In 1852, again under the auspices of the Ecclesiological Society, Thomas Helmore published *The Hymnal Noted*—a clear reference to Merbecke's work. It was a collection of more than one hundred medieval hymns, including Neale's own "O come, O come, Emmanuel," translated from a twelfth-century Latin original. The editor commented:

75. Leaver, "The Prayer Book Noted," 42.

> The omission, at the Reformation, of one entire portion of the ancient ritual treasured up in the Latin devotional books of Western Christendom—the source from which our Book of Common Prayer is derived—though necessary, could not be otherwise than injurious; and although [this] was the only apparent alternative for the avoiding of greater evils . . . the translation into English of the really Catholic Hymns, in such wise as to be capable of being sung to the old Catholic tunes, was a work second only in importance to the translation of the Psalter, the Offices, and the Liturgy.[76]

The Hymnal Noted included Gregorian chant, like the sequence *Dies Irae* ("Day of wrath") from the Requiem Mass, as well as extracts from the Sarum Rite. Hymns in the original Latin and in English translation were listed according to the liturgical calendar. An extended version incorporated musical harmonies to support four-part polyphony and/or organ accompaniment. Scores were provided in both the medieval four-line stave and the modern five-line stave.

The Catholic Revival produced a flurry of hymn writing. The works of Neale, Oakeley, Keble, and Roland Palmer have already been mentioned. Compositions by Tractarians Newman and Isaac Williams found their way into the *English Hymnal,* as also did Gladstone's "O Lead My Blindness by the Hand." John Henry Hopkins, Jr., son of the American bishop, wrote the carol "We Three Kings." Richard Frederick Littledale translated "Come Down, O Love Divine" from a medieval Italian source; it is commonly sung to Ralph Vaughan Williams's tune, "Down Ampney." Russian composer Sergei Rachmaninoff became the musical patron of All Saints', Margaret Street, after a visit to London in 1924, and provided the parish with Masses, canticles, and hymns.

The nineteenth century ushered in another golden age of English church music with the work of John Stainer (1840–1901), Hubert Parry (1848–1918), Charles Villiers Stanford (1852–1924), and many others. Major support for sacred Anglican music was provided by the foundation of the School of English Church Music by Sydney Nicholson in 1927. The school, later renamed the Royal School of Church Music, is the largest church music organization in Britain and has branches in the United States, Canada, and elsewhere.

76. Helmore, *Accompanying Harmonies,* i.

SERVICE AND SOCIAL CONSCIENCE

Serving the poor and disadvantaged has always been a Christian responsibility, and Frederick Denison Maurice (1805–72) and other Anglicans laid the foundations of Christian Socialism. Service found a natural place in the new Anglican religious orders. It was a primary concern of the Community of St John the Baptist, the Sisterhood of St Mary and St Modwenna, the Sisterhood of the Church of the Holy Communion, the Order of the Holy Cross, the Anglican Franciscan order, and other orders.[77] Missionary work traditionally had a service dimension. "Indian schools" operated in the United States and Canada by Anglican and other religious organizations in the nineteenth century provided educational opportunities—sadly at the cost of suppressing indigenous cultures.[78] Important service ministries also emerged at the parish level throughout the Anglican Communion.

Social justice was not foremost in the minds of the early Tractarians and ritualists. But a strong social conscience arose unexpectedly in Anglo-Catholic parishes and among prominent laypeople. Anglo-Catholic clergy in Britain often sought appointments to new parishes in the expanding industrial areas or to struggling inner-city churches, where ritual practices could be introduced without opposition from conservative vestries. Bishops gladly complied; troublesome ritualists could be sent to poor parishes where they could "do no harm," while well-endowed parishes were reserved for more favored clergy.

The Church of England never had much success evangelizing the poorer classes.[79] But working-class people were drawn to Anglo-Catholic worship. Perhaps it was a response to the unfamiliar pastoral attention. No doubt people also saw the colorful ceremony as a relief from the harshness of their everyday environments. Parishioners at a number of London churches protested when attempts were made to eliminate ritual.[80] Ritualist clergy and lay assistants won praise for their work in some of the most depressed areas of Britain. St Peter's, London Docks,

77. Welfare programs in Canada were channeled through faith-based groups until the 1940s.

78. Hayes, *Anglicans*, 31–35.

79. The lack of success was not surprising since the church was identified in many people's minds with the rich and powerful, and working people were forced to sit at the back of the church

80. See the discussion in Reed, *Glorious Battle*, 161–62, 165–66.

gained recognition for its well-attended Sunday services for children. Anglo-Catholics found themselves in the forefront of the church's social ministry.

Bishop Forbes reached out to marginalized people in Scotland, and his rank made him particularly effective. His diocese of Brechin included the industrial city of Dundee, and he focused much of his effort on alleviating the plight of the urban poor. Among much else Forbes established a home for prostitutes, a convalescent house, and an orphanage.[81]

Among prominent laymen, Gladstone demonstrated a strong social conscience. In the 1840s he began walking the streets of London, urging prostitutes to change their ways and offering them rehabilitation. Despite criticism, he continued his one-man ministry for decades, even after becoming prime minister. Gladstone founded the Church Penitentiary Association for the Reclamation of Fallen Women and aided the House of Mercy at Clewer.

Alexander Mackonochie organized an extensive pastoral ministry in the 1860s at St Alban's, Holborn. With two curates and lay assistants he founded schools, soup kitchens, mothers' meetings, and clothing funds. The parish organized a working men's club, where members—200 by 1871—could meet for meals, recreation, and education.[82] The idea quickly expanded to the national level. In 1876 the English Church Union supported creation of the Church of England Working Men's Society. Within twelve years it claimed 285 branches and nearly 10,000 members. Activities were frequently reported in the *Church Times*. Mobilizing such a large number of laypeople was not inconsequential in furthering the Anglo-Catholic cause. On occasions, members of the society demonstrated in support of ritualist clergy and provided bodyguards for those in danger.[83]

Through their service endeavors, clergy from privileged backgrounds acquired first-hand experience of the impact of the Industrial Revolution and associated social ills. Some became activists, and the Christian Social Union was one of the outcomes. The organization was founded in 1889 by Canon Henry Scott Holland of St Paul's Cathedral, London, with help from Charles Gore.[84] Its mission was "to provide

81. Forbes, *A Memoir*, 13.

82. Reed, *Glorious Battle*, 163.

83. Ibid., 163–67.

84. Holland was an associate of Tractarian Henry Liddon and a contributor to Gore's *Lux Mundi*.

direction to the new social gospel" and to "investigate areas in which moral truth and Christian principles could bring relief to the social and economic disorder of society." The Union's journal, *The Commonwealth*, published articles on a broad range of topics related to social justice. A number of bishops became members over the years, including William Temple, archbishop of Canterbury in the 1940s. Temple authored the influential book *Christianity and Social Order* (1942).[85]

In the United States a group of laymen founded the Chapel of St James the Less in 1860 and used it as a base for missionary work among the poor of New York City.[86] The Church Association for the Advancement of the Interests of Labor was founded in 1887; soon it had branches throughout the nation and the support of nearly fifty bishops.[87]

James Huntington, founder of the Order of the Holy Cross, spent time working incognito as a farm laborer to familiarize himself with the plight of the working poor.[88] Henry Sylvester Nash of the Episcopal Theological School explored the basis of social consciousness in *The Genesis of the Social Conscience* (1897) and *Ethics and Revelation* (1899). During World War I, Chicago priest Irwin St John Tucker became so involved in socialist activities that he was imprisoned under the Espionage Act.[89] The 1919 General Convention adopted a resolution affirming that "service to the community as a whole, rather than individual gain, [should be] the primary motive in every kind of work."[90]

REFLECTIONS

The external forms of religion certainly can become empty and meaningless. Church buildings can become shrines to forgotten gods, ritual superstitious proceduralism, vestments symbols of clerical ego, gestures pharisaical, decorations tasteless, and music distractive. But those pitfalls can be avoided. Intelligent and careful attention to externals enhances the religious experience and creates more perfect vehicles for the receipt of divine grace.

85. William Temple was the son of Bishop Frederick Temple.

86. DeMille, *The Catholic Movement*, 109.

87. Holmes, *A Brief History*, 127. The organization had no connection with the Church Association in England.

88. DeMille, *The Catholic Movement*, 143–44.

89. Holmes, *A Brief History*, 128. See also the *New York Times*, March 9, 1918.

90. DeMille, *The Episcopal Church*, 39–40.

The architectural revival and Ritualist Movement were inspired by the belief that worship, particularly the Eucharist, deserves a setting of beauty and grandeur. Fine church buildings, ceremony, and music heighten the solemnity of worship; they also express proper adoration of the transcendent God and the immanent Christ. Morgan Dix of Trinity Church, New York City, commented that the Catholic Revival "revived the lost idea of worship."[91] Anglo-Catholics believe that investment of the very best of human resources in the liturgy rewards not only participants but people everywhere.

The nineteenth-century ritualists may have been deliberately provocative. Some intentionally imitated Roman Catholic practices, and a few converted to Rome. But most were committed Anglicans who sincerely believed that the revival of medieval practices would allow Anglicanism to attain its full potential. Opponents believed that enhanced ritual undermined what the Reformation had accomplished; but destiny was not on their side, and all they could do was slow the process. By the 1880s opposition was weakening. Morgan Dix declared that "the work of the past half century cannot be undone. It shall proceed, in larger outcome, and a wider reach; it shall appear to be the preamble of a vaster movement preparing the nation for the Second Coming of the Lord."[92]

Sacred ritual clearly satisfied a hunger in clergy and laity alike. Anglo-Catholics came from all social classes and walks of life. Opponents criticized ritualism on the grounds that it appealed chiefly to women and effeminate men. They contrasted clergy, acolytes and choristers in their "petticoats" with rugged evangelists striding through the mission fields and with decent men of letters preaching in their Geneva gowns. They ignored the fact that virile men in the Roman Empire wore chasubles. The comment about women—intended to be derogatory—ignored statistics showing that the male–female ratio was about the same in ritualist and nonritualist parishes.[93]

Ritualism succeeded mainly because opponents grew old and died. The Royal Commission of 1904–6 noted that scarcely anyone remembered the austere worship of a century earlier.[94] A whole new generation of clergy

91. Dix, M., *The Oxford Movement*, 20.

92. Ibid.

93. The same is probably true today. In any event, such a comment would need to be refocused since women play active roles as acolytes, deaconesses, priests, and bishops.

94. Reed, *Glorious Battle*, 131–33.

and laity had grown up taking the "glory and beauty" of Anglican worship for granted. Moreover, traditional parties had fragmented, the church faced new challenges, and new partisan groupings were emerging.

The Tractarians and early ritualists set out to transform the Church of England. The realization that others did not embrace their vision was both mystifying and abhorrent. Idealism eventually gave way to pragmatism: "More and more [Anglo-Catholics] were at least temporarily abandoning the original goal of remaking the Church of England and fighting simply to be allowed to exist as a party within it."[95] The shift in expectations tapped into latitudinarian sentiments within the church and softened opposition.

Ironically, by the end of the nineteenth century Anglicanism *was* transformed, to a degree that neither the early Anglo-Catholics nor their opponents anticipated. Only a minority of parishes identified themselves as Anglo-Catholic, but most Anglican churches embraced practices that had provoked riots a few decades earlier. As a historian of the Scottish Episcopal Church observed:

> Early in the century, churches were very plain and without chancels. The only vestment worn by the clergy was the black gown. The services were without musical accompaniment. The psalms were always read . . . . Yet, at the close of the century, it was customary to find surpliced choirs and musical services, with the accompaniment of finely-tuned organs, and monthly or weekly celebration of Holy Communion, and in places a daily Eucharist . . . . The Church had recovered its Catholic heritage.[96]

Anglicanism had always sought a *via media* between Protestantism and Roman Catholicism. But now it resembled the latter much more than the former. The church had religious orders and devotion to Mary, even private confession and Requiem Masses. Some Anglicans had aspirations for some kind of union with Rome, or possibly Constantinople.

In 1865 the ECU expressed hope for the reunification of Christianity, particularly rapprochement with Rome.[97] Those aspirations were dashed in 1896 when Pope Leo XIII rejected the validity of Anglican orders and its apostolic succession. Leo's encyclical claimed that the 1549 ordinal failed to specify the sacerdotal role in the sacrifice of the Mass and to

95. Ibid., 68–69.
96. Goldie, *A Short History*, 99.
97. Reed, *Glorious Battle*, 260.

specify the episcopal responsibility for ordaining priests. Subsequent editions of the Prayer Book neither restored the necessary intent of ordination nor repaired the interruption in the succession.[98]

According to the ruling, Anglican clergy would have to accept not only re-ordination but also re-confirmation, whereupon "their Mother, the Church, will welcome them, and will cherish with all her love and care those whom the strength of their generous souls has, amidst many trials and difficulties, led back to her bosom."[99] Needless to say, the encyclical was not received well by Anglicans, who firmly believed their sacraments to be legitimate and the apostolic succession unbroken.

No hope remained for union with Rome in the foreseeable future. In 1922, however, the patriarch of Constantinople affirmed the validity of Anglican orders, offering new prospects for union with Eastern Orthodox churches.[100] Anglicans also began to realize that they had more in common with Eastern than Roman Christianity.

The Anglo-Catholic ministry to the poor can be compared and contrasted with John Wesley's evangelism of the eighteenth century. Both offered alternatives to the monotonous reading of Daily Offices and dry Anglican preaching. But whereas the Wesley brothers offered the emotional stimulus of congregational singing, Anglo-Catholics offered the aesthetic stimulus of sacred ceremony. Ritualism, as Molesworth observed, "appealed to the eyes of men, and produced strong excitement, especially among the working classes, who are more prone to be stirred by ritualistic innovations than by doctrinal novelties."[101]

Concern for social justice spread throughout the Anglican church and beyond. Ministering to poor and disadvantaged people is now a normal part of the church's mission. Outreach may be particularly important for Anglo-Catholics to overcome any elitist tendency or temptation to live in an idealized reconstruction of the Middle Ages. Nostalgia must never divert us from living and expressing our faith in the modern world. Few challenges are as great—or as compelling—as addressing the social and economic opportunities that exist in our neighborhoods and across the globe.

98. Leo XIII, *Apostolicae Curae*, §31.

99. Ibid., §39.

100. DeMille, *The Episcopal Church*, 59.

101. Molesworth, *History*, 355.

8

Anglo-Catholicism Today

THIS FINAL CHAPTER EXAMINES modern Anglo-Catholicism's most important beliefs and practices. As always, the liturgy and the Eucharist take center stage. We shall see that the liturgies of England, Scotland, the United States, and Canada all now offer forms of the Communion Service that affirm—though still to different degrees—an objective understanding of the real presence and the sacrificial intent of the Eucharist. We shall also see the extent to which Anglican understanding of the Eucharist and other matters has converged with Eastern Orthodox and Roman Catholic teachings.

The chapter begins with a brief review of developments in the twentieth century, including liturgical revisions and ecumenical dialogue. The chapter includes some comments on worship in relation to the divine glory and the larger aspects of the redemption. It ends with a discussion of Marian devotion and mariology in modern Anglicanism.

Inter-denominational relations have greatly improved over the last one-hundred years, along with a willingness to share insights on liturgical and doctrinal issues. We shall give expression to this sense of catholicity by citing works by Eastern Orthodox, Roman Catholic, and other writers when their insights pertain to our story.

DEVELOPMENTS OF THE TWENTIETH CENTURY

Anglo-Catholicism was firmly established by the turn of the twentieth century, but its success was reinforced over the next several decades. Anglo-Catholic Congresses were held in London "to extend the knowledge of

Catholic Faith and Practice at home and abroad."[1] Their more practical purpose was to bring together prominent theologians, church leaders, and others to address topics of interest to the growing, and increasingly self-confident, Anglo-Catholic community. The first congress in 1920 focused on the Church, and the third, in 1927, on the Eucharist. Thousands of people attended.

Congresses were held in various parts of the world in 1933 to mark the centennial of John Keble's assize sermon that launched the Tractarian Movement. A High Mass celebrated at the White City arena in London was attended by 50,000 people, "probably . . . the largest Anglican congregation which had ever been assembled for worship."[2] The same year, the group that organized the London congresses merged with the English Church Union. Over time, interest in large congresses waned, however, and the ones held after World War II attracted little attention. By then Anglo-Catholicism was taken for granted, and few people remembered its birth pains.

Ecumenical Dialogue

The very term "catholic" suggests a unified Christianity, and interest steadily grew in exploring ecumenical possibilities. In 1920 the Lambeth Conference re-affirmed the Chicago–Lambeth Quadrilateral as a basis for ecumenical dialogue and also issued an "Appeal To All Christian People" on behalf of "the Holy Catholic Church in full communion with the Church of England."[3] Anglo-Catholics, like their high-church predecessors, were most interested in union with the Roman and Eastern Orthodox Churches.

Despite Rome's rejection of the validity of Anglican orders in 1896, Viscount Halifax, president of the English Church Union, held several meetings in the 1920s with Cardinal Désiré Mercier, archbishop of Mechelen, Belgium.[4] The latter declared that Anglicanism must be "united" with Roman Catholicism, not absorbed into it. Halifax's initiative was not endorsed by the archbishop of Canterbury, and in 1928 Pope Pius IX distanced himself from any suggestion of "unification."

1. Stone, Preface to *Report*, 9.
2. Rowell, *The Vision Glorious*, 244.
3. Anglican Communion, Lambeth Conference, 1920, §9.
4. See the comments in Griswold, "Listening," §II.

The Second Vatican Council (1962–1965) signaled new openness, and serious ecumenical conversation became possible. In 1966 Archbishop Michael Ramsey of Canterbury—an Anglo-Catholic—and Pope Paul VI agreed to form the Anglican/Roman Catholic International Commission (ARCIC).[5] Its Malta Report of 1968 characterized initial meetings as inspired,

> not only by a spirit of charity and frankness, but also by a growing
> sense of urgency, penitence, thankfulness, and purpose; of urgen-
> cy, in response to the pressure of God's will, apprehended as well
> in the processes of history and the aspirations and achievements
> of men in his world as in the life, worship, witness, and service of
> his Church; of penitence, in the conviction of our shared respon-
> sibility for cherishing animosities and prejudices which for four
> hundred years have kept us apart, and prevented our attempting
> to understand or resolve our differences; of thankfulness for the
> measure of unity which through baptism into Christ we already
> share, and for our recent growth towards greater unity and mutu-
> al understanding; of purpose, in our determination that the work
> begun in us by God shall be brought by his grace to fulfillment in
> the restoration of his peace to his Church and his world.[6]

Over a period of years the commission issued a number of "agreed statements," some of which will be cited herein. The participation of se- nior clergy in the ARCIC gave the statements substantial authority. But the statements were not officially endorsed by the denominations. Also, critics questioned whether real agreement had been reached, or whether skillful ambiguity concealed irreconcilable differences. One problem was that some of the issues under consideration had traditionally di- vided high- and low-church Anglicans. For example, attempts to agree on matters like the Eucharist and Marian devotion had to accommodate internal disagreements as well as bridge the Anglican–Roman Catholic divide. In the circumstances, the commission's statements represented significant achievement.

Frank Tracy Griswold, presiding bishop of the Episcopal Church at the turn of the twenty-first century—another Anglo-Catholic—served as co-chair of the ARCIC's last round of deliberations. Its statement on

---

5. Archbishop Ramsey also supported ecumenical outreach to the Methodist Church, but union proved elusive.

6. Clark & Davey, *Anglican/Roman Catholic Dialogue*, 107–15.

mariology and Marian devotion, issued in 2005, was a work of major importance.[7]

The ARCIC was superseded by the International Anglican–Roman Catholic Commission for Unity and Mission (IARCCUM). Its first agreed statement, issued in 2007, spoke of seeking to overcome "the remaining obstacles to full visible unity." It added: "Discerning a common faith challenges our churches to recognise that elements of sanctification and truth exist in each other's ecclesial lives, and to develop those channels and practical expressions of co-operation by which a common life and mission may be generated and sustained."[8]

High churchmen reached out to the Eastern Orthodox churches in the seventeenth century, and interest increased in the nineteenth and twentieth.[9] The Anglican and Eastern Churches Association was established in 1863, largely at the initiative of John Mason Neale. Recognition of the validity of Anglican orders, by the patriarch of Constantinople in 1922, evoked a favorable response. Six years later the Fellowship of St Alban and St Sergius was formed, with the patriarch and the archbishop of Canterbury serving as joint patrons. Its scholarly journal *Sobornost* is still published.[10]

The Anglican–Orthodox Joint Doctrinal Discussions (AOJDD) resulted from conversations in the 1960s between Archbishop Ramsey and Patriarch Athenagoras of Constantinople. The commission held its first meeting in 1973 and subsequently issued a series of statements. One of its members, Archbishop Basil of Brussels, declared optimistically that "the aim of our Dialogueue is that we may eventually be visibly united in one Church."[11] The Dublin Statement of 1984 affirmed: "The unity of Christians with Christ in baptism is a unity of love and mutual respect which transcends all human division, of race, social status and sex (Gal. 3:28). This unity in Christ is God's gift to the world by which

---

7. ARCIC, Seattle Statement.

8. IARCCUM, Agreed Statement, §96.

9. See for example Frere, "The Eastern Orthodox," 97–101.

10. The Russian word *sobornost*, usually translated as "gathering," or "community," literally means "cathedralness"—wonderfully suggestive of people coming together under the soaring roof of a vast house of worship.

11. AOJDD, Dublin Agreed Statement, preface.

men and women may learn to live in unity with one another, accepting one another as Christ has accepted them."[12]

One of the topics addressed in the AOJDD's Moscow Statement of 1976 was the *filioque* clause in the Nicene Creed, which had been a major cause of the East–West schism of 1054. Rome's modification of "We believe in the Holy Spirit . . . who proceeds from the Father" by insertion of "and the son" [Latin: *et filioque*] outraged the Eastern Orthodox churches and prompted charges of heresy. The Moscow Statement and subsequent Dublin Statement recommended that the clause be deleted. Anglican representatives noted in the latter that "the *Filioque* was not to be regarded as a dogma which would have to be accepted by all Christians."[13] The Lambeth Conferences of 1978 and 1988 urged member churches to consider omitting the clause, and some Prayer Books now put "and the son" in parenthesis, allowing users to express their own understanding of the Trinity. But no definitive ruling has yet been made.

The AOJDD was reconstituted as the International Commission for Anglican–Orthodox Theological Dialogue (ICAOTD). The latter's principal report, the Cyprus Statement of 2006: "The Church of the Triune God," focused on the Holy Spirit's role in the Church. One topic of discussion was Christianity's interaction with the cultures in which it operates. Interaction has not infrequently been detrimental, and "The churches may find themselves called to discern whether their own attitudes and actions require repentance and forgiveness."[14] On the other hand, the commission noted that interaction provides opportunities to serve and raise the consciousness of those cultures.

Dialogue with the Roman and Eastern Orthodox Churches continues, but prospects for union have receded. Major differences remain, including the ordination of women to the Anglican priesthood. Notions of union are now overshadowed by concern for the cohesion of the Anglican Communion. In any event, merger negotiations with Rome, Constantinople, or Moscow would confront an awkward asymmetry: Anglicans view themselves as *belonging* to the one, holy, catholic, and apostolic church; Rome and the Eastern Orthodoxy separately view themselves as being the exclusive expression of that church.

12. Ibid., I, 12.
13. Ibid., II, 46.
14. ICAOTD, Cyprus Agreed Statement, III, 16.

236 THE SACRAMENTAL CHURCH

Ecumenical outreach, however, has paid substantial dividends. Interdenominational polemic has greatly diminished, and mutual understanding is greater than at any time since the eleventh century. Anglican—particularly Anglo-Catholic—religious practices resemble those of Rome. But Anglicanism has found more common ground on theological issues with Eastern Orthodoxy. The statements of the AOJDD/ICAOTD provide a wealth of insight into the confluence of belief as well as into Anglicanism's maturing self-understanding. Importantly for our story, they reveal the extent to which theological concepts which, a century ago, might have been regarded as extreme tractarian thinking, now represent mainstream Anglicanism.

The Anglican Communion was a charter member of the World Council of Churches (WCC), founded in 1948, and Anglicans have contributed substantially to the council's work. The council remains an important forum for ecumenical dialogue. Among its most significant reports was the Lima Document of 1982, "Baptism, Eucharist and Ministry," which included a recommended eucharistic liturgy with potential appeal to multiple denominations. Some of its recommendations have been followed in the revision of Anglican liturgies.

The Anglican Communion is in full communion with the Old Catholic Church, allowing for exchange of the Eucharist and mutual recognition of ministerial orders. Similar agreements have been reached by individual Anglican provinces. For example, the Episcopal Church is in full communion with the Evangelical Lutheran Church of America, and the Anglican Church of Canada with the Evangelical Lutheran Church in Canada. Recently the Episcopal Church and the Moravian Church established full communion.[15] The Church of England and the Scottish Episcopal Church are in partial communion with the Evangelical Lutheran Churches of Estonia, Lithuania, Sweden, Norway, Iceland, and Finland.[16]

The Scottish Episcopal Church and the Church of Scotland held exploratory merger talks in the 1980s. A proposed agreement, which included the acceptance of an episcopate by the Church of Scotland, was ratified by that church's General Assembly but was rejected by the presbyteries.

15. The Moravians owe their origins to the Czech reformer Jan Hus.
16. "The Porvoo," 3–34.

Liturgical Research

Liturgical research by the Nonjurors found its way into the Scottish liturgies of the eighteenth century. But research greatly expanded in the nineteenth and twentieth centuries. Of critical importance was discovery in 1848 of the *Apostolic Tradition*, a manual of third-century CE religious practices attributed to the Roman theologian Hippolytus.[17] It included one of the earliest known eucharistic rites. For fifty years the work remained largely unknown, but then the "Hippolytan rite" became a standard resource for liturgical revision.

Of the many scholars who have contributed to liturgical research, three—all members of religious orders—deserve special mention. Odo Casel (1886–1948), a Benedictine monk at the monastery of Maria Laach, Germany, earned two doctorates, published numerous works, and served as editor of fifteen volumes of the *Yearbook for Liturgical Science*. A brief summary of Casel's work can be found in *The Mystery of Christian Worship* (1962).[18] Casel has been lauded as the father of the Liturgical Movement in Roman Catholicism; one of its goals was to encourage greater lay participation in the Mass.

Arthur Gabriel Hebert (1886–1963), a Kelham Father, promoted the Liturgical Movement within Anglicanism and was particularly interested in the social implications of liturgical renewal. He had many contacts with liturgical scholars on the continent of Europe, including high-church Swedish Lutherans. Two of Hebert's most influential works were *Liturgy and Society* (1935) and *The Parish Eucharist* (1936). Hebert is credited with encouraging the adoption of Holy Communion as the principal Sunday worship service. Further encouragement came from Associated Parishes, co-founded by Masseh Hamilton Shepherd, Jr. (1913–90). Shepherd and other members of the organization were instrumental in preparing the 1979 Episcopal *BCP*.[19]

Gregory Dix (1901–52), an Anglican Benedictine monk at the now-defunct Nashdom Abbey, Buckinghamshire, published a critical edition of the *Apostolic Tradition* in 1937. His most influential work was *The Shape of the Liturgy* (1945), which inspired liturgical revisions in both the Anglican and Roman Churches. Although other scholars have

17. Most historians now question that attribution; but the value of the text is not diminished.

18. Casel, *The Mystery*.

19. Shepherd was influenced indirectly by Casel's work.

questioned the historical accuracy of some of his claims, Dix's influence remains substantial. The bishop of Oxford eulogized him as "the most brilliant man in the Church of England." Dix concluded from his studies that the Last Supper was not, as traditionally assumed, a Jewish *Seder*, or Passover meal;[20] it was a *chaburah*, or religious gathering of friends.[21] That conclusion is reflected in the institution narrative in a modern version of the eucharistic prayer which begins: "On the night before he died [Jesus] had supper with his friends."[22]

Dix also concluded that the primitive Church did not have a single eucharistic rite, but the several rites in use shared a recognizable format, or "shape":

- Offertory: the "taking" of bread and wine
- Consecration: eucharistic dialogue ("The Lord be with you . . . .") and institution narrative
- Fraction: the breaking of the bread
- Communion: receipt of the elements by the celebrant and congregation.[23]

The fourfold shape was established before the epistles and gospels were written and before an intellectual understanding of the eucharist emerged.[24] Indeed, the intellectual understanding probably emerged from the worship experience, affirming the principle of *lex orandi lex credendi*. Dix's shape has acquired new relevance because of the proliferation of options in modern liturgies. If cohesion exists at all in Anglican worship, it must be found elsewhere than in wording.

The Lambeth Conferences of 1958 and 1968 provided guidelines, based on Dix's work, for the reform of eucharistic liturgies. Over the next several decades those guidelines were followed in England, Australia, Canada, New Zealand, South Africa, Scotland, and the United States. In 1995 the International Anglican Liturgical Consultation (IALC) followed up with a proposed structure for the Communion Service as a whole:

- The Gathering of God's People
- Proclaiming and Receiving the Word

20. That assumption is supported by the synoptic gospels but not by John.

21. Dix, G., *The Shape*, 50ff.

22. *CW*, 196. Prayer E. Comparable statements appear in Prayers G and H.

23. Dix, G., *The Shape*, 103–40.

24. Ibid., 2–6.

- Prayers of the People
- Gathering at the Lord's Table
- Going Out as God's People.[25]

Dix's fourfold shape would fit into "Gathering at the Lord's Table."

Prayer Books and Alternative Liturgies

The proposed *Book of Common Prayer* of 1927/8 sought to respond to the Catholic Revival. By that time other liturgies were in use in England, with or without ecclesiastical approval. Some Anglo-Catholic clergy used translations of the Sarum Rite, which had appeal because it was "English." Others used the *English Missal* (1912) or *the Anglican Missal* (1921), both based on the Roman rite. A few used the Latin Tridentine Mass. Parliament's rejection of the proposed *BCP* ended hopes of a new authorized version. Instead, the Church of England began publishing alternative liturgies for use alongside the time-honored 1662 Prayer Book.

Although the Scottish Episcopal Church and the Anglican Church of Canada did not face the hazards of parliamentary approval, they too issued alternative liturgies. In every case those alternative liturgies won broad acceptance and largely replaced the older *BCPs*.

Liturgical revisions in the twentieth century were motivated by pressures within the national churches, influence of the Liturgical Movement, the outcome of ecumenical dialogue, the results of liturgical research, and desire for contemporary relevance. The two last factors were sometimes in conflict: replicating ancient liturgies might appeal to scholars but might not necessarily satisfy ordinary people. Most modern liturgies offer optional forms of the Communion Service and other rites. Whereas Cranmer sought uniformity of worship, individual clergy and parishes can now choose from an array of options. Yet controversy still rages over such issues as the use of contemporary language and inclusive pronouns. Some conservatives question whether liturgical revision is needed at all.

The Church of England published the *Alternative Service Book* (*ASB*) in 1980 and *Common Worship* (*CW*) in 2000. The latter comes in three volumes, the first offering multiple versions of the Communion Service and the others for daily prayer and pastoral services. The Scottish Episcopal Church issued a comprehensive eucharistic liturgy,

25. Dowling, "The Eucharist," 461.

the *Scottish Liturgy of 1982*. New forms for Morning and Evening Prayer were issued in 1988, and revised rites for baptism and confirmation in 2006. The Anglican Church of Canada issued the *Book of Alternative Services* (*BAS*) in 1985 to supplement its 1962 *BCP*. One of the *BAS*'s strengths is a lengthy introduction discussing the history of the liturgy and its place in the life of the church. Another is the provision of musical settings of prayers and responses for congregational use.[26]

The Episcopal Church in the United States published an entirely new *Book of Common Prayer* in 1979. During its preparation the Standing Liturgical Commission employed poets as well as liturgists to create pleasing and durable contemporary language.[27] Several experimental liturgies were field-tested. A notable change was the inclusion of psalms in the Communion Service, thus incorporating some of the flavor of Morning Prayer. The 1979 *BCP* won broad acceptance, and no "alternative liturgy" has been published. But a conservative group, independent of the ECUSA, published the *Anglican Service Book* of 1991, a retro-translation into traditional language. Other conservatives have kept the 1928 Prayer Book.

Navigating through bound volumes of the eucharistic liturgies, with their numerous options, has become so difficult that most parishes now print the entire service in the Sunday bulletin. Preparation from electronic resources is relatively easy.[28] Technological advances may soon make all printed media obsolete, though many people would mourn their passing. Bound volumes are still in the pews, but they are used mostly for rites simpler in format than the Communion Service.

The Communion Service has attracted the most attention and consequently has been the most contentious issue in liturgical revisions. Other parts of the liturgy have retained surprising—and reassuring—stability. Changes have largely been restricted to the use of contemporary language, addition of some new collects, and expansion of the lectionary. The Daily Offices have the same serene beauty they had in Cranmer's time. The two collects from the 1549 Prayer Book, quoted in chapter 3, are still intact. Evening Prayer also includes the much-loved intercession attributed to Augustine of Hippo: "Keep watch, dear Lord, with those who work, or watch, or weep this night, and give your angels charge

26. *BAS ACC*, 7–13; 912–24.

27. Northup, "The Episcopal Church," 362.

28. Kraus. "The *Book of Common Prayer*," 542–43.

over those who sleep. Tend the sick, Lord Christ; give rest to the weary, bless the dying, soothe the suffering, pity the afflicted, shield the joyous; and all for your love's sake."[29]

The Mass, or Holy Communion, has replaced Morning Prayer as the centerpiece of Sunday worship, but Choral Evensong is increasingly popular in parishes that have the resources. Easy transportation allows people to travel relatively long distances to attend Mass, Evensong, or other services at churches of their choice; the "parish" has acquired expanded meaning.[30] Broadcasts and webcasts have brought services to people who might not otherwise have opportunities to experience high-church Anglican worship.

The pastoral offices—baptism, confirmation, marriage, ministration to the sick, the burial service, and so forth—continue to play their traditional roles, as do ordinations and the consecration of church buildings. In some provinces nontraditional liturgies are being developed, such as blessings for same-sex unions.

INITIATION, HEALING AND RECONCILIATION

The doctrine of baptismal regeneration came under assault from Puritans and more recently by George Gorham. Nevertheless, it is accepted by most Anglicans and emphasized by Anglo-Catholics. Australian theologian John Gaden offered an eloquent description of regeneration: "I feel new, made whole. My life has meaning. The darkness has been washed away. I have seen the darkness of death, the gloom of despair. I have stood on the brink of the void of nothingness, but I am alive. Nothing can terrify me now . . . . I am Christ's and Christ is mine. Nothing can separate me from his life and love. His Spirit is with us, refreshing, comforting, insistently urging us to live."[31]

In Anglican tradition baptism is viewed not as a private ceremony for the child or adult and immediate circle but as a public one in which the candidate, to quote Article XXVII, is "grafted into" the church. Baptisms are now usually performed during the Sunday morning Mass.

29. *BCP* ECUSA 1979, 124.

30. The parish to which the present author belongs draws members from three states.

31. Quoted in Rowell et al., *Loves Redeeming Work*, 758. Gaden grew up in England, earned his doctorate at General Seminary in New York City, but spent most of his life in Australia.

Congregants may be asked to renew their own baptismal vows or affirm collective responsibility for nurturing the baptized person's spiritual development.[32] Freed from concerns that a child must be baptized as soon as possible after birth, baptisms may be scheduled on auspicious days, such as the feast of Christ's baptism, the Easter Vigil, and Pentecost.

Revisions of the baptismal liturgy have been molded by new understanding of the theology of initiation. Christian initiation traditionally was seen as a series of rites of passage: baptism, confirmation, and first communion; marriage and ordination to the ministry were viewed as further rites of passage. Infant baptism was regarded as the norm, and first communion was delayed until children had received proper instruction. Adult baptism was treated as an exception, necessitating a separate sacramental rite. Confirmation was neglected in the post-Reformation period but regained popularity in the nineteenth century[33] and once again became a gateway to first Communion.

Much has changed over the last several decades. The rites for infant and adult baptism have converged. Moreover, baptism at any age is increasingly seen as providing full initiation into the church, with all associated rights and privileges. To quote the IARCCUM: "We consider baptism a sacrament of initiation instituted by Jesus Christ, by which we are incorporated into the life of his body, the Church."[34] In its Toronto Statement of 1991 the IALC declared: "Baptism is complete sacramental initiation and leads to participation in the eucharist. Confirmation and other rites of affirmation have a continuing pastoral role in the renewal of faith among the baptized but are in no way to be seen as completion of baptism or as necessary for admission to communion."[35]

Baptism has also recovered much of its pre-Reformation ritual and symbolism. In its Boston Statement of 1985 the IALC encouraged the "copious use of water," rather than mere sprinkling.[36] The baptismal rite of the Episcopal Church invokes the Holy Spirit to effect the candidate's spiritual regeneration: *"Then the Bishop or Priest places a hand on the person's head, marking on the forehead the sign of the cross [using chrism*

---

32. For example *BCP* ECUSA 1979, 303–5.

33. Holeton, *Initiation*, 305.

34. IARCCUM, Agreed Statement, §33.

35. Holeton, *Initiation*, 303.

36. Ibid., 304.

if desired] and saying to each one: 'N., you are sealed by the Holy Spirit in Baptism and marked as Christ's own for ever.'"[37]

Invocation of the Spirit and use of chrism suggest a return to the ancient practice in which baptism and confirmation formed a single sacrament. The 2006 Scottish baptismal rite includes the "Giving of light": "*A lighted candle is given as the president says*: 'N., the light of Christ scatter the darkness from your heart and mind.'" To which the people respond: "Christ go before you to guide your steps. / Christ be within you to kindle your vision. / Christ shine from you to give joy to the world."[38] The presentation of a lighted candle has been adopted by other provinces. In some cases the candle is lit from the paschal candle, "drawing attention to the paschal dimension of baptism."[39]

Sacramental healing has been practiced in the Eastern Orthodox Churches since early times. The sacrament of holy unction, or *euchelaion*, is solemnized on the Wednesday of Holy Week but can be administered in abbreviated form whenever a person is seriously ill; it is not reserved for the dying. Based on the premise that body and soul are inseparable, the purpose of holy unction is to restore health as much as to prepare sick persons for the journey to come.[40]

The revival of a healing ministry in the West, after more than a thousand years of neglect, was one of the notable achievements of modern Christianity. Faith healing was practiced by charismatic groups as early as the eighteenth century; but the revival of sacramental healing is less than a century old, and the Anglican Church played a leading role.[41] In 1924 a committee of the Lambeth Conference declared that healing was "part of the redemptive work of our Lord."[42] A later study in 1953 recommended an expansion of the healing ministry and "increasing understanding and cooperation between [clergy] and the medical profession."[43]

Sacramental healing services are now offered on a regular basis, often in a eucharistic setting. The prayer accompanying the laying-on of hands in the 1979 Episcopal *BCP* is as follows: "[N], I lay my hands

37. BCP ECUSA 1979, 308.

38. *Holy Baptism* 2006, 7.

39. Meyers, "Rites of Initiation," 497.

40. Ware, *The Orthodox Church*, 296–97.

41. Nash, J. F., "Esoteric Healing."

42. *The Ministry of Healing.*

43. *The Church's Ministry.*

upon you in the Name of the Father, and of the Son, and of the Holy Spirit, beseeching our Lord Jesus Christ to sustain you with his presence, to drive away all sickness of body and spirit, and to give you that victory of life and peace which will enable you to serve him both now and evermore." *Common Worship* provides the following prayer for anointing the sick person with oil: "*N*, I anoint you in the name of God who gives you life. Receive Christ's forgiveness, his healing and his love. May the Father of our Lord Jesus Christ grant you the riches of his grace, his wholeness and his peace."[44] Holy Communion is normally administered after the anointing.

Anglicans seek forgiveness for sin in the Daily Offices, the Communion Service, and private confession. Confession and absolution are healing rites. Eastern theologians point out that the Greek verb *sozo*, usually translated in the West as "to save" and forming the root of *soteriology*, the theory of salvation, originally meant "to heal."[45] In its Cyprus Agreement the ICAOTD commented on the Holy Spirit's role in forgiveness and healing: "This healing of humanity implies the healing of all creation. We cannot understand the being, structure, mission, worship, and ministry of the Church apart from God's trinitarian existence."[46] Moreover, the healing of human weakness goes beyond forgiveness for past misdeeds; it creates unlimited possibilities for the future: "Forgiveness is about opening humanity to the future and to a new quality of human relationships . . . It is about healing the past and realising the new humanity in Christ."[47]

The Cyprus Statement added that "[T]he ultimate purpose of the Church . . . is nothing less than to bring human beings into communion with the life the Holy Trinity itself. That is what the Greek fathers and more modern Orthodox theologians called *theosis*."[48] The concept of theosis, or deification, will be discussed in more detail later.

THE EUCHARIST

Doctrinal understanding of the Eucharist has been discussed in earlier chapters from both a theological and a liturgical standpoint. The pres-

44. *CW: Pastoral Services*, 21.

45. *Sozo* appears in several scriptural passages, for example Mark 5:23. "Sacred," "save," "salve," and "salvation" are all derived from the same Indo-European root.

46. ICAOTD, Cyprus Agreed Statement, I, 21.

47. Ibid., II, 29.

48. Italicization in original.

ent discussion focuses on the liturgical developments of the last one-hundred years and on statements of the ecumenical commissions. These semi-authoritative statements add a new dimension, not only placing Anglican beliefs and attitudes in a larger context but also documenting current thinking by influential members of the Anglican Communion. As always, attention to nuances of wording in the liturgy is important in discerning theological understanding.

The following examples will show the extent to which Anglican understanding of the Eucharist has evolved during the period and the degree of convergence among Anglican, Eastern Orthodox, and even Roman Catholic positions. The Scottish and American liturgies, which reflect the work of the Caroline Divines and Nonjurors as well as Orthodox influence, offer eucharistic prayers that affirm the objective real presence and sacrificial intent of the Eucharist. The Church of England has moved in the same direction, though not to the same degree. The Anglican Church of Canada tends to offer both "Scottish/American-" and "English-style" liturgies.

The Real Presence

An intellectual understanding of the Eucharist is not essential to the religious experience. But we are thinking beings, and the theology of the Eucharist is important from both a theoretical and a practical standpoint; what we believe influences how we behave. Most Anglo-Catholics believe that Christ is sacramentally present on the altar and consequently are moved to express adoration during the Mass. But they are not unanimous on whether the real presence is localized in the eucharistic elements or pervades the Communion Service in a more general way. Belief in a localized, objective real presence justifies reservation of the Sacrament.

The Eucharist is about *transformation*—possibly of the elements, but certainly of communicants and the church. Receptionism discounts the possibility of transformation of the elements. Transubstantiation distracts attention from the people's transformation and attempts to reduce transformation of the elements to a chemical formula. The objectivism explored by the Caroline Divines need not imply transubstantiation; the body and blood of Christ may be related to the bread and wine in some other way.[49] Or if, as Lancelot Andrewes believed, transformation occurs,

49. For example, Luther affirmed a "sacramental union" in which Christ is present "in, with, and under" the bread and wine.

it may take some form other than the substitution of one "substance," in the Aristotelian sense, for another.

An objectivist understanding does not resolve the issue of whether the real presence is effected at a specific instant in the Communion Service or takes effect more gradually. Anglicans generally follow Eastern Orthodox tradition in favoring gradualism. The AOJDD declared in its 1976 Moscow Report: "The consecration of the bread and wine results from the whole sacramental liturgy."[50] Even the ARCIC conceded that "Christ is present and active . . . in the entire eucharistic celebration."[51]

As noted earlier, the inclusion of an *epiclesis* in the eucharistic prayer, and its placement and wording, provide important clues to eucharistic understanding. The epiclesis asks God the Father to send the Holy Spirit to bless and sanctify the elements—and, in "strong forms," to give effect to the real presence. By examining the epiclesis and other components of the eucharistic prayer, chapter 5 traced the high-church understanding of the eucharist through the Scottish liturgies to the American 1789 *BCP*. An epiclesis was reintroduced into the Church of England liturgy in the Proposed Book of 1927/8, for the first time since 1549. It was retained in the more recent alternative liturgies, including most options in Rite A of the *Alternative Service Book* and Order One of *Common Worship*.

Table 8.1 compares the epicleses in *The Anglican Missal*;[52] *ASB* Rite A, Prayer 1;[53] and *CW* Order One, Prayer B.[54] The first two ask that the elements "may be *unto us*, the Body and Blood" of Christ (emphasis added), possibly suggesting a receptionist understanding. But their placement before the institution narrative—where the epiclesis was in the 1637 "Laud's Book"—could imply belief that the bread and wine are transformed upon utterance of the words of institution. Roman Catholicism affirms that belief but did not include an explicit epiclesis in the Mass until after the Second Vatican Council.

50. AOJDD, Moscow Agreed Statement, IV, §29.

51. ARCIC, Windsor Statement, §7.

52. *Anglican Missal*, C27.

53. *ASB*, "Holy Communion: Rite A, First Eucharistic Prayer."

54. *CW*, "Liturgy of the Sacrament: Order One, Prayer B," 189–90.

TABLE 8.1. EPICLESES IN ENGLISH EUCHARISTIC LITURGIES

The Anglican Missal (1921)	*Alternative Service Book*, Rite A, Prayer 1 (1980)	*Common Worship*, Order 1, Prayer B (2000)
Hear us, O merciful Father, we beseech thee: and with thy Holy Spirit and Word vouchsafe to bless and sanctify these thy gifts, and creatures of Bread and Wine, that they may be unto us, the Body and Blood thy most dearly beloved Son Jesus Christ.	Accept our praises, heavenly Father, through your Son our Saviour Jesus Christ; and as we follow his example and obey his command, grant that by the power of your Holy Spirit these gifts of bread and wine may be to us his body and blood.	(Before the words of institution) Lord, you are holy indeed, the source of all holiness; grant that by the power of your Holy Spirit, and according to your holy will, these gifts of bread and wine may be to us the body and blood of our Lord Jesus Christ. (After the words of institution) Send the Holy Spirit on your people and gather into one in your kingdom all who share this one bread and one cup, so that we, in the company of [N and] all the saints, may praise and glorify you for ever, through Jesus Christ our Lord.

Prayer B of *CW* Order One contains a double, or split, epiclesis, a rare feature shared by the eucharistic liturgy proposed by the World Council of Churches. The "consecratory epiclesis," placed before the institution narrative, asks that the Holy Spirit give effect to the real presence. That placement could be interpreted as adding weight to the words of institution; on the other hand, "may be *unto us*, the Body and Blood" of Christ (emphasis added) might imply receptionism. The "communion epiclesis," that follows the words of institution, asks the Father to "Send the Holy Spirit on your people and gather into one in your kingdom [and to] praise and glorify" God. None of the epicleses in Order One asks that the elements may *be* or *become* the body and blood of Christ.

Order Two of *Common Worship* follows the tradition of the 1552 and 1662 Prayer Books and omits the epiclesis.

Table 8.2 shows three epicleses in the Scottish/American tradition.[55] All five eucharistic prayers in the current 1982 Scottish Liturgy ask that the elements "may be the Body and Blood" of Christ. Eucharistic Prayer B in the 1979 American *BCP* asks the Father "to send your Holy Spirit upon these gifts that they may be the Sacrament of the Body of Christ and his Blood of the new Covenant." The Canadian *BAS* of 1985 contains optional forms modeled on both the English and the Scottish models. Most affirmative of an objective understanding is Prayer 6, which asks that the "Holy Spirit may descend upon us and these gifts, sanctifying them and showing them to be . . . the bread of life and the cup of salvation, the body and blood of your son Jesus Christ."

TABLE 8.2. EPICLESES IN SCOTTISH/AMERICAN EUCHARISTIC LITURGIES

Scottish Episcopal Church *Scottish Liturgy* (1982), Prayers 1–4	Episcopal Church (U.S.) *Book of Common Prayer* (1979), Rite II, Prayer B	Anglican Church of Canada *Book of Alternative Services* (1985), Prayer 6
Hear us, most merciful Father, and send your Holy Spirit upon us and upon this bread and this wine, that, overshadowed by his life-giving power, they may be the Body and Blood of your Son, and we may be kindled with the fire of your love and renewed for the service of your Kingdom.	We pray you, gracious God, to send your Holy Spirit upon these gifts that they may be the Sacrament of the Body of Christ and his Blood of the new Covenant. Unite us to your Son in his sacrifice, that we may be acceptable through him, being sanctified by the Holy Spirit.	Father, we pray that in your goodness and mercy your Holy Spirit may descend upon us, and upon these gifts, sanctifying them and showing them to be holy gifts for your holy people, the bread of life and the cup of salvation, the body and blood of your Son Jesus Christ.

The Church of England now accommodates, within the pluralism of its optional forms of the Communion Service, a stronger affirmation of the objective real presence than existed in the 1662 Prayer Book. A distinction remains, however, between the English and the Scottish/

55. *Scottish Liturgy*, §18. BCP ECUSA 1979, 369. BAS ACC, "Holy Eucharist," 209.

American forms. The latter continue to offers greater support for ortho- dox high-church and Anglo-Catholic eucharistic understanding.

Eastern Orthodox liturgies have always contained strong epicleses. The ones in the liturgies of St John Chrysostom and St Basil specifically ask that the Holy Spirit give objective effect to the real presence. For example, the former asks: "Send down Thy Holy Spirit upon us and upon these gifts here offered. And make this bread the precious Body of Thy Christ." In both cases the epiclesis follows the words of institution, consistent with the Eastern belief in gradualism. In its Moscow Report the AOJDD emphasized that the epiclesis is "the culminating and decisive moment in the consecration."[56] Interestingly, the liturgy of St Basil asks the Spirit to "reveal this bread to be the precious Body of our Lord and God and Savior Jesus Christ, and that which is in this chalice to be the precious Blood of our Lord and God and Savior Jesus Christ." "Reveal" might suggest that transformation had already been effected by the words of institution.

The prayer of administration, said during distribution of Holy Communion, is another indicator of eucharistic understanding. *Common Worship* offers the terse: "The body of Christ. The blood of Christ."[57] The *Scottish Liturgy of 1982* offers: "The Body of Christ given for you. The Blood of Christ shed for you." The 1979 American Prayer Book provides three options, including the simple but effective: "The Body of Christ, the bread of heaven. The Blood of Christ, the cup of salvation." The Canadian 1985 *BAS* offers both the 1982 Scottish and the 1979 Episcopal forms.

Communicants are rarely expected to respond to the prayer of administration, except possibly with "Amen." But the Sarum Rite required them to recite a lengthy prayer (Table 8.3). *The Anglican Missal* requires a shorter prayer, but one that could still be time-consuming in the modern environment of numerous communicants.

56. AOJDD, Moscow Agreed Statement, IV, §29.
57. *CW*, "Words at the Giving": Prayer 2, 295.

TABLE 8.3. PRAYERS RECITED BY COMMUNICANTS

Sarum Rite	The Anglican Missal
Hail evermore most holy Flesh of Christ: Sweeter far to me than all else beside. May the Body of our Lord Jesus Christ be to me a sinner, the way and the life. In the Name of the Father, and of the Son, and of the Holy Ghost. Hail evermore celestial drink, Sweeter far to me than all else beside. May the Body and Blood of our Lord Jesus Christ be profitable to me a sinner, for an eternal remedy unto everlasting life. Amen. In the Name of the Father, etc. I give Thee thanks, O Lord, Holy Father, Almighty, Eternal God; Who hast refreshed me by the most sacred Body and Blood of Thy Son our Lord Jesus Christ, and I pray that the sacrament of our salvation, which I, an unworthy sinner, have received, may not turn to my judgment and condemnation, according to my deserts, but may be available to the profit of my body and soul, unto everlasting life. Amen.[a]	Grant O Lord, that what our mouths have taken, our minds may receive unalloyed; and what comes to us in time, may be our healing in the endless years. May this Flesh which I have taken, and thy Blood which I have drunk, O Lord cleave unto my heart; and grant that no spot of sin abide in me, whose meat has been thy true and holy sacraments; Who livest and reignest for ever and ever. Amen.[b]

a. *Ordinary and Canon*, 19–20.
b. *Anglican Missal*, C52

Belief in the objective real presence justifies reservation of the sacrament for administration to the sick. The Church of England made provision for reservation in its 1927/8 Proposed Book, and most other liturgies also do so.[58] The Episcopal Church offers a prayer commissioning the eucharistic minister who will administer the sacrament.[59] In the

58. Dowling, "The Eucharist," 472.
59. *BAS* ACC, "Distribution of Holy Communion," 325.

Communion of the Sick, the *Anglican Service Book* follows Roman practice by referring to the host as "the Blessed Sacrament."[60]

The ARCIC proclaimed that it had "reached substantial agreement on the doctrine of the eucharist."[61] It affirmed: "Communion with Christ in the eucharist presupposes his true presence, effectually signified by the bread and wine which, in this mystery, become his body and blood."[62] Given the long history of contentious disagreement over transubstantiation, that statement was highly significant. More generally Anglicans have leaned toward the mystical eucharistic understanding of Eastern Orthodoxy. The Eastern Churches never embraced transubstantiation, and the 1976 Moscow Report of the AOJDD declared: "The deepest understanding of the hallowing of the elements rejects any theory of consecration by formula."

Individual Roman Catholics have shared their own reservations about transubstantiation. In the 1960s the Belgian theologian Edward Schillebeeckx proposed two new concepts: *transsignification*, the significance of the consecrated elements in the minds of participants, and *transfinalization*: the purpose for which the elements are used.[63] He presented the proposal to Vatican II, but Pope Paul VI rejected it.[64] The Swiss theologian Hans Urs von Balthasar (1905–88) did not challenge his Church's teaching but declared that the mystery of the Eucharist transcends dogma. In a statement that Richard Hooker would have endorsed he said:

> It is evident that the "mystery" cannot be "explained," neither the "transubstantiation" of bread and wine into Flesh and Blood nor the other far more important happening which can analogously be called "transubstantiation" of Christ's Flesh and Blood into the organism of the Church (and of Christians as her members). What is important is not that we know *how* God does it, but that we know *that* and *why* he does it. It is on this that the stress must fall in the formation of liturgy.[65]

60. *ASB*, "Order for the Communion of the Sick," 304.

61. ARCIC, Windsor Statement, §12.

62. Ibid., §6.

63. See for example Macquarrie, *A Guide*, 12.

64. Paul VI, *Mysterium Fidei*, §11.

65. Balthasar, *The Glory*, I, 574. Parenthesis and italicization in original.

Jesuit priest and paleontologist Pierre Teilhard de Chardin (1881–1955) viewed celebration of the eucharist as an activity of global or cosmic dimensions. When the priest utters the words of institution, he said, they "extend beyond the morsel of bread over which they are said: they give birth to the mystical body of Christ. The effect of the priestly act extends beyond the consecrated host to the cosmos itself."[66]

Eucharistic Sacrifice

Most forms of the eucharistic prayer contain some reference to sacrifice. Whether the Mass should be viewed as a sacrifice or oblation, and precisely what is offered to God, have long been subjects of disagreement among Anglicans and between Anglicans and members of other sacramental traditions. Much depends on whether *anamnesis* means "remembering an event" or "reliving an experience." Viewpoints differ over whether the Eucharist simply recalls Christ's sacrifice on the cross or in some way participates in that sacrifice.

Roman practice has always been to offer up the eucharistic elements, before and after consecration, in a ritual act of sacrifice. The "offertory" originally had that meaning, whether or not it was accompanied by a plate collection. For example, the Sarum Rite asked: "Wherefore, O most merciful Father, we most humbly pray and beseech Thee, through Jesus Christ Thy Son our Lord, that Thou wouldest vouchsafe to accept and bless these Gifts, these Presents, these holy unspotted Sacrifices."[67] Later in the Mass, the consecrated elements are offered up expressly to link the Eucharist with Christ's sacrifice on Calvary.

Cranmer and fellow reformists rejected the notion of sacrifice, even of self-oblation. However, the latter, prefaced by cautionary language, found its way back into the English liturgy in the twentieth century. Prayers A and C of *Common Worship*, Order One, acknowledge that "we are unworthy, through our manifold sins, to offer you any sacrifice," but they ask that God "will accept this the duty and service that we owe." They also refer to "our sacrifice of thanks and praise."

Prayer B cautiously includes the elements: "As we offer you this our sacrifice of praise and thanksgiving, we *bring before you* this bread and this cup and we thank you for counting us worthy to stand in your

---

66. Quoted in Chardin, *Hymn*, 13.

67. *Ordinary and Canon*, 11.

presence and serve you" (emphasis added). Three of the five eucharistic prayers in the *Scottish Liturgy of 1982* unambiguously link offering of the elements to a self-oblation; the relevant prayer is incorporated into the institution narrative: "Made one with him, we offer you these gifts and with them ourselves, a single, holy, living sacrifice." Three of the four eucharistic prayers in the 1979 Episcopal Prayer Book, Rite Two, contain similar language. For example, Prayer B states, immediately before the epiclesis: "[W]e offer our sacrifice of praise and thanksgiving to you, O Lord of all, presenting to you . . . this bread and this wine."[68]

The Scottish liturgies relate self-oblation to the Last Supper and Christ's sacrifice on Calvary. Commenting on the SEC's *Experimental Liturgy of 1977*, the so-called "Orange Book," one writer noted: "The self-offering of Jesus made possible the self-offering of the church, when united with him in his dedication to God's purpose for creation. Moreover, the self-offering of Christ and the church were to be seen as *one* holy and living sacrifice, not two."[69] The preamble to the Communion Service in the Canadian *BAS* concedes that "Cranmer's liturgy failed to give adequate expression to the unity between the Church's offering and the offering of Christ expressed in the ancient liturgies and in the patristic theology of the 'whole Church.'"[70]

Eucharistic Prayer D in the 1979 Episcopal *BCP* and Prayer 6 in the Canadian *BAS*—both based on the liturgy of Basil of Caesarea—boldly affirm: "[W]e now celebrate the memorial of our redemption . . . offering to you from the gifts you have given us this bread and this cup."[71]

In the *Anglican Service Book* the priest says: "Pray, brethren, that this sacrifice and yours may be acceptable to God the Father Almighty." To which the people respond: "May the Lord receive this sacrifice at thy hands, to the praise and glory of his Name, both to our benefit and that of all his holy Church."[72] The same book explains: "The Mass is 'our sacrifice of praise and thanksgiving.' By acknowledging the Mass as sacrifice, we remember that Jesus freely gave himself in love that we might have true life in him. The sacrifice of the Mass 'participates' in the offering of Jesus at the Last Supper, in the offering of Jesus on the Cross, and in the

---

68. *BCP* ECUSA 1979, 369.

69. Tellini, "The Scottish Episcopal Church," 420. Emphasis in original.

70. *BAS* ACC, 179.

71. Ibid., 209.

72. *Anglican Service Book*, 259.

continual offering of Jesus to his Father in Heaven. It also reminds us that we, too, are to live sacrificially."[73]

In an address to the First Anglo-Catholic Congress in 1920, C. J. Smith, dean of Pembroke College, Cambridge, traced belief in the eucharistic sacrifice through the patristic writings. He insisted that "the sacrifice is not only connected with the death of Christ, but also with His resurrection and ascension . . . . [I]t is so because the Christ who is offered in it is the Christ who not only died in sacrifice, but also who rose and ascended and presents His sacrifice in heaven."[74] "The reality of the sacrifice," Smith continued, "is a direct consequence of the reality of sacramental Presence of our Lord. The oblations of bread and wine which we offer at the offertory, become, by virtue of their consecration, an oblation infinitely greater; become—we believe, not knowing how— the Body and Blood of Christ Himself."[75]

According to the sacrificial understanding of the Eucharist, the priest acts as agent for Christ, the high priest. Christ's priestly role was mentioned several times in the Epistle to the Hebrews; for example: "we have a great high priest, that is passed into the heavens, Jesus the Son of God" (Heb 4:14). Anglo-Catholics tend to agree. Michael Ramsey, writing before he became archbishop of Canterbury, explained: "If [the Eucharist] be called a worship of sacrificial offering, it is so because it is through Christ who is high-priest."[76] Prayer C, Rite Two, in the Episcopal Prayer Book asks: "Accept these prayers and praises, Father, through Jesus Christ our great High Priest."[77] "The highest acts of every religion," Casel asserted, "are prayer and sacrifice."[78] "[W]ithout this mystery," he continued, "the Church would be an offerer without sacrifice, an altar with no gift, a bride cut off from her bridegroom, unconsecrated, knowing no way to the Father."[79]

The ARCIC and IARCCUM understandably trod carefully in addressing sacrificial intent. The former acknowledged that "Christ's redeeming death and resurrection took place once and for all in history." Yet, it

73. Ibid., 236.

74. Smith, "The Sacrifice of the Altar," 128.

75. Ibid., 135.

76. Ramsey, The Glory of God, 94.

77. BCP ECUSA 1979, 372.

78. Casel, The Mystery, 71.

79. Ibid., 21.

continued, "God has given the eucharist to his church as a means through which the atoning work of Christ on the cross is proclaimed and made effective.... Christ instituted the eucharist as a memorial (anamnesis) of the totality of God's reconciling action in him."[80] The IARCCUM reaffirmed: "By memorial, Anglicans and Catholics both intend not merely a calling to mind of what God has done in the past but an effectual sacramental proclamation, which through the action of the Holy Spirit makes present what has been accomplished and promised once-and-for-all."[81]

An important point raised by Dean Smith's discussion—with which Casel no doubt would have agreed—is that in ancient times the focus of attention was less on the slaying of the victim than on the community's collective sacrificial act. Similarly, the Christian community—the congregation and the church—can participate in Christ's sacrifice without any suggestion that he is slain each time the Eucharist is offered. As the IARCCUM noted: "In the eucharistic celebration Christ's one sacrifice is made present for us."[82] If this point is grasped, much of the traditional disagreement between Anglicans and Roman Catholics becomes moot. We shall return to this issue shortly.

Mainstream Anglican understanding of the Eucharist now includes some notion of sacrifice. The very worthy concept of self-oblation is almost universal, while Anglo-Catholics and many others believe that offering the eucharistic elements validly links the Eucharist with Christ's sacrifice at the Last Supper and on the cross.

ADORATION AND THE GLORY OF GOD

Eucharistic Adoration

In an essay marking the centenary of the Tractarian Movement, American philosopher Frank Gavin declared that "*adoration* is the supreme gift of the Anglo-Catholic Movement to Anglo-American Christianity."[83] Adoration, he asserted, is only meaningful in the context of belief in a transcendent God: a God whose essence extends beyond our own projected ideals. Finite beings are moved to adore a beneficent, transcendent God. Correspondingly, belief in the real presence of the

---

80. ARCIC, Windsor Statement, §5. Parenthesis in original.

81. IARCCUM, Agreed Statement, §40.

82. Ibid.

83. Urban, "The Need," §3. Emphasis in original.

body and blood of Christ in the Eucharist—an immanent manifestation of that beneficence—creates an impulse to beautify the setting in which it occurs and the ritual that surrounds its celebration.

The Catholic Revival succeeded in restoring—and possibly exaggerating—the beauty of pre-Reformation ceremony in the Communion Service. The "holy table" is back in the chancel, though not always against the east wall of the church. Following the Liturgical Movement and Vatican II, the Mass in both Roman Catholic and Anglican churches is often celebrated facing the people. Altar draperies and clerical vestments in the liturgical colors, symbolic gestures, burning of candles, and ringing of bells are now standard practices. Processions of vested acolytes and choristers, chanting of responses, and use of incense are common in the Sung Eucharist, or High Mass.

Elevation of the consecrated host and chalice is almost universal in Anglo-Catholic churches—and common in other Anglican churches—whether or not the real presence is believed to be localized or to manifest at that instant. The rubrics of the Sarum Rite prescribed the priest's gestures in minute detail; for example, the words of institution "*ought to be spoken with one breath, and under one utterance, without any pause. After these words, let the priest bow to the host, and afterwards raise it above his forehead, that it may be seen by the people, and reverently let him replace it before the chalice in the manner of a cross made by the same. And then let him uncover the chalice and hold it between his hands, not disuniting his thumb from his forefinger, save only while he blesses.*" We are reminded of John Purchas's *Directorium Anglicanum* of 1868. Detailed choreography is more often left to individual priests. Genuflection before and/or after the elevation is common but not universal in the Anglo-Catholic Mass.

Anglicans normally kneel to receive the Sacrament, and, despite the Black Rubric's assurance, the practice implies adoration. The rubrics for Order One of *Common Worship* state that "local custom may be followed and developed in relation to posture." Yet it urges: "The people should stand for the reading of the Gospel, for the Creed, for the Peace and for the Dismissal. Any changes in posture during the Eucharistic Prayer should not detract from the essential unity of that prayer. It is appropriate that, on occasions, the congregation should kneel for prayers of penitence." Order Two suggests: "It is appropriate for the people to kneel for the opening prayer and Commandments, the Prayers of

Intercession, the Confession, Absolution and Comfortable Words, the Prayer of Consecration and prayers after the distribution."[84] Anglo-Catholics genuflect or bow before the high altar upon entering or leaving the church, signaling that Christ has been present on the altar, even if the Sacrament is not reserved in the tabernacle.

Adoration of the reserved Sacrament remains controversial, even among Anglo-Catholics. A significant number of parishes, however, offer Benediction of the Blessed Sacrament, modeled on the Roman rite. Perpetual adoration, in which teams of volunteers keep watch for hours or days, is another practice adopted from Roman Catholicism. It can result in powerful experiences; de Chardin described how the host in the monstrance seemed to expand to encompass the whole of creation:

> [T]he flow of whiteness enveloped me, passed beyond me, over-ran everything. At the same time everything, though drowned in this whiteness, preserved its own proper shape, its own autonomous movement; for the whiteness did not efface the features or change the nature of anything, but penetrated objects at the core of their being, at a level more profound even than their own life. It was as though a milky brightness were illuminating the universe from within, and everything were fashioned of the same kind of translucent flesh.[85]

As the vision faded, Chardin remarked, "I heard then the *Ave verum* being sung."

In some forms of the eucharistic prayer the *Sanctus* is prefaced by a reference to the heavenly hosts. For example: "[W]e offer you our praise, with angels and archangels and the whole company of heaven, singing the hymn of your unending glory."[86] The reference may be more than just devotional hyperbole. The twelfth-century mystic Hildegard of Bingen reported a vision of angels during the Mass:

> [W]hen a priest clad in sacred vestments approached the altar to celebrate the divine mysteries, I saw that a great calm light was brought to it from Heaven by angels and shone around the altar until the sacred rite was ended and the priest had withdrawn from it. And when the Gospel of peace had been recited and

84. *CW*, Introductory Notes.

85. Chardin, *Hymn*, 45. De Chardin attributes the experience to "a friend," but it is generally assumed to have been his own experience.

86. *Scottish Liturgy*, §18. See also Prayers A and B of the *BCP* ECUSA 1979.

the offering to be consecrated had been placed on the altar, and the priest sang the praise of Almighty God, "Holy, Holy, Holy, Lord God of Hosts," which began the mystery of the sacred rites, Heaven was suddenly opened and a fiery and inestimable brilliance descended over that offering and irradiated it completely with light, as the sun illumines anything its rays shine through. And, thus illuminating it, the brilliance bore it on high into the sacred places of Heaven and then replaced it on the altar, as a person draws in a breath and lets it out again; and thus the offering was made true flesh and true blood, although in human sight it looked like bread and wine.[87]

The Pseudo-Dionysius, sixth-century father of Christian angelology, described the divine beauty streaming down from the godhead through a hierarchy of angels.[88] In our own time, Geoffrey Hodson (1886–1983) and other clairvoyantly gifted people have reported visions of angelic participation in the Mass. Hodson, a priest in the Liberal Catholic Church, observed "the presence and attention" of "music angels" during singing of the *Agnus Dei*, commenting: "They are also chanting." The work of the those angels, he explained, "is almost entirely devotional, having been associated with such music in ancient days."[89]

Aesthetics and Drama

Anglo-Catholics emphasize the aesthetic dimension of worship, regarding it not only as a way to enhance participants' experience but as a proper response to the glory of God. Beauty, Balthasar argued, "dances as an uncontained splendor around the double connection of the true and the good and their inseparable relation to one another."[90] The beauty invested in sacred ritual and in church architecture and decoration provides a glimpse, however dim, of the beauty of the heavenly realms. When the emissaries of Vladimir I of Russia returned from Constantinople, after attending the Great Liturgy (High Mass) in the basilica of Hagia Sophia, they reported: "We knew not whether we were in heaven or on earth."[91]

87. Hildegard, *Scivias*, 237.

88. Pseudo-Dionysius, *The Celestial Hierarchy*, ch. 3, 153–55.

89. Hodson, *Clairvoyant Investigations*, 90–92. The Liberal Catholic Church claims the apostolic succession through the Old Catholic Church.

90. Balthasar, *The Glory of the Lord*, i, 18.

91. Ware, *The Orthodox Church*, 264.

The rite for dedication of a church in the Episcopal Church *BCP*, thanks God "for the gifts of your people, and for the work of many hands, which have beautified this place and furnished it for the celebration of your holy mysteries."[92] Celebration of the Mass, in which the very Son of God is present, would seem to merit investment of the very best of human resources.

Ceremony is intended to stand out from the affairs of everyday life, evoking eager anticipation, demanding rapt attention, and leaving rich memories. Through appeal to the senses it brings the whole person into active participation. Sacred ritual also evokes a sense of divine drama. The Liturgy of the Sacrament captures the drama of Christ's "blessed passion and death, his glorious resurrection and ascension [and] the coming of his Kingdom."[93] The Liturgy of the Word captures the drama of his birth, baptism, ministry, transfiguration, death, and resurrection, and the continuing drama of his ascension and the descent of the Holy Spirit. The liturgy of Holy Week and other major festivals, the marriage and burial services, and the rite for consecration of bishops explore a particularly broad range of human emotions.

The musical setting of the monastic daily liturgy, in Casel's words, "proceeds from the very heart of worship . . . . If every kind of music rises on the one hand from deep emotion, away from the triviality of daily life . . . , on the other hand it possesses a deep vision of harmony and beauty in rhythm and number. The plenitude of God's power and the up-raising of the mind bring us into his freedom and order and lead to music, and music in pure, classical form."[94]

Settings of the psalms and related antiphons set the mood of the service and the liturgical season: "The choral music . . . which is sung to the psalm," Casel continued, "changes according to the musical tone of antiphon. One can see how simple and yet great are the means which the Church uses her, the alleluia, for example, brings an Easter note to the whole office and exalted and joyful aura."[95] The psalms contain "an immense and inexhaustible sea of teaching, prayer, poetry and wisdom for living."[96] Settings of the Mass by the Renaissance, Baroque, and

92. *BCP* ECUSA 1979, 573.
93. *Scottish Liturgy*, §18.
94. Casel, *The Mystery*, 78.
95. Ibid., 82.
96. Ibid.

many modern composers are cultural treasures as well as profound statements of faith.

Sacred ritual creates a "form," or vessel, into which the divine presence and grace can flow. Its power is enhanced by repetition on a daily, weekly or annual cycle.[97] Each enactment is both a recapitulation and a new spiritual experience. To quote Massey Shepherd, it affords us "ever new opportunities for a fresh start."[98]

Christ's incarnation—along with his death, resurrection and ascension—spanned multiple levels of reality. On the mundane level it occurred in first-century Palestine, but at higher levels it lay outside space and time. A bishop in the Greek Orthodox Church commented: "The Holy Liturgy is something that embraces two worlds at once, for both in heaven and on earth the Liturgy is one and the same—one altar, one sacrifice, one presence."[99]

In a real sense the incarnation is taking place now. Shepherd added: "Every season and every holy day . . . is for us an advent, a coming in the present time of God's mighty acts of old in His Christ and in His saints. When we 'make memorial' of them we relive them as though we ourselves were the very historic participants in the drama."[100] To recognize the timelessness of sacramental ritual helps resolve debate over whether *anamnesis* means "recollection" or "reactualization." It should also help allay residual fears that the sacrificial intent of the Eucharist somehow contradicts the once-offered "full, perfect, and sufficient sacrifice, oblation, and satisfaction, for the sins of the whole world."

Participation in the Divine Glory

Archbishop Ramsey declared that the crucifixion should be viewed not as a disaster or disgrace but, inextricably linked with the resurrection and ascension, as the glorious fulfillment of the redemptive process. God, he noted, "who created the world for his glory will glorify His creatures and lead them to glorify Him. The end is a new creation, forged from out of the broken pieces of a fallen creation, filled with glory and giving glory

97. Eliade, *The Myth*, especially 34–35.

98. Shepherd, *The Worship*, 264.

99. Ware, *The Orthodox Church*, 265.

100. Shepherd, *The Worship*, 265.

to its maker."[101] If the Eucharist, he added, "be called a worship of glorifying, it is so because it is through Christ who glorifies the Father."[102]

Judaism acknowledged the divine glory in the transcendent *Kavod*: "Give unto the Lord the glory due unto his name: bring an offering, and come before him: worship the Lord in the beauty of holiness" (1 Chr 16:29), and "[L]et the beauty of the Lord our God be upon us: and establish thou the work of our hands upon us" (Ps 90:17). The divine glory could also be localized in places like the Holy of Holies (1 Kgs 8:6–11) or in people's hearts. Rabbinic writers coined the term *Shekinah* to refer to the immanent, indwelling glory of God.[103]

In the New Testament, when the angel announced Christ's birth to the shepherds, "the glory of the Lord shone round about them" (Luke 2:9). The fourth gospel proclaimed that "the Word was made flesh, and dwelt among us, and we beheld his glory, the glory as of the only begotten of the Father, full of grace and truth" (John 1:14). "Dwelt among us" may have been an intentional reference to the Shekinah.[104] At the transfiguration Peter, James, and John saw Christ in his divine glory (e.g., Mark 9:2–8). The resurrection, Balthasar declared, "pours out its 'sublime splendor' (*kavod, doxa, gloria*) over the whole sphere of the Church and of the bestowal of grace."[105] In the church the immanent glory is manifest in the sacraments, particularly the Sacrament of the Altar.

The Pseudo-Dionysius depicted God as the source of pure beauty, bestowed upon the righteous through the mysteries.[106] The *Gloria* proclaims: "We praise you, we bless you, we worship you, we glorify you, we give thanks to you for your great glory." And recited or chanted psalms end with "Glory be to the Father, and to the Son, and to the Holy Spirit." After giving thanks for "the brightness of the vesper light," one of the optional verses in Evening Prayer asks that God "would shine into our hearts the brightness of your Holy Spirit."[107]

Ramsey declared that "the eucharistic worship of the Church is on its godward side a participation in God's glorifying of the Father, and on

101. Ramsey, *The Glory of God*, 89.

102. Ibid., 94–95.

103. Nash, J. F., "The Shekinah."

104. Ramsey, *The Glory of God*, 58–60.

105. Balthasar, *The Glory of the Lord*, 38. Parenthesis and italicization in original.

106. Pseudo-Dionysius, *The Celestial Hierarchy*, iii.

107. *BCP* ECUSA 1979, 110.

its manward side a receiving of God's glory—the glory of the Cross."[108]
The Eucharist "unites those who partake with the glory of Christ as He
now is—risen [and] ascended."[109] Ramsay, who had studied Eastern
Orthodox theology, was aware that notions of humanity's participation
in the divine glory are embraced by the eastern concept of *theosis*, or
"deification." Deification goes beyond western notions of grace to express
a state of identification with the Divine. Scriptural support comes from
2 Peter 1:4, and patristic support was provided by Irenaeus, Clement of
Alexandria, and Athanasius. The last famously declared: "He [the Logos]
was made man that we might be made god."[110]

More recently the concept of deification has been explored by the
Russian Orthodox theologians Vladimir Lossky and Sergei Bulgakov,
and, with more of a stretch, by the Wesley brothers.[111] Bulgakov (1871–
1944) argued that the incarnation was motivated not only by the need
for human redemption but more importantly by God's plan for the glori-
fication of humanity. In response, "Man desires to become a son of God
and enter into that glory of creation, and he is predestined to this. Out of
natural man, he is called to become a god-man."[112] That goal became possible when divine and human nature were united in Christ. Deification
obviously cannot be achieved by unaided human effort. Nevertheless,
the doctrine's optimism—contrasting with Augustine's and Calvin's view
of the human condition—would have appealed to the Celts.

Our deification obviously lies in the future; but how long do we
have? Reflection on our life expectancy, as well as our own inadequacies,
could produce despair. Then again, opportunity for spiritual growth
may extend beyond death. As noted in chapter 6, Newman and others
explored the possibility of an intermediate state—other than a punitive purgatory—between physical death and resurrection. The AOJDD
linked the concept of post-mortem sanctification to traditional beliefs
in Eastern Orthodoxy: "[I]n the view of the Orthodox and also of many
Anglicans, further progress and growth in the love of God will continue
for ever. After death, this progress is to be thought of in terms of healing

108. Ramsey, *The Glory of God*, 98.

109. Ibid.

110. Athanasius, *On the Incarnation*, 54. See also Louth, *The Origins*, 76; and
Christensen, "The Problem," 23–31.

111. Christensen, "John Wesley," 219–29.

112. Bulgakov, *The Lamb of God*, 187.

rather than satisfaction or retribution . . . . The traditional practice of the Church in praying for the faithful departed is to be understood as an expression of the unity between the Church militant and the Church triumphant, and of the love which one bears to the other."[113]

MARIAN DEVOTION AND MARIOLOGY

Marian devotion was revived by the Caroline Divines after neglect in the immediate post-Reformation period. It gained momentum with the work of Keble and the later Newman and was popular among Anglo-Catholics by the end of the nineteenth century. Clearly Marian devotion expressed a deep-seated aspiration. But it confronted resistance in the Anglican psyche and is still unsettling for many today.

Developments in Roman Catholicism did not help. The dogmas of the immaculate conception (1854) and the assumption (1950) hurt the revival of Anglican devotion to Mary as much as they harmed ecumenical initiatives. The former asserted that Mary was conceived without original sin, the latter that she was taken up, body and soul, into heaven at the end of her earthly life. The immaculate conception and assumption had been topics of piety since the Middle Ages, but, lacking scriptural support, they were considered matters of private judgment. Rome's unilateral declaration of their infallibility, angered Anglicans and other Christians.

Notwithstanding the resulting tension, Anglican and Roman Catholic attitudes toward Mary continued to converge. As the ARCIC noted: "[M]any Anglicans were drawn into a more active devotion to Mary, and Roman Catholics discovered afresh the scriptural roots of such devotion."[114] That rediscovery confirmed a more balanced treatment of Marian devotion since Vatican II. The commission also noted: "This study has led us to the conclusion that it is impossible to be faithful to Scripture without giving due attention to the person of Mary."[115] Commenting on the Marian dogmas, the ARCIC noted: "[W]e can affirm together that God has taken the Blessed Virgin Mary in the fullness of her person into his glory [and that] Mary, as *Theotokos*, holds the

---

113. AOJDD, Dublin Agreed Statement, III, 72.

114. ARCIC, Seattle Statement, §65.

115. Ibid., §77.

pre-eminent place within the communion of saints and embodies the destiny of the Church."[116]

On questions of mariology, Anglicans have found that they can relate more readily to Eastern Orthodox teachings. Eastern theologians question the need for the immaculate conception because they attach little significance to original sin—a western doctrine that dates from the scholastic era. And in place of the assumption, they prefer to speak of Mary's *dormition*, or "falling asleep." August 15, the traditional feast of the assumption/dormition, is listed in Anglican calendars as the feast of "St Mary the Virgin." The collect for the feast in the *Scottish Liturgy* declares: "O God, you have taken to yourself the blessed Virgin Mary, mother of your incarnate Son. May we who have been redeemed by his blood share with her the glory of your eternal kingdom."[117]

Anglican devotion focuses on Mary's role in the incarnation, thereby minimizing the risk of mariolatry. Through Mary, Christ came into the world; she provided the means by which the divine and human natures were united. Anglicans could agree with Balthasar: "In Mary heaven and earth finally converge, here the finite encounters the infinite. Heaven, being masculine, takes the initiative and bestows its infinity on the earth; the earth, endowed with the quality of infinity, responds accordingly and brings forth her fruit."[118] An Eastern Orthodox hymn affirms Mary's place in the angelic hierarchy: "Mother of our God. More honorable than the Cherubim . . . more glorious than the Seraphim."[119]

Some versions of the eucharistic prayer refer to Mary. For example, Prayer 6 in the Canadian *BAS* asks "[G]rant that we may find our inheritance with the Blessed Virgin Mary, with patriarchs, prophets, apostles, and martyrs . . . and with all the saints."[120] The *Magnificat*, which survives in Evening Prayer in most Anglican liturgies, includes the memorable words: "[B]ehold, from henceforth all generations shall call me blessed" (Luke 1:48). Pronunciation and associated understanding of "blessed" is left to individual preference.

Archbishop Donald Coggan of Canterbury, not usually considered high-church in sympathies, posed an interesting question concerning

116. Ibid., §58.
117. *Scottish Liturgy*, §21.
118. Balthasar, *Engagement with God*, 39.
119. "Meet It Is," from the liturgy of St John Chrysostom.
120. *BAS ACC*, 208, 210.

the relationship between Mary and Christ: "Who knows the influence of a mother on her unborn child? Here is a world of mystery which is still not wholly understood. But is it not possible that something of the concept of dedicated servanthood which was at the heart of this young pregnant woman 'got through' to the child as yet unborn, and became an integral part in the shaping of his manhood and his ministry?"[121] He added, insightfully: "There may be more in this than has been generally recognized." Indeed there may! Despite Newman's warning in Tract 71, the argument that Mary retains special influence with her son is cited to justify Marian intercession.

As noted earlier, John Keble was open to notions of intercession. Bishop Griswold included an intercessionary prayer in a book of devotions: "Mary, our sister, Mother of the Word Incarnate . . . . Pray for us that your courage and endurance may find a home in our hearts, and let your loving intercession embrace all those who grieve and bear the wound of loss."[122] Dialogue with Eastern Orthodox theologians has helped clarify the issue of intercession. In its Dublin Statement the AOJDD explained:

> All prayer is ultimately addressed to the Triune God. We pray to God the Father through our Lord Jesus Christ in the Holy Spirit. The Church is united in a single movement of worship with the Church in heaven, with the Blessed Virgin Mary, 'with angels and archangels, and all the company of heaven.' The Orthodox also pray to the Blessed Virgin Mary and Theotokos and the saints as friends and living images of Christ . . . . The Blessed Virgin Mary played a unique role in the economy of salvation by virtue of the fact that she was chosen to be Mother of Christ our God. Her intercession is not autonomous, but presupposes Christ's intercession and is based upon the saving work of the incarnate Word.[123]

Anglo-Catholics have revived the medieval practice of pilgrimages. The shrine at Walsingham in Norfolk, England, is once again a favored destination.[124] When Alfred Hope Patten, a priest of the Order of St Andrew, was appointed vicar of Walsingham in 1921, he commissioned a statue of Our Lady of Walsingham, modeled on the seal of the medieval priory. He installed it in the parish church of St Mary's and offered

---

121. Quoted in Rowell et al., *Loves Redeeming Work*, 703.

122. Griswold, *Praying*, 135.

123. AOJDD, Dublin Agreed Statement, III, §§66, 75.

124. The Roman Catholic shrine was restored in 1897.

regular Marian devotions. Pilgrims came in increasing numbers, and in 1931 the statue was moved to the present building. David Michael Hope, master of the Guardians of the Shrine, the shrine's trustees, from 1982 to '93, became archbishop of York.

More recently, a group of Anglicans and Roman Catholics restored the shrine of Our Lady of Ipswich in neighboring Suffolk. When a newly commissioned statue of Mary was dedicated in 2002, the ceremony was attended by contingents from the Eastern Orthodox and Methodist churches. Devotions at the shrine include prayers for Christian unity.

Marian devotion within the Anglican Communion now has a number of supporting organizations, including the Society of Mary, formed in 1931 from two earlier societies. The society, not to be confused with the Roman Catholic religious order of the same name, now operates in many countries. These organizations work to popularize devotions, like the Rosary, *Angelus* ("The angel of the Lord declared unto Mary"), and *Regina Coeli* ("Queen of Heaven Rejoice"), which were once used only in Roman Catholicism.

FINAL REFLECTIONS

Anglo-Catholicism emphasizes God's transcendence and the profound mystery of Christ's birth, transfiguration, death, and resurrection. The resurrection, in Richard Meux Benson's words, was "the beginning of a new Creation, the exaltation of man's nature to a region of spiritual power that is altogether new . . . . The whole human being of our Lord Jesus was glorified by the Resurrection."[125]

The gulf between us and the transcendent God is bridged by the incarnation, by Mary Theotokos, by the angelic hosts, by the visible church, and by the sacraments. Bishop Grafton declared: "[The Church] had Christ for its Founder, the Apostles for its authorized Ministers, the Sacraments for its means of grace . . . . It was a spiritual living Organism, through which Christ, ever present in it, acted. An Organism in which the Holy Ghost dwelt. An Organism by whose Ministry and Sacraments the life and light of Christ was conveyed to individuals. An Organism which was to be eternal and was to be the Bride of Christ."[126]

---

125. Quoted in Rowell et al., *Loves Redeeming Work*, 451.
126. Grafton, *Pusey and the Church*, 244.

Geoffrey Rowell described the Catholic Revival as "a transformation of the self-understanding and self-expression of Anglicanism."[127] To view Anglo-Catholicism as a "sect" within Anglicanism is to miss its greatest contribution. Rather it should be viewed as an array of options that Anglicans can explore to enhance their religious experience. No particular set of practices and beliefs is anointed as canonical. Each person must approach the sacred mysteries with humility and reverence, seeking guidance and hoping for glimpses of the divine reality. Anglicans, however, have received *permission* to do and believe things previously considered "off limits." Anglicans can believe in the objective real presence and sacrificial nature of the Eucharist. They can engage in acts of adoration, join a monastery, or pray to Mary *while remaining fully Anglican*. The liberating effect has been enormous, allowing people to respond to such impulses without fear of betraying their tradition.

The range of options provided in modern liturgical texts dismays many people; but in the pragmatic spirit of Anglicanism, it has enabled people of all leanings to find liturgical forms that express their aspirations. The eucharistic tradition of the Scottish Episcopal Church, which passed into the liturgies of North America, has now reinvigorated the liturgy of the Church of England. Anglicanism is becoming, in the full sense of the word, a sacramental church. We are indebted to the Caroline Divines, Nonjurors, Tractarians, ritualists, and many others whose labor and resolve in the face of great difficulties made this possible.

Anglicans are reaching out to Lutheran and other traditions that are claiming their own sacramental heritages. The convergence between Anglicanism and Roman Catholicism and the even stronger convergence between Anglicanism and Eastern Orthodoxy are far-reaching in significance. Matters that divided the communions over the centuries have not all been resolved, and unity still eludes us. But mutual understanding is at a level that would have been unthinkable a century ago.

Prayerful contact with other branches of Christianity, with a commitment to understand their long traditions and deeply held beliefs, has given us a greater understanding of our own traditions and beliefs. Anglicans have benefited greatly from contact with the mystical theology of the Eastern tradition, providing much-needed balance to western intellectualism. A more mystical approach to the Eucharist and other mysteries of our faith is proving particularly fruitful. Mysticism also has

127. Rowell, *The Vision Glorious*, 251.

considerable ecumenical potential. When Bishop Henry Hill of Ontario was appointed co-chair of the AOJDD, he moved to an ecumenical Benedictine priory where Roman Catholic, Orthodox, Anglican, and other Christians shared a communal life of contemplation. Silent prayer, he commented, "unites us more deeply than our schisms can divide." May similar ideals apply within the Anglican Communion.

Anglo-Catholicism offers an alternative to what William Urban called "the soul-destroying oppositions of Fundamentalism and Humanism."[128] Fundamentalism clings to a naïve pietism and scriptural literalism in the face of human progress and common sense. Humanism—and its offspring, liberal Protestantism—have demythologized Christianity to the point where it is devoid of mystery, spirituality, and symbolism. Fundamentalism and liberalism both ignore the rightful place of adoration, aesthetics, and transcendent mystery in worship; they have destroyed a sense of "the sacred." The one offers nothing more than emotional stimulation, the other nothing more than intellectual stimulation. We pray that, one day, they may be drawn back to a sacramental appreciation of Christianity.

Anglo-Catholicism is often seen as elitist and self-serving. But the sacraments, the extension of Christ's incarnation, are not just vehicles of personal sanctification; they also carry the charge of discipleship. From the ritualists' work in inner-city parishes, Anglo-Catholicism's social conscience has developed and expanded. What is received through worship is channeled into the church's external ministries. With Christ's blessing, we are sent out to serve with this prayer on our lips: "Father, your steadfast purpose is the completion of all things in your Son. May we who have received the pledges of the kingdom, live by faith, walk in hope and be renewed in love, until the world reflects your glory and you are all in all; through Jesus Christ our Lord. Amen."[129] Anglicanism has recovered its ancient richness and moves into the twenty-first century, adoring God, witnessing to Christ, and serving humanity. Thus the story of the sacramental church goes on.

128. Urban, "The Need," §5.
129. *Scottish Liturgy*, §24.

Bibliography

"A Brief History of the Scottish Episcopal Church." SEC. Online: http://www.scotland
.anglican.org/index.php/about/history/.

*A Communion Office, Taken Partly from Primitive Liturgies and Partly from the First
English Reformed Common Prayer Book.* London: J. Smith, 1718.

"A History of the Diocese of Brechin." Online: http://new.thedioceseofbrechin.org/
index.php?page=history.

*Act for the Establishment of Religious Public Worship in this Province and for Suppressing
Popery.* Province of Nova Scotia, 1758.

Act for Uniformity of Service and Administration of the Sacraments throughout the Realm.
London, January 21, 1549.

Alexander, J. Neil. "The Shape of the Classical Book of Common Prayer." In *The Oxford
Guide to the Book of Common Prayer*, 64–72. Oxford: Oxford University Press,
2006.

Alternative Service Book. London: Church House Publishing, 1980.

"An Admonition to all Ministers Ecclesiastical." In *Two Books of Homilies*, 151. Oxford:
The University Press, 1859.

Andrewes, Lancelot. *Preces Privatae*, 1675. Trans. F. E. Brightman. London: Methuen,
1903.

Anglican Communion. *Lambeth Conference Resolutions Archive*, 1920. Online: http://
www.lambethconference.org/resolutions/1920/.

Anglican Communion. *Lambeth Conference Resolutions Archive*, 1968. Online: http://
www.lambethconference.org/resolutions/1968/.

Anglican Missal. London: Society of SS Peter & Paul, 1921.

Anglican Service Book. Rosemont, PA: Church of the Good Shepherd, 1991.

Anglican–Orthodox Joint Doctrinal Discussions. Dublin Agreed Statement: *The Mystery
of the Church*, 1984.

———. Moscow Agreed Statement: *The Church as Eucharistic Community*, 1976.

Anglican–Roman Catholic International Commission. Seattle Statement: *Mary: Grace
and Hope in Christ*, 2005.

Anglican–Roman Catholic Joint Preparatory Commission. Windsor Statement: *Agreed
Statement of Eucharistic Doctrine*. London: SPCK, 1981.

Anselm of Canterbury. *Third Great Prayer to Mary*. Trans. J. Roten, Marian Library.
Dayton, OH: University of Dayton.

Armentrout, Donald S., & Robert B. Slocum. *Documents of Witness*. New York: Church
Hymnal, 1994.

Arnold, Thomas. *Principles of Church Reform*. London: Fellowes, 1833.

Athanasius of Alexandria. *On the Incarnation.* Trans. "a religious of C.S.M.V." Crestwood, New York: St Vladimir's Seminary Press, 1993.

Avis, Paul. What is "Anglicanism"? In *The Study of Anglicanism*, revised ed., 459–76. Minneapolis, Minnesota: Fortress, 1998.

Balthasar, Hans U. von. *Engagement with God.* Trans. J. Halliburton. Fort Collins, Colorado: Ignatius, 1975.

———. *The Glory of the Lord: A Theological Aesthetics*, vol. 1. Fort Collins, Colorado: Ignatius Press, 1961.

Bede, Venerable. *Ecclesiastical History of the English People.*

Bertie, David M. *Scottish Episcopal Clergy, 1689–2000.* Edinburgh: Clark, 2000.

Bishops' Statement on the Polity of the Episcopal Church, §III. Anglican Communion Institute, April 2009.

Blake, William. *Jerusalem.* In *Milton a Poem*, 1804

Book of Alternative Services. Toronto: Anglican Book Centre, 1985.

Book of Common Prayer and Administration of the Sacraments and Other Rites for the Use of the Church of Scotland, Edinburgh: Young, 1637.

Book of Common Prayer and Administration of the Sacraments and other Rites and Ceremonies as Revised and Proposed to the Use of the Protestant Episcopal Church, 1785.

Book of Common Prayer. ACC. Toronto: Anglican Book Centre, 1962.

Book of Common Prayer. Church of England, 1549, 1552, 1662. Online: http://justus .anglican.org/resources/bcp/england.htm.

Book of Common Prayer. ECUSA. New York: Church Hymnal, 1979.

Book of Common Prayer. PECUSA. Philadelphia: Lippincott, 1789.

Book of Occasional Services. New York: Church Publishing, 2004.

Book Proposed to be Annexed to the Prayer Book Measure. London: University Press, 1927.

Borthwick, J. Douglas. *History of the Diocese of Montreal 1850–1910.* Montreal: Lovell, 1910.

Bouwsma, William J. "The Spirituality of Renaissance Humanism." In *Christian Spirituality: High Middle Ages and Reformation.* New York: Crossroads, 1988.

Boyce, Philip. *Mary: The Virgin Mary in the Writings of John Henry Newman.* Leominster, England: Gracewing, July 2001.

Bramhall, John. "Schism Guarded." *Works of Archbishop Bramhall.* Oxford: Parker, 1845.

Bright, William. *Early Chapters in English Church History*, 3rd ed. Oxford: Clarendon Press, 1997.

Brooks, Chris, & Andrew Saint. *The Victorian Church: Architecture and Society.* Manchester: Manchester University Press, 1995.

Brown, Michelle P. *The Lindisfarne Gospels: Society, Spirituality, and the Scribe.* Toronto: University of Toronto Press, 2003.

Caldwell, John. *The Oxford History of English Music.* Oxford: Oxford University Press, 1991.

Calivas, Alkiviadis C. "The Sacramental Life of the Orthodox Church." Greek Orthodox Archdiocese of America. Online: http://www.goarch.org/ourfaith/ourfaith7106/.

Campbell, Charles. *History of the Colony and Ancient Dominion of Virginia.* Philadelphia: Lippincott, 1860.

"Canon Carter of Clewer." *Church Quarterly Review* (vol. 53, article IX, 1902) 416–32.

Carabine, Deidre. *John Scottus Eriugena*. Oxford University Press, 2000.

Casel, Odo. *The Mystery of Christian Worship*, 1932. English translation 1962. Reprint with Introduction by A. Kavanagh. New York: Crossroads, 1999.

Certain Sermons or Homilies Appointed to be Read in Churches, 1562. Reprint, Oxford: The University Press, 1859.

Chandler, Michael. *An Introduction to the Oxford Movement*. New York: Church Publishing 2003.

Chardin, P. Teilhard de. *Hymn of the Universe*. Trans. G. Vann. London: Collins, 1965.

Cheshire, Joseph B. *The Church in the Confederate States*. New York: Longman's 1912.

Chorley, E. Clowes. *The New American Prayer Book: Its History and Contents*. New York: Macmillan, 1929.

Christensen, Michael J. "John Wesley: Christian Perfection as Faith Filled with the Energy of Love." In *Partakers of the Divine Nature*, 219–32. Grand Rapids, Michigan: Baker Academic, 2008.

—————. "The Problem, Promise, and Process of *Theosis*." In *Partakers of the Divine Nature*, 23–31. Grand Rapids, Michigan: Baker Academic, 2008.

Church, R. W. *The Oxford Movement*. London: Macmillan, 1891.

Clark, Alan C., & Colin Davey. *Anglican/Roman Catholic Dialogue: The Work of the Preparatory Commission*. Oxford: Oxford University Press, 1974.

Common Worship. London: Church House Publishing, 2000.

Communion-Office for the Use of the Church of Scotland. Edinburgh: Drummond, 1764.

Concordat 1784 between the Scottish Bishops and Dr. Samuel Seabury. Online: http://bishop.jmstanton.com/smu/smu_docs_Concordat.htm.

Copeland, William J., *et al*. *Library of Anglo–Catholic Theology*, 95 vols. Oxford: Parker, 1841–1853.

Corsi, Pietro. *Science and Religion: Baden Powell and the Anglican Debate: 1800–1860*. Cambridge: Cambridge University Press, 1988.

Cosin, John. *The History of Popish Transubstantiation*. Reprinted as Tract 27. *Tracts for the Times*, Project Canterbury. Online: http://anglicanhistory.org/tracts/tract27.html/.

Council of Constance. Session VIII. May 4, 1415.

Craig, Barry L. *Apostle to the Wilderness*. Madison, New Jersey: Fairleigh Dickinson University Press. 2005.

Crockett, William R. "Holy Communion." In *The Study of Anglicanism*, revised ed. Minneapolis, Minnesota: Fortress, 1998.

DeKoven, James. *Letter to the Clergy and Laity of Illinois*, Sept. 1875. Online: http://anglicanhistory.org/dekoven/letter1875.html/.

DeMille, Charles E. *The Catholic Movement in the American Episcopal Church*, 1941. Reprint, Eugene, Oregon: Wipf & Stock, 2005.

—————. *The Episcopal Church Since 1900*. New York: Morehouse–Gorham, 1955.

Dix, Gregory. *The Shape of the Liturgy*, 1945. Reprint, New York: Seabury, 1982.

Dix, Morgan. "A Sermon for the Times." Trinity Church, New York City, April 25, 1867. New York: Pott & Amery, 1867.

—————. *The Oxford Movement*, 3rd ed. Chicago: Living Church, 1884.

Dorman, Marianne. "Andrewes and the Caroline Divines' Teachings on the Blessed Virgin Mary." Ecumenical Society of the Blessed Virgin Mary, 2000. Online: http://anglicanhistory.org/essays/dorman3.pdf/.

Douglas, George W. "Anne Ayres." *Project Canterbury: Essays in Appreciation*, 1913. Online: http://anglicanhistory.org/women/ayres/douglas1913.html/.

Dowling, Ronald. "The Eucharist." In *The Oxford Guide to the Book of Common Prayer*, 460–75. Oxford University Press, 2006

Eliade, Mircea. *The Myth of the Eternal Return*. Princeton New Jersey: Princeton University Press, 1954.

Ewer, Ferdinand C. *Catholicity in its Relationship to Protestantism and Romanism*. New York: Putnam's Sons, 1878.

———. *What is the Anglican Church?* 2nd ed. Chicago: Living Church Co., 1883.

Farmer, David H. *The Age of Bede*, revised ed. London: Penguin Classics, 1998.

Forbes, George H. *A Memoir of Alexander, Bishop of Brechin*. London: Masters, 1876.

Fox, Matthew. *Sheer Joy*. New York: Tarcher/Putnam, 1992.

Frank, Mark. "Sermon on the feast of the Annunciation of the Blessed Virgin Mary." Project Canterbury. Online: http://anglicanhistory.org/lact/frank/v2/sermon30.html/.

Frere, W. H. "The Eastern Orthodox Church." In *Report of the First Anglo-Catholic Congress*, 97–101. New York: Macmillan, 1920.

Fulford, Francis. "Address of Metropolitan." Project Canterbury. Online: http://anglicanhistory.org/canada/fulford/address1861.html/.

Gaskoin, Charles J. B. "Nonjurors." In *Encyclopedia of Religion and Ethics*, 394–96. Edinburgh: Hastings, 1917.

General Convention of the Episcopal Church, Resolution C006, 2009.

Gildas. *On the Ruin and Conquest of Britain*, §66. Online: http://www.fordham.edu/halsall/basis/gildas-full.html/.

Gillis, Clive. *The History Of The Coronation Oath*. Belfast, Northern Ireland: European Institute of Protestant Studies, 2003.

Goldie, Frederick. *A Short History of the Episcopal Church in Scotland*, revised ed. Edinburgh: St Andrews, 1976.

Gore, Charles. "Christ and Society": *Halley Stewart Lectures*, 1927. Online: http://www.anglocatholicsocialism.org/csu.html/.

———. *Lux Mundi: A Series of Studies in the Religion of the Incarnation*. London, Murray, 1891.

Gorham v. Bishop of Exeter, The Judgment of the Judicial Committee of Privy Council. London, March 8, 1850.

Grafton, Charles C. *A Journey Godward*. Milwaukee, WI: The Young Churchman, 1910.

———. *Pusey and the Church Revival*. Milwaukee, Wisconsin: The Young Churchman, 1908.

———. *The Lineage of the American Catholic Movement*. Milwaukee, Wisconsin: The Young Churchman, 1911.

Gregory, Jeremy. "The Prayer Book and the Parish Church: From the Restoration to the Oxford Movement." In *The Oxford Guide to the Book of Common Prayer*, 93–105. Oxford University Press, 2006.

Griswold, Frank T. "Listening with the Ear of the Heart." Presentation to Trinity Institute, New York City, May 1998. Reprinted in *Cross Currents* (Winter 1998–9).

———. *Praying Our Days*. New York: Morehouse, 2009.

Hardinge, Leslie. *The Celtic Church in Britain*, 1972. Reprint, Brushton, New York: Teach Services, 1995.

Hayes, Alan L. *Anglicans in* Canada. Champaign, Illinois: University of Illinois Press, 2004.

Haywood, Marshall de L. *Lives of the Bishops of North Carolina*. Raleigh, North Carolina: Williams, 1910.

Hefling, Charles. "Scotland: Episcopalians and Nonjurors." In *The Oxford Guide to the Book of Common Prayer*, 166–75. Oxford University Press.

Hein, David, & Gardiner H. Shattuck. *The Episcopalians*. Westport, Connecticut: Prayer Publishers, 2004.

Helmore, Thomas. *Accompanying Harmonies to the Hymnal Noted*. London: Novello, 1852.

Hildegard of Bingen. *Scivias*. Trans. C. Hart & J. Bishop. Mahwah, New Jersey: Paulist, 1990.

Hobart, John Henry. "The Origin, the General Character, and the Present Situation of the Protestant Episcopal Church in the United States." Address to General Convention, PECUSA, May 1814.

Hodson, Geoffrey. *Clairvoyant Investigations*. Wheaton, Illinois: Theosophical Publishing House, 1984.

Holmes, David L. *A Brief History of the Episcopal Church*. Valley Forge, Pennsylvania: Trinity, 1993.

Holy Baptism 2006. Edinburgh: General Synod of the Scottish Episcopal Church, 2006.

Homily II: "A Sermon of the Misery of All Mankind." In *Two Books of Homilies*, 16–23. Oxford: The University Press, 1859.

Homily IV: "A Short Declaration of the True, Lively, and Christian Faith." In *Two Books of Homilies*, 36–47. Oxford: The University Press, 1859.

Homily XX (second vol.): "Repentance and True Reconciliation unto God." In *Two Books of Homilies*, 525–35. Oxford: The University Press, 1859.

Hook, Walter F.. *An Ecclesiastical Biography Containing the Lives of Ancient Fathers and Modern Divines*. London: Rivington, 1848.

Hooker, Richard. *A Learned discourse of Justification*, 1585. Online: http://www.ccel.org/ ccel/hooker/just.toc.html/.

———. *Of the Laws of Ecclesiastical Polity*, book V, 1597. In Isaac Walton. *The Works of . . . Richard Hooker*, 7th ed., vol. II, 1–535. Oxford: The University Press, 1888.

Hopkins, John H. *The Law of Ritualism*. New York: Hurd & Houghton, 1866.

Hunt, Gaillard. "Story of a Great Southern Bishop." *New York Times* (Jan. 25, 1908).

Huntington, William R. *The Church Idea, an Essay toward Unity*. New York: Dutton, 1870.

Hutton, William H. *William Laud*, 3rd ed. London: Methuen, 1905.

Ignatius of Antioch *Epistle to the Smyrnaeans*, viii. Online: http://www.ccel.org/ccel/ schaff/anf01.v.vii.html/.

Inglis, Charles. "The Duty of Honouring the King." Project Canterbury. Online: http:// anglicanhistory.org/charles/inglis.html/

"International Anglican Liturgical Consultations." IALC. Online: http://www .anglicancommunion.org/resources/liturgy/docs/ialcreview.cfm/.

International Anglican–Roman Catholic Commission for Unity and Mission. Agreed Statement: *Growing Together in Unity and Mission*. 2007.

International Commission for Anglican–Orthodox Theological Dialogue. Cyprus Agreed Statement: *The Church of the Triune God*. 2006.

Jackman, Sydney W. *Deviating Voices: Women and Orthodox Religious Tradition.* Cambridge: Lutterworth, 2003.

Jeanes, Gordon. "Cranmer and Common Prayer." In *The Oxford Guide to the Book of Common Prayer*, 21–38. Oxford: Oxford University Press, 2006.

Jewell, Frederick S. *The Special Beliefs and Objects of Catholic Churchmen.* Milwaukee, Wisconsin: The Young Churchman, 1886.

Jewell, John. *The Apology of the Church of England.* Trans. Lady Ann Bacon, 1564. Reprint, London: Cassell, 1888.

Johnson, John. *The Theological Works of the Rev. John Johnson.* Oxford: Parker, 1847.

Jolly, Alexander. *The Christian Sacrifice in the Eucharist.* Aberdeen, Scotland: Brown, 1831.

Julian of Norwich. *Showings*, Paris Manuscript, folios 9–10v, 1580. Reprint, Mahwah, New Jersey: Paulist, 1977.

Jülicher, Adolf. *An Introduction to the New Testament.* Trans. J. P. Ward. London: Smith, Elder, 1904.

Keble, John. *Assize Sermon July 14, 1833.* London: Mowbray. Online: http://anglicanhistory.org/keble/keble1.html/.

Kelway, Albert C. *George Rundle Prynne: A Chapter in the Early History of the Catholic Revival.* London: Longmans Green, 1905.

Kip, William I. *The Double Witness of the Church*, 23rd ed. New York: Dutton, 1886.

Kirby, W. J. Torrance. *Richard Hooker and the English Reformation.* Dordrecht, Netherlands: Kluwer Academic, 2003.

Kraus, Donald. "The Book of Common Prayer and Technology." In *The Oxford Guide to the Book of Common Prayer*, 541–44. Oxford: Oxford University Press, 2006.

Langford, H. W. "*The Non-Jurors and the Eastern Orthodox.*" Proc. Durham Conf., Fellowship of St Alban and St Sergius, June 1965.

Lathbury, Thomas. *A History of the Convocation of the Church of England.* London: Harrison, 1842.

Latimer, *Sermons by Hugh Latimer*, Cambridge: Cambridge University Press, 1844.

Law, William. *Three Letters.*

Leaver, Robert A. "The Prayer Book Noted." In *The Oxford Guide to the Book of Common Prayer*, 39–43. Oxford: Oxford University Press, 2006.

Leo XIII. Encyclical: *Apostolicae Curae* ("On the Nullity of Anglican Orders"). Vatican, 1896.

Liddon, Henry P. *Life of Edward Bouverie Pusey.* London: Longmans Green, 1893.

Long vs. Bishop of Cape Town: Decision of the Privy Council. London: Butterworths, 1866.

Louth, Andrew. *The Origins of the Christian Mystical Tradition*, 2nd ed. Oxford: Oxford University Press, 2007.

Luther, Martin. "The Fruits of Faith–Our Spiritual Service." In *Sermons of Martin Luther*, vii, 7–19. Grand Rapids, MI: Baker, 2000.

———. *Works of Luther.* Weimar Edition. Trans. J. Pelikan. St Louis, Missouri: Concordia, 1960.

MacCulloch, Diarmaid. *The Reformation.* London: Penguin, 2003.

Macquarrie, John. *A Guide to the Sacraments.* New York: Continuum, 1998.

Magna Carta, §1. Trans. N. Vincent. National Archives. Online: http://www.archives.gov/exhibits/featured_documents/magna_carta/translation.html/.

Maltby, Judith. "The Prayer Book and the Parish Church: From the Elizabethan Settlement to the Restoration." In *The Oxford Guide to the Book of Common Prayer*, 79–92. Oxford: Oxford University Press, 2006.

Magocsi, Paul R. *Encyclopedia of Canada's Peoples*. Toronto: University of Toronto Press, 1999.

Maurice, Frederick D. *The Kingdom of Christ*. London: Darton & Clark, 1838.

Meyers, Ruth A. "Rites of Initiation." In *The Oxford Guide to the Book of Common Prayer*, 485–99. Oxford: Oxford University Press, 2006.

Middleton, Arthur. *Eminent English Churchmen*. Project Canterbury. Online: http://anglicanhistory.org/essays/middleton/.

Molesworth, William N. *History of the Church of England from 1660*. London: Kegan, Paul, Trench, 1882.

Moorman, J. R. H. *A History of the Church in England*, 3rd ed. New York: Morehouse, 1963.

Mozley, James B. *The Primitive Doctrine of Baptismal Regeneration*. London: Murray, 1856.

Muhlenberg. William A., et al. Memorial to the Bishops of the Protestant Episcopal Church. 1853. Online: http://bishop.jmstanton.com/smu/pdf_files/Muhlenberg_Memorial_linenum.pdf/.

Nash, J. O. & Charles Gore. *William Law's Defence of Church Principles*, 2nd ed. Edinburgh: Grant, 1909.

Nash, John F. "The Shekinah: The Indwelling Glory of God." *The Esoteric Quarterly* (Summer 2005) 33–40.

———. "Esoteric Healing in the Orthodox, Roman and Anglican Churches." *The Esoteric Quarterly* (Spring 2007) 37–50.

———. *Christianity: the One, the Many*, two vols. Bloomington, IL: Xlibris, 2007.

Newman, John H. "Advertisement to the Tracts." November 1, 1834. Project Canterbury. Online: http://anglicanhistory.org/tracts/advertisement.html/.

———. "The Intermediate State, " Sermon III, 25. In *John Henry Newman: Parochial and Plain Sermons*. Fort Collins, Colorado: Ignatius, 1997.

———. *Apologia pro Vita Sua* ("A Defense of One's Life"). London: Dent, 1864.

———. *Lectures on The Prophetical Office of The Church, Viewed Relatively to Romanism and Popular Protestantism*. London: Rivington, 1837.

Nockles, Peter B. *The Oxford Movement in Context*. Cambridge: Cambridge University Press, 1994.

Northup, Lesley A. "The Episcopal Church in the U.S.A." In *The Oxford Guide to the Book of Common Prayer*, 360–68. New York: Oxford University Press, 2006.

Ollard, Sidney L. *A Short History of the Oxford Movement*. London: Mowbray, 1915.

Ordinary and Canon of the Mass According to the Use of the Church of Sarum. Trans. J. T. Dodd. London: Masters, 1872.

Ottley, Robert L. *Lancelot Andrewes*, 2nd ed. London: Methuen, 1894.

Overton, John H. *The English Church in the Nineteenth Century: 1800–1833*. London: Longmans Green, 1894.

———. *The Nonjurors: Their Lives, Principles, and Writings*. New York: Whittaker, 1903.

———. *William Law, Nonjuror and Mystic*. London: Longmans Green, 1881.

Palmer, William P. "Ecclesiastical Vestures." In *Antiquities of the English Ritual*, appendix. London: Rivington, 1832.

————. *A Treatise on the Church of Christ*. London: Rivington, 1838.

Parker, John W. *Essays and Reviews*. London: Parker, 1860.

Pascoe, Charles F. *Classified Digest of the Records of the Society for the Propagation of the Gospel in Foreign Parts: 1701–1892*, 4th ed. London: SPG, 1894.

Paul VI. *Mysterium Fidei*. Encyclical. Vatican, September 1965.

Pearson, John. *Exposition of the Creed*, 6th ed. Oxford: Clarendon Press, 1877.

Pegis, Anton C. *Introduction to St Thomas Aquinas*. New York: Modern Library, 1948.

Perry, John, *et al*. *A Time to Heal*. London: Church House Publishing, 2000.

Pfatteicher, Philip H. "The Prayer Book and Lutheranism." In *The Oxford Guide to the Book of Common Prayer*, 222–26. Oxford: Oxford University Press, 2006.

Philpotts, Henry. *Letter to Charles Butler*, 1825. Reprint, Charleston, South Carolina: BiblioLife, 2010.

Pius V. *Regnans in Excelsis*. Bull. Vatican, 1570.

Podmore, Thomas. *A Layman's Apology for Returning to Primitive Christianity*. Manchester: James Lister, 1745.

Prichard, Robert. *A History of the Episcopal Church*, revised ed. New York: Morehouse, 1999.

Provincial Synod of Canada. Address to the Archbishop of Canterbury, Sept. 16, 1865.

Prynne, George R. *The Eucharistic Manual: Instructions and Devotions for the Holy Sacrament of the Altar*. London: Masters, 1864.

Pseudo-Dionysius. *The Celestial Hierarchy*. In *Pseudo-Dionysius: the Complete Works*, 143–91. Trans. C. Luibheid. Mahwah, New Jersey: Paulist Press, 1987.

Purchas, John. *Directorium Anglicanum: a Manual of Directions for the Right Celebration of the Holy Communion*. London: Masters, 1868.

Pusey, Edward B. *An Eirenicon: The Church of England. A Portion of Christ's One Holy Catholic Church, and a Means of Restoring Visible Unity*. London: Rivington, 1865.

Pusey, Edward B., *et al*. *Library of the Fathers*, 50 vols. London: Rivington, 1838–85.

Ramsey, A. Michael. "Charles C. Grafton, Bishop and Theologian." Lecture at Nashotah House, September 26, 1967. Project Canterbury. Online: http://anglicanhistory .org/amramsey/grafton.pdf/.

————. *The Glory of God and the Transfiguration of Christ*, 1949. Reprint, Eugene, Oregon: Wipf & Stock, 2009.

Rankin, James. *A Handbook of the Church of Scotland*, 4th ed. Edinburgh: Blackwood, 1888.

Reed, John S. *Glorious Battle*. Nashville, TN: Vanderbilt University Press, 1996.

Remains of the Late Reverend Richard Hurrell Froude, M.A., two vols. London: Rivington, 1838.

Report of the Royal Commission on Ecclesiastical Discipline. London, 1906.

Roberts, G. Bayfield. *The History of the English Church Union, 1859–1894*. London: Church Printing House, 1895.

Robertson, Alec. *Requiem*. London: Cassell, 1967.

Rosman, Doreen M. *The Evolution of the English Churches*. Cambridge: Cambridge University Press, 2003.

Rowell, Geoffrey . *The Vision Glorious*. Oxford: Oxford University Press, 1983.

Rowell, Geoffrey, *et al*. *Love's Redeeming Work: The Anglican Quest for Holiness*. Oxford: Oxford University Press, 2001.

Russell, H. Lloyd. "The Intermediate State, and Prayer for the Departed." *Sermon, All Soul's Day, 1885*. London: Guild of All Souls, 1885.

Rutherford, Edward. *Sarum*. New York: Ballantine, 1987.

Schaff, Philip. *History of the Christian Church*, revised ed. New York: Scribner, 1910.

Scherer, Paul. *Lord John Russell: A Biography*. Cranbury, New Jersey: Associated University Presses, 1999.

Scott, Gilbert. *Personal and Professional Recollections*. London: Sampson, et al., 1879.

Scott, Walter. *Guy Mannering: Or the Astrologer*, two vols. Boston: Estes & Lauriat, 1893.

Scottish Liturgy. Edinburgh: Scottish Episcopal Church, 1982.

Shepherd vs. Bennett, 1869. *Law Journal Reports for the Year 1870: Ecclesiastical Cases* (vol. 39, 1870) 1–10.

Shepherd, Massey H., Jr. *The Worship of the Church*, 1952. Excerpts in *Documents of Witness*, 262-266. New York: Church Hymnal, 1994.

Smith, C. J. "The Sacrifice of the Altar." *Report of the First Anglo–Catholic Congress*. New York: Macmillan, 1920.

Spinks, Bryan. "From Elizabeth to Charles II." In *The Oxford Guide to the Book of Common Prayer*, 44–55. Oxford: Oxford University Press, 2006.

Sprague, William B. *Annals of the American Pulpit*. New York: Carter, 1859.

Stakemeier, E. *De Mariologia et Oecumenismo*. Rome: Balic, 1962.

Stanwood, Paul G. "The Prayer Book as Literature." In *The Oxford Guide to the Book of Common Prayer*, 140–9. Oxford: Oxford University Press, 2006.

Stephen, Thomas. *History of the Church of Scotland: From the Reformation to the Present Time*, vol. 4. London: Lendrum, 1845.

Stevenson, Kenneth. "The Prayer Book as "Sacred Text." In *The Oxford Guide to the Book of Common Prayer*, 133–9. Oxford: Oxford University Press, 2006.

Stevenson, W. Taylor. "Lex Orandi–Lex Credendi." In *The Study of Anglicanism*, revised ed., 187–202. Minneapolis, Minnesota: Fortress, 1998.

Stevick, Daniel B. "Canon Law." In *The Study of Anglicanism*, revised ed., 216–45. Minneapolis, Minnesota: Fortress, 1998.

Stone, Darwell. Preface to *Report of the First Anglo–Catholic Congress*, 9–10. New York: Macmillan, 1920.

Strong, James. *Cyclopedia of Biblical, Theological and Ecclesiastical Literature*, vol. viii. San Francisco: Harper, 1894.

———. *The Doctrine of a Future Life*. New York: Hunt & Eaton, 1891.

Strong, Rowan. *Alexander Forbes of Brechin: the First Tractarian Bishop*. Oxford: Oxford University Press, 1995.

Taylor, Gordon R. *Sex in History*. Jackson, Tennessee: Vanguard, 1954.

Taylor, Jeremy. *The Whole Works of the Right Reverend Jeremy Taylor*, vol. 6, revised ed. London: Longman *et al.*, 1852.

Taylor, John W. *The Coming of the Saints: Imaginations and Studies in Early Church History and Tradition*. New York: Dutton, 1907.

Tellini, Gianfranco. "The Scottish Episcopal Church." In *The Oxford Guide to the Book of Common Prayer*, 420–25. Oxford: Oxford University Press, 2006.

"The Abbey of Glastonbury." *The Saturday Magazine* (Oct. 1835) 139–41.

The Church's Ministry in Healing. London: Archbishops Council, 1958.

The Constitution of the Protestant Episcopal Church in the United States of America. New York: Protestant Episcopal Church, 1789.

The Ministry of Healing. London: Lambeth Conference, 1924.

"The Porvoo Common Statement." *Concordia Theological Quarterly* (Jan.–April 1997) 3–34.

Thirty-Nine Articles. Online: http://anglicansonline.org/basics/thirty-nine_articles .html/.

Thomas, Charles. *Christianity in Roman Britain to AD 500.* Berkeley, California: University of California Press, 1981.

Thompson, J. H. "The Conditions of Christ's Presence with Church Synods, " 1858. ProjectCanterbury.Online:http://anglicanhistory.org/canada/thompson_conditions .html/.

Thorndike, Herbert. *An Epilogue of the Tragedy of the Church of England.* 1659.

————. *The Theological Works of Herbert Thorndike,* vol. 5. Oxford: Parker, 1854.

Towle, Eleanor A. *Alexander Heriot Mackonochie: A Memoir,* 2nd ed., 1890. Reprint Charleston, South Carolina: BiblioLife, 2009.

Tract 5: "A Short Address to his Brethren on the Nature and Constitution of the Church of Christ, and of the Branch of it Established in England, by a Layman." *Tracts for the Times.* Project Canterbury. Online: http://anglicanhistory.org/tracts/tract5 .html/.

Tract 7: "The Episcopal Church Apostolical." *Tracts for the Times.* Project Canterbury. Online: http://anglicanhistory.org/tracts/tract7.html/.

Tract 15: "On the Apostolical Succession in the English Church." *Tracts for the Times.* Project Canterbury. Online: http://anglicanhistory.org/tracts/tract15.html/.

Tract 21: "Mortification of the Flesh a Scriptural Duty." *Tracts for the Times.* Project Canterbury. Online: http://anglicanhistory.org/tracts/tract21.html/.

Tract 26: "The Necessity and Advantage of Frequent Communion." *Tracts for the Times.* Project Canterbury. Online: http://anglicanhistory.org/tracts/tract26.html/.

Tract 34: "Rites and Ceremonies of the Church." *Tracts for the Times.* Project Canterbury. Online: http://anglicanhistory.org/tracts/tract34.html/.

Tract 54: "Sermons for Saints' Days and Holidays. No II. The Annunciation of the Blessed Virgin Mary." *Tracts for the Times.* Project Canterbury. Online: http:// anglicanhistory.org/tracts/tract54.html/.

Tract 67: "Scriptural Views of Holy Baptism." In *Tracts for the Times,* vol. II, part II, 4th ed., 1–393. London: Rivington, 1840.

Tract 71: "On the Controversy with the Romanists." *Tracts for the Times.* Project Canterbury. Online: http://anglicanhistory.org/tracts/tract71.html/.

Tract 80: "On Reserve in Communicating Religious Knowledge." *Tracts for the Times.* Project Canterbury. Online: http://anglicanhistory.org/tracts/tract80.html/.

Tract 89: "On the Mysticism Attributed to the Fathers of the Church." *Tracts for the Times.* Project Canterbury. Online: http://anglicanhistory.org/tracts/tract89/.

Tract 90: "Remarks on Certain Passages in the Thirty-Nine Articles." *Tracts for the Times.* Project Canterbury. Online: http://anglicanhistory.org/tracts/tract90/.

Tytler, Patrick F. *History of Scotland,* vol. 6. Edinburgh: Tait, 1837.

Urban, William M., "The Need of a Catholic Philosophy Today, " In *Liberal Catholicism and the Modern World,* Milwaukee, Wisconsin: Morehouse, 1933.

Vincentius of Lérins, *The Commitorium,* Cambridge Patristic Texts.

Walker, William. *The Life of the Right Reverend Alexander Jolly, D.D., Bishop of Moray,* 2nd ed. Edinburgh: Douglas, 1878.

Walker, Williston. *A History of the Christian Church,* revised ed. New York: Scribner, 1959.

Walsh, Walter. *Secret History of the Oxford Movement*. London: Church Association, 1899.

Walton, Guy. *A Short History of St Luke's Church, Hope, Warren County, New Jersey*. St Luke's Episcopal Church, 2006.

Ware, Timothy. *The Orthodox Church*, 1963. Reprint, London: Penguin, 1997.

Wesley, John. "Duty of Constant Communion." In *Sermons for Several Occasions*, vol. 2, 349–56. New York: Lane & Sandford, 1842.

———. Letter to Miss B, April 17, 1776. In *The Works of the Rev. John Wesley*, New York: Harper, 1827.

White, James F. "Prayer Book Architecture." In *The Oxford Guide to the Book of Common Prayer*, 106–15. Oxford: Oxford University Press, 2006.

Wilde, C. B. "Hutchinsonianism, Natural Philosophy and Religious Controversy in Eighteenth Century Britain." *History of Science* (vol. xviii, 1980).

Williams, Peter, & Barbara Owen. *The Organ*. New York: Norton, 1980.

Williams, Rowan. *Anglican Identities*. Cambridge, Massachusetts: Cowley, 2003.

Wood, Andy. *The 1549 Rebellions and the Making of Early Modern England*. Cambridge: Cambridge University Press, 2007.

Woods, Richard J. *The Spirituality of the Celtic Saints*. Maryknoll, New York: Orbis, 2000.

Wright, J. Robert. "Early Translations." In *The Oxford Guide to the Book of Common Prayer*, 56–60. Oxford: Oxford University Press, 2006.

Wright, Lewis. "Anglo-Catholicism in Antebellum North Carolina: Levi Silliman Ives and the Society of the Holy Cross." *Anglican and Episcopal History* (vol. lxix, no. 1, 2002) 44–71.

Wriothesley, Thomas. *A Chronicle of England During the Reigns of the Tudors, From A.D. 1485 to 1559*, vol. 1. Reprint, London: Camden Society, 1875.

Young, Carolyn A. *Canada's First Parliament Buildings*, Montreal, Quebec: McGill-Queen's University Press, 1995.

Index

ABOUT THE AUTHOR

John Francis Nash was born in the United Kingdom but has lived in the United States since the 1960s. He earned his Ph.D. from the University of London and holds other degrees from British, Belgian, and American institutions. A varied career led him from scientific research to business and eventually to higher education. Since "retiring," after thirty years in academia, he has focused on writing and teaching in religious philosophy. He was founding editor of *The Esoteric Quarterly,* an international peer-reviewed journal of esoteric philosophy. His lifetime output of publications includes fourteen books and 150 papers and articles in multiple fields.

Dr. Nash grew up in the secure religious environment of pre-Vatican II Roman Catholicism. After a long spiritual journey he became an Episcopalian and is an active member of St Mary's Parish, Asheville, North Carolina, a church that was founded in the Anglo-Catholic tradition. His interests include sacred choral and organ music.